PurposeFull

How businesses and not-for-profits do better as *purpose-driven* organisations

PurposeFull: How businesses and not-for-profits do better as *purpose-driven* organisations © Paul Bird 2021

ISBN: 978-1-922578-31-0 (paperback)

Published in Australia by Paul Bird and InHouse Publishing.

www.inhousepublishing.com.au

INHOUSE PTY LTD PUBLISHING

NATIONAL LIBRARY OF AUSTRALIA

A catalogue record for this book is available from the National Library of Australia

Contents

www.purposefull.com.au

Purpose is not an initiative; it is a way of business. It must be core to the decisions, conversations, and behaviors across all levels to be authentic and deliver the wealth of advantages it promises. Now, more than ever, companies must cultivate the power of purpose if they are to succeed in a world where the opportunities—and responsibilities—of business have never been greater.

PwC, Putting Purpose to Work, June 2016

I think corporate Australia, if it's to fix the reputations it has out there, needs to be vocal on social issues. That's what good businesses do. They are part of society; they help promote societal change and help promote what's good for our people.

Alan Joyce, CEO Qantas

Without a sense of purpose, no company, either public or private, can achieve its full potential.

Larry Fink, BlackRock

Charities must never lose sight of why they exist and must demonstrate how their charitable purpose drives everything they do.

Charity Commission for England and Wales[1]

If we don't invest in the planet, and in things our people are telling us, there won't be a lot of growth.

Mike Cannon-Brookes, Co-CEO, Atlassian

Today, businesses are distinguished not by what they do, but what they stand for, what they mean.

Simon Longstaff, CEO, Centre for Ethical

Purposeful businesses will be essential contributors to solving the global challenges of the 21st century, best expressed in an integrated way by the UN Sustainable Development Goals.

The British Academy[2]

There's a growing body of research that says these purpose-driven firms—ones that place their top commitment to something other than generating profits—are more profitable for their investors in the long run.

Korn Ferry

Being able to articulate that purpose to your employees, customers, suppliers and other stakeholders is how an organisation galvanizes people and inspires them.

Beyond Bank[3]

Companies that do good, do well.

Mark Kramer[4]

We cannot solve our social and environmental challenges by merely tinkering with our existing system.

Sir Ronald Cohen[5]

Everyone has a second job in life—the job of leaving the world a better place.

Chris Richardson,
Chief Economist, Deloitte Access Economics[6]

To Tracey, Georgie, India and Stephen.

For everyone working with and supporting purpose-driven organisations. Your skill, passion, commitment and drive are an inspiration to us all.

In memory of
David Thompson AM, Chris Hawken and
Ian (Macca) McDonald.

Introduction

A life is not important except
in the impact it has on other lives.

Jackie Robinson

I am standing in the middle of a village on a tropically hot and steamy day, talking to a distraught man sat slumped and forlorn on a chair outside his house. Life carries out around him with excited children running around women sitting cross-legged on a mat, talking and preparing the vegetables for the evening meal. The sadness runs deep on his face; his eyes glazed and hollow.

His left leg from the knee down is hideously swollen and disfigured, five times the size of his other leg. In constant pain, he had been the proud head of the family and active elder of the community. Unable to work, he is now ostracised as useless and needy. A burden.

As a child, and in common with millions of other children around the world, he had been bitten by a mosquito, the world's most deadly animal. It had injected a roundworm parasite carried in the blood of another infected human. Living for six to nine years, the worm nests in the lymphatic vessels and disrupts the normal function of the lymphatic system, producing millions of immature larvae that circulate in the blood during their lifetime.

Called lymphatic filariasis, or elephantiasis, 893 million people living in tropical areas are in need of treatment for this disease. But the good news is that this is one disease that can be easily eliminated from the face of the Earth with three cheap and widely available drugs given once a year for up to six years. Alternatively, to break the cycle, the fruit-flavoured tablets can be given to children by teachers annually at school.

I was in the country to meet members of the *Global Programme to Eliminate Lymphatic Filariasis*, which was set up in 2000 to coordinate efforts to eradicate the disease by 2020. I came with commitments from companies to donate the drugs required. But, like so many basic health priorities in developing countries, progress has been painfully slow. Currently, of the seventy-two endemic countries, only fourteen have been validated by the World Health Organization to have succeeded.

At a cost of a billion US dollars to wipe this disease off the face of the planet, I came home from my visit to the news that the cost of the redevelopment of a railway station in my city had cost more.

The former Lord Mayor of Melbourne and Chairman of Channel 7, Ivan Deveson AO, talks about the stone in your shoe. It niggles at you, touches a nerve and grates on your conscience. It is those things that make you feel uncomfortable, prick your conscience and make you want to act. It gives you the energy, passion and commitment to respond.

With eight of ten Australian adults donating over $12 billion a year to causes, at least fourteen million of us have these stones. As employees, customers, clients, investors, partners and donors, we want to work for, buy from, collaborate with and support organisations that can respond to our stones through their purpose. As Peter Fisk explains, 'purpose is good for business. Purpose-driven companies are more ambitious, they attract the best talent, inspire richer innovation, make faster decisions, are more trusted, have greater loyalty, and attract more investment.'[7] McKinsey, meanwhile, points out that a 'compelling purpose attracts talent and unleashes its potential', but that 'superficial branding efforts around purpose that are not anchored in the organisational DNA only serve to undermine leadership credibility'.[8]

After all, Australians now expect action from business with over eighty per cent believing that business has a responsibility to do social good,[9] seventy per cent agreeing that large companies should place equal importance on economic, environmental and social performance, and over three-quarters supporting business leaders that speak out on social and environmental issues.[10]

With one in eight business leaders thinking that purpose is central to their business's success but less than half of them saying that their organisational purpose is a guidepost to their decision-making,[11] this book shows how all organisations can become *PurposeFull*.

Globally, consumers are four to six times more likely to purchase, protect and champion purpose-driven companies,[12] whilst, although there is near unanimity in the business community about the value of purpose in driving performance, less than half of the executives surveyed said their company had actually articulated a strong sense of purpose and used it as a way to make decisions and strengthen motivation. Only a few companies appear to have embedded their purpose to a point where they have reaped its full potential.[13]

In Australia today, two of our four societal institutions—business and not-for-profits—are trusted to be both ethical and competent.[14] The ability of both sectors to work together on a common purpose will determine the social and environmental impact that can and will be achieved. *PurposeFull* gives the roadmap needed to do so.

After thirty years of working in the private and not-for-profit sectors, alongside governments in Africa, Australia, Europe and Asia, I have been privileged to work for purpose-driven organisations and have learnt much from many inspiring people—from villagers up in the hills with three-thousand-year-old rice terraces in northern Philippines forming a credit cooperative to safeguard them from traffickers offering cash loans for their children; to young people recovering from chronic drug and alcohol issues serving the head of the government department that funds their rehabilitation program his daily flat white; to farmers in Bosnia tending their fields at night to avoid snipers while they plant seed potatoes donated by the German people; to multinational corporate managers weeping in front of child brides in Uganda; to Indigenous trainee chefs passionately showing off their culture to a hundred corporate CEOs through the stories of native ingredients in their dishes; to the retired builder treating young trainees with tough love on their first day on a construction project in Melbourne, as their first job and the first time they have been treated as someone other than a welfare recipient.

Using my experiences across the globe and the latest research, this book articulates and explains why *PurposeFull* organisations are the defining business model and the competitive advantage for both the private and not-for-profit sectors, and how these organisations can deliver outstanding outcomes to all their stakeholders.

I believe that *PurposeFull* organisations will be at the heart of both our society and economy into the future with their constituents, customers and clients as the engine of social, economic and environmental change.

Why PurposeFull?

> It is wonderful what great strides
> can be made when there is a
> resolute purpose behind them.
>
> *Sir Winston Churchill*

It wasn't the seventy-year history, slick tailored suits, best salaries or its reputation as a driven, global and progressive firm that only took the best graduates that got me at the information session at my university, my ninth in two weeks (well, there was free food and drink at each session).

At the end of sixteen years of education and a serious lack of disposable income, it was the mention of getting paid to travel. The induction course was in Spain. After that, the global training college in Chicago beckoned.

Having spent the previous summer as an intern at Peat Marwick (now KPMG), I at least had a track record of photocopying, filing and making coffee (thankfully though the brown suit didn't last) and I was invited to join *The Firm*.

In the beautiful city of Segovia, we had a Greek history lesson and learnt the eternal truth of the self-fulfilling prophecy—our belief in the outcome will ensure it comes true. In other words, we have the power to determine our own destiny. Armed with this belief, we have an unshakeable confidence in our abilities and endless optimism.

This was heady stuff for the thrusting, competitive and gifted young executives. We were told that we were the top two per cent of the population. We felt like the masters of the universe. The world was at our feet.

Rather than a cape, the strict dress code demanded dark Italian-made suits, tailored white shirts, silk ties and leather-soled business shoes.[15] In four weeks, we had successfully been reincarnated as Andersen Androids. We were devout followers of the Andersen Way. We were *The Firm*.

The accountancy firms operate a pyramid scheme. The grunts, as we were known, are at the bottom and do most of the work, led by a supervisor, who reports to a manager, who is accountable to a partner. As each level has less people, competition is fierce to make the next grade with the race to generate the most chargeable hours and so the most profit for the partners—who decide who gets promoted.

On a diet of work, eat, study, sleep, repeat, I didn't see much daylight for four years, but loved The Firm's philosophy of pushing responsibility down as far as possible. I was a supervisor at the end of my first year, on the audit of Taylor Made, the golfing supplies company, a year ahead of my friends in other firms.

Over the next four years, clipboard in hand, I went down London's sewers to inspect the repairs, binged on free rejected chocolate bars at Mars in Bendigo, picked up a police car's flashing light at Bosch in Germany, glimpsed into the brave new world of information technology at Oracle, and got to understand more about the world of agribusiness than I ever wanted to know (of which, more later).

I revelled in the approach The Firm had to always look for improvements in the business during the audit, not as a value add to justify the fees, but as a genuine way to develop and harness our expertise and support our client. We were expected to develop a knowledge of the business's industry, as well the company itself, and produce a 'Blueback' report to management of our findings, which Arthur had introduced fifty years earlier as a first for the profession.

This was the era of Reaganomics and Thatcherism—market deregulation, small government, lower taxes, labour mobility, fee-for-service social services and education, and the liberation of the entrepreneurial spirit. With Margaret Thatcher's view of *'who is society? there is no such thing!'*, the individual was freed from the shackles of regard for others to go forth, beat the competition and claim their prize. Gordon Gecko decreed that *money never sleeps* and *greed is good,* and the US stock market averaged a handsome seventeen per cent annual return.

These entrepreneurial juices were also flowing at The Firm, in what would demonstrate the culture of unaccountability, arrogance and greed that fifteen years later would lead Arthur Andersen to its demise at the hands of the US authorities.

To mark the end of the audit, the manager hosted a celebratory dinner to thank the audit team and the client's staff. The cost of the dinner was billed to the client in their audit fees as sundry incidentals. In a 'work hard, play hard' culture these dinners became folklore. The goal was to beat the record for the highest amount spent per person. The choicest restaurants with the most expensive food and drink were the order of the day, and the subject of much gossip and status around the office.

Looking back, there was cult-like belief in the Andersen Way with the overriding purpose to induct more and more Andersen Androids to the sect. This introspective culture meant that there was a growing gap between the expectations of the outside world, including clients and regulators, and the behaviours displayed by the partnership. At the end, The Firm was indicted over Enron by the US Assistant Attorney General Michael Chertoff, who 'was infuriated by what he saw as arrogance and a lack of desire to change'.[16] Five months later, The Firm ceased to exist.

Having qualified as a chartered accountant and desperate to see more of the world, my next stop was managing KPMG's practice in West Africa, based in The Gambia. In addition to the setting for Alex Halley's *Roots*, with hot dry weather for eight months of the year, the country's beaches are home to Scandinavian tourists as cheaper than heating their homes in their winter. I don't know what was more perplexing to the Gambians—underwhelmed African Americans wandering around looking for signs of their heritage or large, topless, pale women grilling themselves on sun beds. Being ever enterprising, the latter did provide a lucrative business opportunity for toned young Gambian men offering sex at a very affordable price.

KPMG came with a suite of manuals and a different feel. All KPMG offices were required to be operated the same way and to the same quality. It shouldn't matter if you walked into the Birmingham, Baltimore, Bangkok or Banjul offices.

The enormity of this task started with the oversized international brand manual. With no sign writers in the country, we got a local artist to paint the KPMG logo on the front of the office, which somewhat resembled the required slanted boxes and shade of blue, especially from a distance.

The emphasis on quality, not maximising profit from each job, enabled time to build relationships, focus on what was important to the client and ensure the work was thorough. Alongside the statutory compliance requirement of the audit, I genuinely felt that the purpose of the firm was to support clients to achieve their goals.

This translated into anything I could do to add value across West Africa—designing menus for beachside cafes, privatising a national bank for the government to comply with the conditions of World Bank financing, running a national airline as administrator, modelling timetables for a State-owned bus company, re-establishing a national audit office (after the director had left the country after raiding the agency's bank account), assessing local partners for international not-for-profits, establishing the first community microcredit schemes, and reviewing international development projects funded by US and European governments.

As a small team of fifteen, we could all see every day how we were supporting business, government and communities in social and economic progress in such a poor sub-Sahel region.

But how do you instil this purpose and empower over two hundred thousand staff in 155 countries. As a purpose-led organisation, KPMG's purpose today is themed *Inspire Confidence. Empower Change* to encourage staff to recognise and celebrate the meaning and positive impact of the work they do. Partners and employees were asked to create and share digital posters, giving staff two extra paid days off if they met the ten thousand stories goal by Thanksgiving. In the end, they ended up with forty-two thousand posters.[17] With 'I combat terrorism' from their work preventing money laundering and 'I help farms grow' by supporting financing with credit systems, the tag line on the posters said: *KPMG. We're/you're here for a purpose*.

As a result, ninety per cent of staff reported an increase in their pride in KPMG and the rise in morale saw the firm jump seventeen positions on *Fortune* magazine's annual '100 Best Companies to Work' list and made KPMG the no.1-ranked Big Four firm for the first time in its history.[18]

Capitalism meets purpose

Today's companies—with separate legal personality, limited liability, transferable joint stock, delegated management and investor ownership—owe their existence to the English joint stock charters in the seventeenth century and the ability to incorporate a joint stock company under the Joint Stock Companies Act 1844, followed by the Limited Liability Act 1855.

So launched the most successful system in our history—capitalism—an economic system in which a country's businesses and industry are controlled and run for profit by private owners. This continued to be the prevailing wisdom of the twentieth century, from the Friedman doctrine, 'there is one and only one social responsibility of business—to use its resources and engage in activities designed to increase its profits'[19] to the US Business roundtable stating in 1997 that 'the paramount duty of management and of boards of directors is to the corporation's stockholders. The interests of other stakeholders are relevant as a derivative of the duty to stockholders'.

Whilst this profit motive has led to the most wealth, highest standard of living and longevity that we have ever seen, with the global poverty rate gradually declining to below ten per cent, two catastrophic and widespread systematic side effects of capitalism harm and threaten our very species—income inequality and climate change. The former was predicted by Sir Winston Churchill, who recognised 'the inherent vice of capitalism is the unequal sharing of blessings'. The latter was shown by economist Joseph Schumpeter in 1942 with 'creative destruction' leading to capitalism eating itself.[20]

Whether it is the death of workers from factory fires in Bangladesh or mesothelioma from inhaling asbestos fibres, the environmental damage caused by oil spills or burning fossil fuels to make electricity, the underpayment of wages or use of child labour, stealing the savings of pensioners or charging them fees after they have died, history is littered with the tragic results of maximising profit at the expense of people and the planet.

So, is it any wonder then that the Royal Commission into Misconduct in the Banking, Superannuation and Financial Services Industry found pervasive 'greed—the pursuit of short term profit at the expense of basic standards of honesty'[21] and in response to the Commission's interim findings, National Australia Bank argued that it did not owe its superannuation customers an 'overarching obligation' to act in their interests.

Except in this day and age not only does the customer expect to be treated with respect and fairness, the shareholders, staff, government and the wider public demand that companies act responsibly for the benefit of society and the environment, as KPMG found with lower financial returns accepted by most investors if a company always acted ethically towards customers, employees and the community.[22]

If not, the immediacy and pervasiveness of online news and social media, as well as the odd Royal Commission and Annual General Meeting, will find them out. This growing corporate activism by employees, customers, clients and the public has seen the demise of many a corporate reputation and their CEO.[23]

With the corporate wheel turning twenty-two years later, the US Business Roundtable, with 181 of America's most influential CEOs, announced an epiphany. They completely redefined the purpose of business to embrace the many stakeholder interests involved:[24]

While each of our individual companies serves its own corporate purpose, we share a fundamental commitment to all of our stakeholders. We commit to:

- Delivering value to our customers. We will further the tradition of American companies leading the way in meeting or exceeding customer expectations.
- Investing in our employees. This starts with compensating them fairly and providing important benefits. It also includes supporting them through training and education that help

develop new skills for a rapidly changing world. We foster diversity and inclusion, dignity and respect.

- Dealing fairly and ethically with our suppliers. We are dedicated to serving as good partners to the other companies, large and small, that help us meet our missions.
- Supporting the communities in which we work. We respect the people in our communities and protect the environment by embracing sustainable practices across our businesses.
- Generating long-term value for shareholders, who provide the capital that allows companies to invest, grow and innovate. We are committed to transparency and effective engagement with shareholders.

Each of our stakeholders is essential. We commit to deliver value to all of them, for the future success of our companies, our communities and our country.

This stance was reinforced by the *Davos Manifesto 2020: The Universal Purpose of a Company in the Fourth Industrial Revolution* which stated 'The purpose of a company is to engage all its stakeholders in shared and sustained value creation. In creating such value, a company serves not only its shareholders, but all its stakeholders – employees, customers, suppliers, local communities and society at large.'

This is confirmed by the ninety-one per cent of Australians who believe that stakeholders, not shareholders, are most important to long-term company success,[25] as has been widely championed by Larry Fink, the head the world's largest asset manager, BlackRock, saying 'purpose is not the sole pursuit of profits but the animating force for achieving them. Profits are in no way inconsistent with purpose—in fact, profits and purpose are inextricably linked'.

Purpose matters. In a global survey, at least eighty per cent of executives said a strong sense of purpose drives employee satisfaction, enables the organisation's ability to transform, delivers higher quality products/services and creates greater customer loyalty.[26]

A 2018 survey of the top US Fortune 1,000 CEOs and C-suite executives found that four in five agree that a company's future growth and success will hinge on a values-driven mission that balances profit and purpose; and three-quarters believe these companies will have a competitive advantage over those that do not.[27]

Meanwhile, a study of eight thousand global consumers and seventy-five companies found that ninety-four per cent of consumers said it is important that the companies they engage with have a strong purpose. Eighty-three per cent said companies should only earn a profit if they also deliver a positive impact. However, only thirty-seven per cent of consumers believe companies today have a clear and strong purpose.[28]

Similarly, in 2020, Deloitte found that seventy-nine per cent of businesses regarded 'fostering a sense of belonging in the workplace was important to their organisation's success in the next 12–18 months, but only 13 per cent said they are very ready to address this'.[29]

Purpose also enables improved financial performance with purpose-led companies being found to 'outperform the market by 5–7 per cent per year, grow faster and have higher profitability'.[30] According to the Global Leadership Forecast 2018, purposeful companies outperform the market by forty-two per cent.[31]

This shouldn't be surprising, we just needed to heed Jim Collins and Jerry Porras in 1994, who found that visionary companies, 'who have woven themselves into the very fabric society', performed six and fifteen times better than their comparison companies and general market, respectively, between 1926 and 1990.[32]

However, whilst a global survey of executives found that there is near unanimity in the business community about the value of purpose in driving performance, less than half of the executives surveyed said their company had actually articulated a strong sense of purpose and used it as a way to make decisions and strengthen motivation. Only a few companies appear to have embedded their purpose to a point where they have reaped its full potential.[33]

At the same time, with reputations at risk and CEOs jumping on the purpose train, companies are turning to their marketing department to come up with a desperately needed purpose or a revamped corporate social responsibility strategy to advertise their renaissance. The result can be readily exposed as tokenistic *virtue signalling* or *purpose washing*, as PepsiCo found out when their Join the Conversation advert was accused of trivialising Black Lives Matter and was forced to withdraw it with a public apology.

Through six steps, this book outlines how business can truly be *PurposeFull* and harness this competitive advantage to achieve better financial returns alongside social and environmental outcomes by engaging all their key stakeholders.

Rediscovering purpose

Not-for-profits face their own challenges with declining public trust; falling fundraising returns in an increasingly competitive market; loss of government funded services to budget cuts, mainstreaming of service systems and private sector competition; ageing supporter bases; and generating sufficient margins to finance its core operations and essential IT systems.

Government is officially agnostic in the tendering of its services between for-profit and not-for-profits. It adheres to strict procurement policies and processes to ensure transparency and value for money for the taxpayer. In reality, however, it views the private sector as more competent as responsive, accountable and cost efficient in spending taxpayer's money to deliver its services. At the same time, business doesn't answer back or publicly criticise government.

Most charities started life as one or a small group of people that saw an abuse of human or environmental rights or insufficient services to address needs, combined with the unwavering belief that this right and need should and could be addressed. This could be the right to adequate health, shelter, education, food, employment or care to alleviate poverty, homelessness, suffering and enable justice, dignity, safety and opportunity.

They built relationships, influenced, listened to their constituents and grew a supporter base, seeking more support and resources for their work to meet the need. They behaved as networks and were outspoken on the tragic circumstances, desperate need and their innovative solutions.

As more people heard about them, they got more referrals, outstripping their ability to raise the donations needed to fund the rising cost. After going to see their local parliamentarian, they were advised to seek government funding and decided to work with established government funded agencies, as well as, tender for their own government service contracts.

As time went on, the proportion of government funding increased and they became more structured and professional, in line with government standards and public expectations. Now reliant on the public purse, they were reluctant to speak up against the government for fear of biting the hand that feeds them.

With a growing emphasis on risk management, the outputs demanded from government increased and the services covered a broader cohort. The not-for-profit's staff found themselves working with larger and more impersonal caseloads, rising administration and a declining proportion of the clients that they originally worked with. Staff felt compromised when they were not able to give sufficient time to utilise their skills to achieve the best outcomes for the people they supported. They increasingly felt like the government bureaucrats that were managing them more closely.

The pressure of more deliverables with the same or less funding (especially if not indexed annually) resulted in cost cutting to those organisational activities that did not contribute to the contracted outputs, such as research and evaluation, leaving the not-for-profit less capable of measuring its outcomes or impact. The proceeds of its fundraising, which were previously used to finance innovative pilots and partnerships, now had to contribute to the shortfall in the funding needed to deliver its contracted services. As a result, fundraising became a lot harder, competing against new and exciting initiatives promoted by competitors.

The agency had to spend more on marketing to try to keep up, but as donations fell, administration and fundraising cost ratios rose, making the not-for-profit even less attractive to prospective supporters.

The fixed-term service contracts, constant restructuring of their government department and political cycles meant that the board, management and staff were in a state of perpetual uncertainty and anxiety for their income, jobs and clients, not knowing if the contracts would change or be renewed. This made long-term planning impossible.

The charity had changed from a networker to a producer as a service provider displaying many of the traits of its government masters and ever more trying to match its not-for-profit and private sector competitors in a zero-sum game. The focus was now on achieving short-term contractual outputs rather than sustained, long-term impact in order to fulfil its purpose.[34]

Meanwhile, to reduce administration and risk, and with the cost of its services rising above the growth in revenues, the government had to reform its services by mainstreaming and amalgamating with a smaller number of larger contracts that structured funding according to outcomes achieved or 'payment by results'. These contracts created a wider scope of services and larger geographical areas, payment in arrears, reduced margin for administration and profit, and shifted even more risk to the contractor. These larger contracts suited bigger organisations that could finance the higher cash flow needed, minimise operating costs by investing in new operating systems, offer less generous working conditions and absorb the outcome risk.

The not-for-profit tells the government that it is not in a position to tender for the next contract, resulting in cuts to services and staff redundancies, along with donor and community disillusionment and mistrust.

In 2014, then executive director of the Brotherhood of St Laurence, Tony Nicholson, voiced this concern. 'If we don't begin to re-think now, the way we operate, the next two decades will witness the sector's gradual demise'.[35] His premise was that not-for-profits cannot continue to meet society's current and emerging needs, and so fulfil their purpose, by contracting to the government and, in doing so, having to become ever bigger, efficient, professional and subject to regulation.

Tony concluded that, ultimately, in being beholden to government for their funding and authority to deliver their services, they will die. If not now, at some point in the future they will not be big, efficient or professional enough to win the government's favour. In the meantime, the gap inevitably widens between the needs of its constituents and the response of the government's prescribed and regulated services delivered by the not-for-profit.

I don't blame the government decision makers. Public visibility and expectations are high and there is constant budget pressure with ongoing departmental and service cost savings required.

Whilst this approach has introduced monitored quality standards and enabled consistency of service delivery, the reality is that it has seen the defunding and demise of smaller, locally appropriate, expert services run by not-for-profits that effectively addressed the specific needs of a section of the community, usually those most in need with high and complex needs.

Tony Nicholson's prediction does not have to come true. Just because not-for-profits are founded on a purpose doesn't mean they are *PurposeFull*. This book articulates six steps to demonstrate that *PurposeFull* is the very competitive advantage not-for-profits need to flourish and achieve the long-term sustainability they desperately seek, along with lasting outcomes and unique impact.

At the very least, it will challenge, and hopefully change, the perception that not-for-profits are amateurs and need to be professional and efficient like business, be judged on irrelevant cost ratios, not seen as a career choice by the best and brightest, nor underfunded by governments.

We will see that *PurposeFull* does not mean not-for-profits becoming a business. Far from it. As Jim Collins noted 'we must reject the idea—well intentioned, but dead wrong—that the primary path to greatness in the social sectors is to become more like a business'.[36]

A broad church

Whilst the private and not-for-profit sectors are treated separately here, in reality, most organisations are companies under the Corporations Act 2001 with the former limited by shares and the latter limited by guarantee. The members and guarantors have the same limited liability to the value of their shares or guarantee.

The only legal difference is that not-for-profits cannot distribute their income or assets, including on winding up, to their members (except in good faith for goods, services, expenses provided at least at fair and reasonable rates).

Many Australian companies, such as Atlassian and the Macquarie Group, have a corporate foundation that is established as a trust or company and financed by a gift of cash or shares and a percentage of sales or pre-tax profits. They can also receive government or other foundation grants, fundraise and match workplace giving donations from staff.

The corporate foundation can be registered as a charity to be income tax exempt and attain status as a public benevolent institution (for exemption from the Fringe Benefits Tax for staff) and deductible gift recipient (to allow donations of $2 and more to be tax deductible by the donor).

Unlike the United States or United Kingdom with their fifty-four hundred benefit corporations and fourteen thousand Community Interest Corporations, respectively, Australia does not have a form of incorporation that requires directors to consider the social and environmental impact of their decisions in addition to the shareholders' pecuniary interests. The closest currently is voluntary certification as a B Corporation, which is outlined later.

I subscribe to Peter Drucker's view that *not-for-profit*, and the US equivalent *non-profit*, are negative terms which only tell us only what we are not.[37] In fact, NFL (*Not-For-Loss*) is a better term given that profits, or surpluses, are needed to generate the cash flow needed to invest in people, systems, infrastructure and innovation, as the private sector well understands.

This book illustrates that all organisations, irrespective if they are for-profit or not-for-profit, can be *PurposeFull*. To do so, the following chapters outline six steps:

1. Begin with Belief
2. Live the Dream
3. Demonstrate Impact

4. Work for Change

5. Partner with Purpose

6. Evolve or Else

These six steps are supported by *Starting Guides* at the back of the book which outline the range of actions a company can take to commit, join, engage, employ, train, buy and give to gender equality, diversity and inclusion, Indigenous rights, environmental sustainability, poverty and homelessness, health and animal welfare.

Begin with Belief

We dig beneath the archaeological strata of vision and mission, purpose statements, values and promotional videos to unearth the underlying timeless and closely held beliefs that the organisation stands for. These beliefs are inherent in the way the organisation was established and behaves. The discovery process entails a bottom-up consultation with all the stakeholders of the organisation, including staff, volunteers, customers, clients, board directors, government, suppliers, supporters, investors, financiers, donors, partners, shareholders, members and the community involved.

These beliefs anchor the organisation in these uncertain and changing times, power the purpose, provide the basis for strategic decision-making, drive positive culture and behaviours, demonstrate responsibility and impact, strengthen the brand and customer or client loyalty, develop better products and services and enable enhanced performance.

Live the Dream

Because *PurposeFull* organisations engage a wide range of key stakeholders, not just shareholders, the belief and purpose need to be able to be consistently and visibly realised across constituent groups. If not, a reality gap grows between what it espouses and what it actually achieves, leading to disillusionment and dissatisfaction, the loss of staff, customers and clients, and even the social licence to operate.

Demonstrate Impact

The measurement and reporting of impact is not only essential to demonstrate effectiveness, it enables staff and stakeholders to feel part of achieving the organisation's belief and purpose, creates new financing opportunities to scale up, and drives improvements and innovations in products and services.

Work for Change

The greatest impact *PurposeFull* organisations (PFOs) can make is to influence the positive change of community perceptions, government policy and systems that are aligned to their beliefs and purpose. To do so, PFOs must engage and galvanise stakeholders across sectors to develop and advocate for evidence-based solutions.

Partner with Purpose

No one organisation or sector can address the social and environmental challenges we face today. *PurposeFull* organisations need to be networkers, not just producers, and form mutually beneficial partnerships across the private, government and not-for-profit sectors.

Evolve or Else

In these times of unprecedented change, *PurposeFull* organisations are able to reduce the risks and weather the storms, recognise and take advantage of opportunities, be agile and adapt to the changing circumstances.

We will see in the next six chapters how businesses and not-for-profits have (and have not) harnessed these stages to thrive as *PurposeFull* organisations.

Begin with Belief

I want to work for a company that contributes to and is part of the community. I want something not just to invest in. I want something to believe in.

Dame Anita Roddick, founder of The Body Shop

In the entrance to the Intrepid Group's offices is an unavoidable glowing neon sign that reads '*change the way people see the world*.'

Like generations of travellers before them, Darrell Wade and Geoff (Manch) Manchester experienced the way travel can change the way we see the world and can benefit both the traveller and the communities they visit.

As bad employees but good travellers, they took the odd year off between jobs to travel around Asia or Africa as backpackers on $10-$15 per day. Ten years after having met on their first day at university, Darrell and Manch bought a tip truck from the local council, fitted it out and put it on a Polish ship to London. On Manch's truck driver's licence, they took fourteen travellers paying $2,000 each on a fourteen-month trip through Africa.

On the truck one day, they talked about people that didn't have the time or confidence to plan such trips. They discussed how people could combine the benefits of independent travel—

value for money, being close to culture, taking many different forms of transport, dining at local eateries, and staying in weird and wonderful places—with their limited time and experience to organise a trip.

This idea, unlike the yabby farming and the importation of microlites before it, got the thumbs up from Anna, Darrell's future wife.

Manch took the first tour to Thailand followed by Indonesia and Borneo. Their curiosity and respect for the local people and culture was infectious with the travellers engaged in the community's stories, traditions, rituals and beliefs as they went, rather than just seeing a cultural show over dinner. The adventure was experiencing and learning about other lives, as well as seeing the sights.

In 1993, they were one of the first operators to go into Vietnam, before going into China and India, and then diversifying into the rest of the world following the slowdown in Asian tourism with SARS and bird flu. Through this growth, they donated ten per cent of profits to projects in the communities they visited, augmented by matched donations from travellers to the Intrepid Foundation.

Their business idea created a new genre in the tourism industry—organised adventure travel. Thirty years later, the Intrepid Travel Group, through 'purpose beyond profit', is the largest adventure company in the world with over 400,000 travellers annually on small group, sustainable, experience-rich travel adventures in 120 countries.

A constant has been their unshakeable belief that their style of travel enables their travellers, in meeting and experiencing different people and their cultures, to appreciate both the often-surprising positive differences—such as how welcoming and accepting they are—but also how similar they are. As a result, the Intrepid travellers come back with a deeper understanding and respect for the country and its people, think and act in a different way and get more involved in the world, including returning for another trip.

Homo consumus

Whenever I join an organisation, I ask everyone what the vision and mission is. The record so far is three consecutive words. Nicely displayed in the reception and illustrated with smiling faces of clients or customers, the vision and mission are usually devised by the management team in planning workshops. A painful process with endless word smithing, the end result, albeit well-meaning, inevitably fails to capture a succinct and compelling case for the future and the purpose of the organisation, as eighty per cent of Australian employees agree.[38]

Many corporates simply aim to be the seller of choice in their market as the driver of sales and profit, translating into higher share prices and dividends to their shareholders, whether it is McDonald's that wants 'to be our customers' favorite place and way to eat and drink', Hugo Boss to 'be the most desirable fashion and lifestyle brand in the premium segment of the global apparel market', or 7 Eleven 'to maintain our position as 1st Choice in terms of customer preference and market share'.

To beat the competition and get to number one means to capture the most market share. To do so, management sets stretch goals over and above last year, which leads to a perpetual fixation on daily, weekly, monthly and quarterly sales figures.

Inventory turnover is key, so products are designed with obsolescence (such as printer ink cartridges) and billions are spent on creating and marketing the latest design trends, whether for the next season's fashion, mobile phone colours or the new model of car.

Managers, especially in sales, are incentivised with bonuses to sell more. The business has to create new differentiated products and services at higher prices and bigger margins to more customers. Whilst this can drive innovation to make our lives better, such as new pharmaceuticals, the unbridled pursuit of profit can be dangerous, as we found when the 'smartest men in the room' took Enron from an energy supply company to a major dealer in complex energy products and financial derivatives, until it became able to hide billions of dollars in debt from failed deals and projects to become the largest bankruptcy in US history.

The creation of other financial instruments to make money, such as the repackaging of sub-prime mortgages with a poor credit history into mortgage-backed securities and collateralised debt obligations that concealed the risk of mortgage default, led to the 2008 Global Financial Crisis after becoming worthless due to the dramatic increase in those underlying mortgages defaulting and foreclosing when the favourable initial terms expired, home prices fell, and adjustable rate mortgage interest rates were reset higher.

To increase profit margins there is constant pressure on reducing costs, especially the most expensive item—labour. As a result, over the decades, labour-intensive manufacturing has moved offshore to cheaper wage countries. To reduce fixed costs with permanent employees, we are seeing more temporary and insecure work arrangements, such as casual contracts, with limited or no access to paid leave, irregular and unpredictable working hours, unpredictable pay, and a lack of voice at work on wages and conditions. The result is record underemployment.

We are all consumers. Encouraged by our governments to spend, together with the four years of our lives we spend watching commercials, we buy more stuff to help our economy grow, have jobs for us and our children, and keep our social services going.

We are addicted to consumption, as Clive Hamilton and Richard Denniss noted in their seminal book *Affluenza,* 'our houses are bigger than ever, but our families are smaller. Our kids go to the best schools we can afford, but we hardly see them. We've got more money to spend, yet we're further in debt than ever before'.[39]

To buy more stuff we must work longer. Australia has one of the longest working hours per worker in the Organisation for Economic Co-operation and Development (OECD) countries, just behind Japan and twenty-two per cent more than Germany. It is now un-Australian to say we are not busy, leading to 3.2 billion hours of unpaid overtime worked a year, 134 million days of annual leave accrued, 3.8 million of us not taking a lunch break and 7.4 million adult Australians not getting enough sleep. It is no wonder that stress and anxiety have risen to be the top of our growing mental health issues.

Three billion people worldwide now belong to the 'consumer class'—the group of people characterised by diets of highly processed food, desire for bigger houses, more and larger cars, higher levels of debt, and lifestyles devoted to the accumulation of non-essential goods. This number will grow to five billion by 2030.

As a result, we now live in a world in which more people are obese than underweight[40] and most of the world's population live in countries where obesity kills more people than being underweight. This consumption and our rising population are devouring our planet's resources in increasingly destructive volumes. To maintain our current appetite for resources, we would need the equivalent of 1.75 Earths. If everyone lived like Australians, we would need 5.2 Earths.

Is this really the world we want to, or can, live in?

Buy the product, be the change

Sitting on bean bags in the blue-sky room, there were blank faces gazing at the clouds above after I asked the same question on vision and mission of the head office team.

Former marketing manager, Graeme Wise, and social worker, Barry Thomas, had together built The Body Shop Australia and New Zealand into a formidable world-leading franchise based on Dame Anita Roddick's founding beliefs of animal rights through no animal testing, reusing and recycling (from the post-war frugality of her Italian migrant parents), natural ingredients and the celebration of each person's unique natural beauty, irrespective of their shape, age or size.

From postcard campaigns to ban battery hens to the generously proportioned doll dubbed *Ruby* for the self-esteem campaign ('there are 3 billion women who don't look like supermodels and only 8 who do'), to not using beautiful people in advertising, to celebrating ageing ('if you really didn't ever want to get wrinkles, then you should have stopped smiling years ago!'), these beliefs were the DNA for The Body Shop's owners, staff, suppliers, customers and partners, founding a worldwide movement of conscientious, committed and passionate customers.

We eventually found a framed and lengthy corporate vision and mission in the basement which made little sense. Instead, the beliefs were put, loud and proud, on the entrance pillars of the shops so everyone walking in would see them: Protect Our Planet; Against Animal Testing; Support Community Fair Trade; Activate Self Esteem and Defend Human Rights.

To paraphrase Mahatma Gandhi, all of us, by harnessing ourselves and our organisations, have the belief that we can be the change we want to see in the world. According to leading social researcher, Hugh Mackay AO, the desire for something to believe in is one of the ten desires that drive us.[41] This underlying belief in change creates a powerful purpose and the momentum for a *PurposeFull* organisation.

It is not surprising then that most PFOs have been founded on a belief.

The first *PurposeFull* organisations at the start of the European settlement of Australia in the 1850s, such as the city missions, were established by the belief that the rapidly growing city dwellers should be living in accordance with Christian ordinances, as well as the Christian belief to help the poor enshrined in Jesus' teachings.[42] In turn, religious faith led to the widespread belief in fundamental human rights, leading to the Geneva Declaration of the Rights of the Child of 1924 and the 1948 Universal Declaration of Human Rights.

Whether it is the Smith Family's belief that 'every child deserves a chance', Launch Housing's belief that housing is a basic human right that affords people dignity and everyone has a right to a home, or Variety's belief that all kids deserve a fair go, the belief in human rights forms the basis of social justice that underpins many *PurposeFull* organisations.

Indeed, the belief that all people should be free to have and express their own beliefs has led to a number of *PurposeFull* organisations, most notably Amnesty International which states that 'we believe that together, we can create a world where our most basic human rights are enjoyed by all'. Supporting LGBTQIA+ young people and their mental health, Minus18 believes in an Australia where all young people are safe, empowered and surrounded by people that support them.

The belief that diseases, from cancers to dementias to malaria, can be cured lies at the heart of many health *PurposeFull* organisations, be they not-for-profits raising funds, medical institutions carrying out research or companies developing treatments.

The power of belief has also been shown by sporting organisations since Pheidippides picked the short straw and ran his first and last long-distance event from Marathon to Athens in order to bring the news of a Greek victory over the Persians.

As the most successful sports team in history, the All Blacks harness the central tenants of Māori beliefs to enable personal meaning to a higher purpose. Better people make better All Blacks. It is encapsulated in *mana*, the ultimate goal of great personal prestige and character, possessing strength, leadership, great personal power, gentleness and humility.[43]

South African rugby team's first black captain, Siya Kolisi, had the belief that a win by his side in Rugby World Cup 2019 final in Japan would unite his country, as Nelson Mandela had done when the Springboks won in 1995 after fifty years of apartheid. 'Since I've been alive, I've never seen South Africa like this', Kolisi said. 'Now, with all the challenges we have been through we're not playing for ourselves anymore; we're playing for our people back home'.

The Springboks routed favourites England 32–12 to lift the Webb Ellis trophy. As the All Blacks mental skills specialist Gilbert Enoka noted 'the more you play for, the better you play.[44]

As we will see throughout this book, businesses are increasingly discovering and embedding their social and environmental beliefs across all their stakeholders for their competitive advantage, sustainability and performance, together with safeguarding their social licence to operate.

Whether it is the public exposure of unacceptable treatment of women leading to the belief in women's rights, visible effects of climate change leading to the belief in environmental sustainability, the lack of Closing the Gap progress leading to the belief in Indigenous rights, passing a beggar on the street on the way to work leading to a belief in ending homelessness, an employee suffering mental health or cancer leading to the belief in finding a cure, or customers complaining of your packaging damaging marine life leading to a belief in animal welfare, this book provides a six-step methodology with starting guides to join the growing businesses becoming *PurposeFull*.

Because it is hard wired in us for something to believe in, engagement in the PFO's belief attracts staff, funders and followers, and enables the belonging, passion, commitment and support that defines PFOs.

The power of humanity

The world's largest PFO was created by a Swiss businessman, Henri Dunant, in 1863. Whilst on business, he experienced the influx of casualties coming into the Italian town of Castiglione delle Stiviere from the nearby Battle of Solferino where 300,000 Austrian and Allied soldiers fought for fifteen hours. Dunant was appalled at the unnecessary suffering and death during and after the battle due to the lack of people and organisation to distribute the food, water and medical supplies. He successfully formed local volunteer groups to do so, and in his memoir, called for societies of trained volunteers to care for wounded combatants in times of war.[45]

In the face of each side letting wounded enemy soldiers die rather than being cared for, and with a Judaeo-Christian background, Dunant's fundamental belief that all wounded combatants should receive the same treatment led to the 1864 Geneva Convention, the universally recognised rules of war.

Now in 190 countries, the Red Cross and Red Crescent movement is the largest non-government organisation, comprising millions of staff, members and volunteers.

With a rifle pointed at my face, I experienced the power of the Red Cross and Red Crescent movement in Croatia and Bosnia in 1993 and 1994 during the conflict.

I worked for the Lutheran World Federation, whose emergency program remit was to support the over two million internally displaced people to return to their communities to resume their lives. This approach represented the organisation's belief in self-determination for those affected by the war, creating opportunities for them to restart and repair their lives.

With the harsh winter approaching, travelling with a United Nations convoy of humanitarian supply trucks, we drove through central Bosnia. Every building had either been destroyed or had lumps taken out by shells and bullets. The solid brick and concrete walls looked like rocks had been thrown into melted ice cream. As we drove along, we saw the appalling state of children on the streets, many with tattered clothes and bare feet.

A year before, President Izetbegović had ordered all male citizens between eighteen and fifty-five years of age to report to the Territorial Defence Headquarters and instructed the owners of material resources subject to registration for defence purposes to place such property at the disposal of the military. Industry was closed, except for those making supplies for the army. Women, children and the elderly were left alone with no source of income.

We finished the day at the Tuzla Hotel and walked in to find a dimly lit floor strewn with mattresses and were told to stay away from the windows. Being the only multistorey building in the area, the hotel was a favourite for target practice, as we heard that night.

The next day, we drove past a clothing factory and popped in to see if we could purchase clothing for these children. The gate was locked shut and the place appeared deserted. I pressed the buzzer anyway, and to our surprise the factory manager came out to the open the gate. With nothing getting through the front lines, except limited humanitarian aid, and stocks of materials being sequestered for the military, the factory had to cease production and send the women workers home without wages. The men had already been conscripted for the army.

Out of a sense of duty, he explained that he still came in every day. I asked him whether, if I could get fabric to him at no cost, he could ask the women workers to come back and we could pay piece rates so they would make and distribute warm clothing for the children for the winter. He smiled and we shook hands.

After we got back though, the United Nations convoys stopped. They were no longer being allowed through the front lines. In hope, I bought up all the off-cut rolls of fabric in Zagreb I could find, no matter the colour or textile.

We were working with the Red Cross on using their design to locally manufacture fifty thousand wood burning stoves for central Bosnia for the winter and two months later, we got word from them that a Red Cross convoy might get through. I sent the fabric to their depot, explaining the arrangement with the factory. A month later, the convoy had permission and the Red Cross truck turned up at the Tuzla factory to the tears of joy of the waiting manager.

A brief belief

On our bedroom wall hangs a painting. A gift from my time in West Africa, it shows a proud and beautiful baobab tree silhouetted against the sunset. Native to Africa, the baobab has a thick long trunk and can look like it is planted upside down with what appears to be the roots as its branches. If you look closely at the picture, some of the ends of the branches have hands waving and the trunk has a face. It reminds me of the layers and richness of the African culture and community that I had the privilege to experience for three years. To quote Einstein, 'the more I learn, the more I realize how much I don't know'.

The baobab is a remarkable tree. A prehistoric species which predates both mankind and the splitting of the continents over two hundred million years ago, it grows in the most arid landscapes and can live for up to five thousand years, reach up to thirty metres high and up to an enormous fifty metres in circumference.

It is called the tree of life for good reason. Water is stored in its trunk, its bark can be turned into rope and clothing, its seeds can be used to make cosmetic oils, its leaves are edible, its fruit are nutrient rich, and it provides shade and shelter where little else grows.

In the African culture, it also represents the spiritual centre of the village and the place for its rituals. It is the community's one constant in the midst of constant change—drought, flood, famine, disease, plague. It is the foundation of strength and tradition across the generations.

In these times of dramatic global change and uncertainty—described as VUCA, Volatile, Uncertain, Complex and Ambiguous by the US army—belief is the baobab tree for *PurposeFull* organisations.

With the 2015 Paris agreement committing 195 of the world's governments to limit global warming to well below two degrees Celsius, many companies now explicitly believe in the science of climate change and in setting science-based targets that specify how much and how quickly they need to reduce their greenhouse gas emissions to net zero.

As a collaboration between CDP, World Resources Institute, the World Wide Fund for Nature and the United Nations Global Compact, PFO Science Based Targets initiative champions science-based target setting as a powerful way of boosting companies' competitive advantage in the transition to the low-carbon economy through guidance, tools and technical assistance to facilitate the adoption of science-based targets and incentivise companies to set meaningful targets. To date, over a thousand companies have registered to take science-based climate action and five hundred companies have approved science-based targets, including eleven in Australia.

Akin to car manufacturers racing to mass produce electric vehicles in order to be in the tent of a lower emissions world, oil and gas companies have realised that they must embrace low carbon energy in their products by investing in carbon capture and storage, green hydrogen and massive deployments of wind and solar energy. The industry now even supports a climate policy it once fiercely opposed—pricing emissions of carbon dioxide.

For instance, BP's purpose is now 'reimagining energy for people and our planet. We want to help the world reach net zero and improve people's lives'. In December 2020, BP acquired a majority stake in the largest US forest carbon offset developer Finite Carbon.

The world is watching Big Oil. In May 2021, Royal Dutch Shell was ordered by a court in the Hague to slash its greenhouse gas emissions and investors forced Chevron and Exxon Mobil to do more on climate change.

Lush cosmetics has six beliefs in a *we believe statement*, including 'we believe in long candlelit baths, sharing showers, massage, filling the world with perfume and the right to make mistakes, lose everything and start again' and 'we believe that all people should enjoy freedom of movement across the world'.

In believing that its people are its most important asset, Liberty Financial 'is a community that embraces diversity and advocates for equality'. Its Women in Leadership program provides guidance for female leaders across the business with advice, training and resources, and is endorsed by PFO *Work 180*, an employment platform which pre-screens employers to see how well they support women's careers.

Universal rights

Eleanor Roosevelt is up there as one of the world's greatest human rights activists. When her husband was governor of New York, they took a small boat used by State officials to do inspections to visit the State's institutions—prisons, asylums and hospitals for crippled children. He would discuss what new buildings were needed and, as he had trouble walking due to infantile paralysis, she would go inside to see how it was run and ensure the inmates were getting proper food, medical care and sleeping arrangements.

From him, she learned to observe. In their many train journeys, Franklin would watch crops, how people dressed, how many and the condition of the cars and even the washing on the clothes lines.

As the First Lady, and despite the protocol that 'the President's wife does not go out informally except on rare occasions to old friends', she visited World War I veterans that had been evicted from their encampment by the army. Refusing to have a Secret Serviceman to accompany her everywhere, she was given her own revolver.

With the Quakers, she then went to see the appalling conditions of the coal miners in the company houses in the mining towns in West Virginia. She was told that, after deductions for rent and oil for their lamps, only a dollar was left for the week. With six children in the family, the children only had scraps that 'you or I might give to a dog'.

Eleanor liked the Quakers' model of men and women working on homestead and other projects to use their abilities and develop new skills, mirroring her past experience with her handmade furniture social enterprise to provide an occupation for young men who would otherwise leave the farms for lack of income.

Her passion for young people to have a voice, no matter their background or colour, led to the establishment of the National Youth Administration. Her advocacy that coloured people should have full civil rights led to complaints from southern senators and her strong support for women led to trips around the world to talk to and inspire women's groups, and even setting up her own press conference just for women journalists who were not getting any work.

After her husband's death, she was asked to be a US delegate on the new United Nations General Assembly from her work with the American Association for the United Nations. She believed the United Nations to be the one hope for a peaceful world. She was the only woman on the delegation and feared that if she failed all women had failed and so there would be little chance of women serving in the future.

At the United Nations, as its first chairman the year after the end of World War II, she considered her work on the Human Rights Commission her most important task. The Commission had been tasked with writing the United Nations Declaration of Human Rights and the Covenants. She set a gruelling schedule, finishing at eleven each night and completing it by Christmas 1947 despite the 'vast social and economic differences between the various countries'. The Declaration was proclaimed by the United Nations General Assembly in Paris a year later.

And all this whilst writing a daily newspaper column six days a week for the past twelve years.

As relevant today as ever, the United Nations Declaration of Human Rights set out, for the first time, the fundamental universal rights and freedoms for all, no matter nationality, place of residence, gender, national or ethnic origin, colour, religion, language or any other status. Across all member nations, it sets out human, civil, economic and social rights, asserting these rights are part of the 'foundation of freedom, justice and peace in the world'.

Australia played an important role as one of the eight nations involved in drafting the Universal Declaration, due largely to the influential leadership of Dr Herbert Vere Evatt, the head of Australia's delegation to the United Nations. In 1948,

Dr Evatt became President of the UN General Assembly, the year of the Declaration's ratification.

Over the years, the Declaration has led to legally binding international human rights treaties and the foundation for the following human rights-based beliefs that organisations can adopt.

Gender equality

Strong women leaders such as Julia Gillard AC, Sam Mostyn AO and Julie Bishop have quite rightly elevated gender equality as a national priority. The Australian Government's Workplace Gender Equality Agency (WGEA) notes that 'workplace gender equality is achieved when people are able to access and enjoy the same rewards, resources and opportunities regardless of gender'.

Whilst this applies to all genders, including those that identify as lesbian, gay, bisexual, transgender, gender diverse, intersex, queer, asexual and questioning (LGBTQI+), it is primarily focused on women who 'continue to earn less than men, are less likely to advance their careers as far as men, and accumulate less retirement or superannuation savings'. Women are also the predominant victims of domestic violence and death from men.

As well as a human right, gender equality has shown to increase organisational performance and enhances the attraction and retention of employees. A study of over a thousand leading firms across thirty-five countries and twenty-four industries found that gender diversity relates to more productive companies, as measured by market value and revenue, but only where there is the widespread cultural belief that gender diversity is important.[46]

Despite this, and fifty years since the landmark 1969 equal pay decision that first saw Australian women win the right to be paid the same as men for doing the same work, Australia's full-time total remuneration gender pay gap is 20.8 per cent, meaning men working full-time earn on average $25,679 a year more than women working full time.

The pay gap starts early with university-educated women earning less than men from the very start of their careers, for instance with dental graduates earning $10,700 more in their first full-time job if they are male and female law graduates getting $4,700 less than men. Male architects pocket a $2,400 pay premium for their first full-time job, while female scientists get $3,000 less than men with a degree in maths or science.

PurposeFull organisations can lead the way in ensuring gender equality, especially in their board and management composition, enterprise agreements (such as domestic violence being included in personal leave), flexible work arrangements, leadership behaviours and staff training, including unconscious bias.

There is a compelling business case for more women in organisations, including:

- Companies with more women in senior management score more highly on organisational criteria than companies with no women at the top.
- Companies with more women on their boards have been shown to financially outperform companies that have no women on their boards.
- Companies with women in key board committee roles (such as risk and audit) perform better.
- Women bring different leadership skills and behaviours to the table with teams being smarter, more effective and creative.[47]

Companies in the top quartile for gender diversity on their executive teams were twenty-one per cent more likely to experience above-average profitability, whilst companies with low representation of women and other diverse groups were twenty-nine per cent more likely to underperform on profitability.[48]

Environmental sustainability

Research shows that Australia can achieve net zero emissions before 2050 through the accelerated deployment of mature and demonstrated zero-emissions technologies, together with the rapid development and commercialisation of emerging zero-emissions technologies in harder to abate sectors.

Globally and in Australia, major corporations, investors and governments are already moving to align their strategies with the goal of net-zero emissions.

The pressure for businesses to take action is growing stronger and consumers are moving to support brands that take a stand. Employees, in particular millennials, are seeking to have a meaningful impact through work that aligns with their own values and investors are similarly engaged. In September 2019, an international group of institutional investors—representing some US$4 trillion in assets under management—came together as the Net-Zero Asset Owner Alliance. Collectively, these investors declared that they would transition their portfolios by 2050.[49]

However, the transition will not happen in time without strong action by every level of government, businesses, not-for-profits and families to support technology development, demonstration and deployment.

Many organisations have now made a commitment to achieve net-zero carbon emissions by 2050 or earlier, with ClimateWorks Australia recording commitments on their *net-zero momentum tracker*.

As the world's most pressing challenge that threatens our very existence, all PFOs should play their part in reducing their carbon emissions to net zero by at least 2050, and preferably earlier, with clear milestones to then, as well as use their procurement to buy from similarly committed suppliers and advocate to staff and other stakeholders to take action.

Diversity and inclusion

I'm standing on level two of the Bob Rose stand, named after the greatest player ever to play for Collingwood, showing the club's president, Eddie McGuire AM, around the new headspace centre. As he spoke, he noticed an old honour roll plaque on the wall and proceeded to spend the next twenty minutes telling us about the Collingwood heroes. I've never met a more passionate, proud, generous, knowledgeable and fierce advocate for their organisation. After finishing third last, Collingwood played in back-to-back grand finals within three years of his appointment.

Eight years later and, unfortunately, Eddie ignored crisis management 101—acknowledge, apologise and address—by inexplicably announcing that 'this is an historic and proud day for the Collingwood Football Club' in 'embracing a leadership position on equity' in the face of a damning report finding the Club's response to players and fans experiences of racism to be 'at best ineffective, or at worst exacerbated the impact of the racist incidents', leading to the conclusion of systematic racism within the Club.[50] A week later, Eddie resigned.

Racism is not confined to sport. It pervades our society. Whilst thirty per cent of Australians were born overseas in over two hundred countries and we are seen as a world leader in multiculturalism, there are increasing incidents of discrimination and racism in Australia,[51] creating an underclass of some migrant groups and leading to a self-perpetuating vicious cycle of disadvantage and discrimination.

Whilst eighty-four per cent of Australians believe that multiculturalism has been good for Australia and a majority agree that Australians should 'do more to learn about the customs and heritage of different ethnic and cultural groups in this country,' they also believe that 'people who come to Australia should change their behaviour to be more like Australians'.[52]

The COVID-19 pandemic has seen an increase in the negative sentiment towards national groups from Africa, Asia and the Middle East. Six out of ten Australians believe that 'too many immigrants are not adopting Australian values' and four in five Asian Australians have experienced instances of discrimination.[53]

In 2015, McKinsey found that companies in the top quartile for racial and ethnic diversity were thirty per cent more likely to have financial returns above their respective national industry medians.[54] Three years later, they reported that this had increased to thirty-three per cent and that the inclusion of highly diverse individuals, including LGBTQI+, can be a key differentiator among companies.[55]

Australia's non-heterosexual population aged eighteen and over in 2016 was estimated to have been 592,000,[56] including over one in five high school students. One of the greatest social advances of the last twenty years in Australia has been the decriminalisation of homosexuality, the decrease in community stigma and the increased recognition of people declaring as gender diverse. The marriage equality vote was another step on this journey with a resounding majority of Australians supporting the rights of same-sex couples.

However, discrimination, prejudice and stigma remain, leading to exclusion, abuse and harassment, with LGBTQI+ young people at least five times more likely to attempt suicide and twice as likely to self-harm.[57] Minus18 is a leading PFO for LGBTQI+ young people and a number of PFOs provide training for staff, such as Edge Effect.

Another minority group is the one in five Australians that are estimated to have a disability from genetic disorders, illnesses, accidents, ageing or a combination of these factors. To uphold the rights of people with disabilities, the *Disability Discrimination Act 1992* requires that people with disabilities be given equal opportunity to participate in and contribute to the full range of economic, social, cultural and political activities.

With the unemployment rate for people with disabilities double the national average, businesses who employ people with disabilities benefit from the diverse range of skills, talents and qualifications that people with disabilities have to offer, as well as, higher rates of retention, better attendance and fewer occupational health and safety incidents than those without a disability.[58]

With Australian workers from culturally diverse backgrounds up to three times less likely to experience their workplaces as inclusive, Diversity Council Australia has found a low level of inclusive leadership capability of senior leaders. As a result, organisations are missing out on the benefits of inclusive leadership, including improved job and team performance, higher return on income and productivity, higher levels of innovation, higher sense of employee well-being and feeling valued and respected.[59]

First Nations peoples

After the tragic death of George Floyd at the hands of a white police officer in the US state of Minneapolis in June 2020, tens of thousands turned out at rallies across Australia despite the COVID-19 restrictions. The American Black Lives Matter movement resonated here with the corresponding treatment of Indigenous people and their disadvantage, including the tragic 434 Aboriginal deaths in custody since 1991.

Since 1989, the imprisonment rate of Aboriginal and Torres Strait Islander people has increased twelve times faster than the rate for non-Aboriginal people. Half of the ten- to seventeen-year-olds in jails are Aboriginal and more than thirty per cent of all Aboriginal males come before Corrective Services.

Indigenous Australians remain the most disadvantaged of all Australians with clear disparities between Indigenous and non-Indigenous Australians across all indicators of quality of life.

As our first peoples with the oldest continuous living culture on the planet, PFOs have taken the lead in recognising Aboriginal and Torres Strait peoples and taking action with a Reconciliation Action Plan (RAP) approved by Reconciliation Australia. RAPs follow four graduating stages—Reflect, Innovate, Stretch, Elevate—and outline the organisation's commitment to Indigenous rights and reconciliation through Indigenous recognition, employment and procurement.

Poverty and disadvantage

Article 25 of the Universal Declaration of Human Rights states that 'everyone has the right to a standard of living adequate for the health and well-being of himself and of his family, including food, clothing, housing and medical care and necessary social services'.

Whilst over the last twenty-five years more than a billion people have lifted themselves out of extreme poverty and the global poverty rate is now lower than it has ever been in recorded history, the COVID-19 pandemic is predicated to have pushed seventy-one million people back into extreme poverty.[60]

The world has an abundance of resources but income inequality means the family to which you are born determines your access and share to what you need to live life. The world's richest one per cent, those with more than $1 million, own forty-four per cent of the world's wealth, whilst adults with less than $10,000 in wealth make up 56.6 percent of the world's population but hold less than two percent of global wealth.[61]

The world's income inequity is stark. The twenty-six richest billionaires own as many assets as the poorest 3.8 billion people.

In 2018, Oxfam reported that the wealth of more than twenty-two hundred billionaires across the globe had increased by US$900 billion—or US$2.5 billion a day. The twelve per cent increase in the wealth of the very richest contrasted with a fall of eleven per cent in the wealth of the poorest half of the world's population.[62]

As well as a public health crisis, the COVID-19 pandemic has had a devastating impact on poverty levels and inequality. In the United States, the combined wealth of US billionaires increased by over $637 billion to a total of $3.6 trillion whilst over forty-four million people lost their jobs.

Next to climate change, income inequality is the biggest challenge the world faces today. Its rise is bad for economies and has reduced economic growth by five per cent across OECD countries in the two decades to 2010.[63] It can lead to excessive concentration of power that becomes self-perpetuating, fraying the bonds of social cohesion and trust.[64]

In a country regarded as egalitarian, the reality of income inequality in Australia will come as a shock to many. A person in the highest twenty per cent income group lives in a household with five times as much disposable (after tax) income as someone in the lowest twenty per cent. The highest one per cent live in households that have an average weekly disposable income twenty-six times the income of a person in the lowest five per cent, meaning that the highest one per cent earns as much in a fortnight as the lowest five per cent receives in a year.[65]

The top one per cent of Australians own more wealth than the bottom seventy per cent combined.

With the growing inequitable distribution of wealth, poverty is actual increasing in Australia. Over three million Australians, or over one in eight live in poverty, including 774,000, or over one in six, Australian children.[66] In the last year, more than one in five Australians have been in a situation where they have run out of food and been unable to buy more, with three in ten of these Australians going a whole day each week without eating.[67] At the same time, 7.3 million tonnes of food valued at $20 billion are wasted every year in Australia.

Poverty is cruel and unrelenting. Poverty is a daily battle to meet basic costs, including struggling to pay for food, accommodation, clothing, education, health care, utilities, transport and recreation. The effects of exclusion and isolation, along with stress and other factors, especially family conflict and low parental education, can combine with low income to have an impact on a child's health, development and longer-term educational and employment futures.[68]

Homelessness

In such an affluent country, it is unconscionable that over one hundred thousand Australians will not be sleeping in a home tonight. With domestic violence the highest, and rising, cause of homelessness, 92,300 people who contacted homeless services in 2018 to 2019 did not get support, most of them women.[69]

Tragically, 19,500 children under fourteen years old will be homeless tonight and of the sixty-five thousand children that accessed specialist homelessness services in 2017 to 2018, almost half were due to domestic violence and family breakdown.[70]

From 2011 to 2018, homelessness increased by fourteen per cent nationally and rough sleeping increased by twenty per cent. It is now acknowledged that the Housing First model, which prescribes safe and permanent housing as the first priority for people experiencing homelessness, has efficacy as the foundation to provide ongoing support services to break the cycle of homelessness. However, there has been a lack of investment by governments in social housing for decades and, nationally, there are 140,600 applicants on a wait list for public housing.[71]

Violence against women

The United Nations Declaration on the Elimination of Violence against Women defines violence against women as 'any act of gender-based violence that results in, or is likely to result in, physical, sexual or psychological harm or suffering to women, including threats of such acts, coercion or arbitrary deprivation of liberty, whether occurring in public or in private life'.[72]

The statistics in this country paint a shocking picture. Half of Australian women have experienced violence, partner emotional abuse or stalking since the age of fifteen.[73] On average, one woman a week is murdered by her current or former partner.

With one in three women in Australia experiencing violence in her lifetime and one in five being the victim of sexual violence,[74] the Australian Human Rights Commission states that violence against women continues to be one of the most prevalent human rights abuses in Australia.

In Australia, male intimate partner violence contributes more to the disease burden for women aged between eighteen to forty-four years than any other well-known risk factors like tobacco use, high cholesterol or use of illicit drugs.[75]

It is not surprising then that domestic violence is the single biggest cause of homelessness, and the shortage in crisis accommodation for domestic violence victims often results in many women being turned away or put on waiting lists. As a result, over the last five years, there has been a seventy-five per cent increase in older women sleeping in their cars. The COVID-19 restrictions have only served to make family violence worse with more and severer incidents.

Mental health

Whilst under reported, and on the rise in every country, over one in ten of the world's population, or 792 million people, live with a mental health disorder and more than seventy per cent of them receive no treatment from health care staff.[76]

Today, three million Australians live with anxiety or depression and nearly half of us will have a mental disorder in our lifetime.[77] Suicide remains the leading cause of death for Australians aged between fifteen and forty-four, and every day eight Australians die from suicide and a further thirty people will attempt to take their own life.[78]

In economic terms, untreated mental health conditions cost Australian workplaces approximately $10.9 billion per year, comprising $4.7 billion in absenteeism, $6.1 billion in productivity and $146 million in compensation claims.[79]

Stigma is still a major issue in Australia with three-quarters of people feeling uncomfortable telling their employer that they are experiencing a mental illness.

Over nintety per cent of staff believe that mental health in the workplace is important. But, with only fifty-six per cent of staff believing their most senior leader values mental health and only fifty-two per cent of employees believing their workplace is mentally healthy,[80] PFOs have a critical role to play in acceptance and reducing stigma, providing a safe and conducive workplace and enabling timely and appropriate connection with support through their employee assistance program.

Despite the public advocacy of mental health PFO leaders such as Pat McGorry AO at Orygen and Jeff Kennett AC and Julia Gillard AC at Beyond Blue, there has been a decline of government expenditure on mental health services from $139 per person in 2013 to 2014 to $135 in 2017 to 2018, despite an average per annum increase of over five per cent in the utilisation of hospital services for mental health over this same period.[81]

Recently, however, in Victoria their advocacy has paid off, with mental health being at the centre of the Victorian 2021 budget, committing $3.8 billion over the next four years.

Chronic diseases

With worldwide obesity tripling since 1975, more than two billion adults are overweight, now exceeding those in the world that are underweight. Most of the world's population live in countries where overweight and obesity kills more people than being underweight.

In Australia, two-thirds of adults are overweight or obese with obesity rising by sixty-three per cent over the last twenty-five years to nearly one in three adults. Excess weight is a major risk factor for cardiovascular disease, type 2 diabetes, high blood pressure, sleep apnoea, psychological issues, some musculoskeletal conditions and some cancers.[82]

With an estimated 1.2 million Australian adults living with one or more conditions related to heart or vascular disease, coronary heart disease is the leading cause of death for men.[83]

Most of us would know of someone who has or had cancer. There are over one million people alive in Australia who are either living with or have lived with cancer with 132 Australians dying each day due to cancer. Even though cancer survival rates have increased and cancer mortality rates continue to drop, cancer accounts for around three of every ten deaths in Australia.[84]

Animal welfare

As one of the world's most trafficked mammals with their scales prized in traditional medicine and folk remedies, we all know now what pangolins look like now as suspect number one in the transference of COVID-19 from bats to humans. Australia is no stranger to animal trafficking with the Australian Border Force reporting that more and more Australian reptiles are being smuggled overseas in increasingly sophisticated networks.

Despite seventy-three counties ratifying the Convention on International Trade in Endangered Species of Wild Fauna and

Flora, with a value of between $7 billion and $23 billion each year, illegal wildlife trafficking is the fourth most lucrative global crime after drugs, humans and arms.

I suppose it should be no surprise that animals are treated as commodities in a food manufacturing system that uses factory farming to produce quantity of food over quality of lives. Nonetheless, it is distressing to actually see the conditions. On a tour of an agribusiness, I will never forget seeing and smelling a massive feedlot strewn over hillsides as far as the eye could see with thousands of cattle being fattened up in the last few weeks of their lives. Some animals, unable to support their own weight, just sat in their own excrement.

According to World Animal Protection, chickens served by KFC in Australia are among the millions of chickens raised in factory farms in the country, tightly packed with up to sixty thousand birds being housed in a single shed and unable to express natural behaviours such as roaming around and flapping their wings. Fast-growing breeds are used which means chickens grow to their full size in an average of just six weeks. This accelerated growth rate, combined with low light levels and insufficient space to move, can lead to serious health problems including heart and lung failure, muscle weakness and lameness.

Change is possible though.

In the first years of The Body Shop, Anita Roddick collected millions of signatures to protest against animal testing for cosmetics, resulting in the UK government introducing a ban in 1998.[85] Twenty-two years later, Australia introduced a ban on cosmetic testing on animals so that any new cosmetic ingredients manufactured in, or imported into, Australia will not be able to use information from animal testing to prove safety.

National fast food chains Grill'd and Nandos now purchase RSPCA-approved chicken, as does Coles for its own brand.

The move towards cage free eggs since The Body Shop asked customers to sign postcards twenty years ago has been slow. However, McDonald's, which uses more than ninety-one million eggs a year in Australia, phased out caged eggs at the end of 2017.

Five attributes of belief

Aligned

No organisations I know started out just to make money. The founders of the business had a product or service that they passionately wanted to produce to benefit customers or clients based on their own experiences, such as Nike's running shoes for athletes or Patagonia's steel, rock climbing pitons or Intrepid Travel's small group travel.

As the company grows, it believes, through its core business, that it can seriously tackle social and environmental causes. So, Nike goes beyond running to the belief 'to unite the world through sport to create a healthy planet, active communities and an equal playing field for all'. Yvon Chouinard sees the damage in the rocks he climbs caused by his steel pitons and moves to aluminium chocks leading to Patagonia's belief that it's their 'business to save our home planet'. Intrepid Travel takes a stand on animal rights by banning elephant rides and protects the rights of children by banning their travellers visiting orphanages.

In this way, the belief emanates from the corporate's heritage and not an attempt to invent a purpose to repair a reputation or gain market share as virtue signalling, as we will see in the next chapter.

For not-for-profits, their belief is inherent in their foundation and heritage. However, as we have heard above, it may have been buried for years under layers of government service contracts, corporate visions and missions, and marketing materials. With this book as a guide, the PFO's founding belief can be unearthed and harnessed.

Personal

Any organisation is simply a collection of people, be they employees, suppliers, customers, clients, volunteers, supporters, members and other stakeholders. A belief needs to be able to emotionally connect with all these people so that everyone engages and lives out the cause. A purpose needs to be *felt*.[86]

As a country that prides itself on a 'fair go', we care about the plight of our fellow humans in what we see as an injustice that shouldn't happen in this day and age. As an affluent Australia, how can we stand by and see more four hundred thousand children growing up in poverty, over one hundred thousand Australians experiencing homelessness tonight, mothers escaping domestic violence sleeping in their cars because there is a shortage of emergency accommodation, people dying from curable diseases, the eight Australians that will take their lives today, or the rising rates of racism and discrimination in our communities.

Overseas, modern slavery accounts for forty million people in forced labour, human trafficking, sexual exploitation, debt bondage and forced marriage, with one in four being children. Twenty thousand children will die today from diseases that we prevent in Australia, 689 million still live in extreme poverty, one in four still live without basic toilets and the same proportion of the world's population live without electricity.

Meanwhile, climate change is personal to seventy-eight per cent of Australian youth who are concerned or extremely concerned and feel very strongly that Australia is not doing enough to reduce carbon emissions. They are taking action with two-thirds switching to reusable water bottles and coffee cups, avoiding spending money on unnecessary items, and reducing household waste, water and electricity usage.[87]

So, what is personal to you and your colleagues?

Aspirational

The belief needs to be followed by 'one day' and how the world will be a better place. It is the light on the hill that people can see and be involved in as an aspirational and inspirational future that would benefit them and those they care for.

For instance, Homelessness Australia and the Mercy Foundation believe in ending homelessness, and World Vision Australia believes in eradicating extreme poverty for all people, everywhere, by 2030.

With one in two Australians having at least one chronic condition, all families have experienced suffering and death at the hands of a disease. Be it a cancer, arthritis, dementia, diabetes or asthma, we believe in a day when these diseases will be eradicated.

We all fear getting these diseases, especially later in life, which is why there are hundreds of disease-related charities which believe in finding a cure through funding research, such as the Cancer Council for 'a cancer-free future'.

On 27 September 2015, all 192 member States of the United Nations unanimously resolved 'between now and 2030, to end poverty and hunger everywhere; to combat inequalities within and among countries; to build peaceful, just and inclusive societies; to protect human rights and promote gender equality and the empowerment of women and girls; and to ensure the lasting protection of the planet and its natural resources. We resolve also to create conditions for sustainable, inclusive and sustained economic growth, shared prosperity and decent work for all, taking into account different levels of national development and capacities'.

This *Agenda 2030* is the most ambitious global cooperation yet and includes seventeen Sustainable Development Goals (SDGs) with a total of 169 targets and builds on the achievements of the Millennium Development Goals.

This time the SDGs apply to all countries, including Australia, which report to the United Nations on their progress every three years through a Voluntary National Review. Australia's report was presented in July 2018[88] and it was a privilege to sit on the Department of Foreign Affairs and Trade's advisory group with not-for-profit peak bodies and iconic Australian corporates, such as Australia Post and Qantas.

Australia's progress to the SDGs is reported by the SDG Transforming Australia Project. It notes we have much work to do in the areas of: Newstart welfare payments (SDG 1), obesity levels (SDG 2), domestic violence (SDG 5), energy and water affordability (SDGs 6 and 7), household debt, stagnant wages growth and underemployment (SDG 8), investment in research and development (SDG9), income inequality and distribution of wealth (SDG 10), housing affordability and homelessness (SDG 11), hazardous waste generation (SDG 12), greenhouse gas emissions (SDG 13), Great Barrier Reef hard coral cover (SDG 14), threatened species (SDG 15), sexual assault and prison population (SDG 16) and official development assistance (SDG 17).

Under the belief of environmental sustainability, the world's most pressing aspiration is 'holding the increase in the global average temperature to well below 2°C above pre-industrial levels and pursuing efforts to limit the temperature increase to 1.5°C above pre-industrial levels' under the Paris Agreement.[89]

Enduring

Twenty years ago, in a cold, draughty church hall the executive team of the Brotherhood of St Laurence sat down to devise the vision and mission of the venerable organisation. A much-loved national institution, the Brotherhood was founded in 1930 by Anglican priest and social activist, Father Gerard Tucker.

Famous for his preventative approach—it is better to have a fence at the top of the cliff than an ambulance at the bottom—

the Brotherhood has had a history of evidence-based, action research into the causes of poverty and disadvantage, thereby influencing government policy and practice.

From making films in the 1940s showing the appalling living conditions of the slums in inner Melbourne, to an open letter to Prime Minister Bob Hawke citing the nearly one million children in poverty published on the front page of the newspaper, the Brotherhood has been at the forefront of policy advocacy and establishing innovative responses, such as family planning clinics, family day care and social housing.

The weight of this heritage and expectation was not lost on us. The astute executive director at the time, Bishop Michael Challen, had a keen sense of, and respect for, the Brotherhood's tradition and we spent the morning talking about the ethos that underpinned the organisation.

In the end, we deliberately avoided workshopping a new vision and mission and settled on the one overriding belief that Father Tucker enshrined for the organisation from the start—*an Australia free of poverty*. This enduring belief of the Brotherhood remains today and continues to inspire thousands of people around the country.

Since 1898, Australia's first health food company and the maker of Weet-Bix, Sanitarium Health Food Company has maintained the belief that plant-based diets provide optimal health as outlined in the Bible (Genesis 1:29). Although more motivated today by climate change, over 120 years later, the number of new food products launched in Australia with vegan labelling has almost tripled in the past five years as veganism continues to rise in Australia.

The one thing I've learnt in my years in working with businesses and not-for-profits around the world is that change is slow, incremental and occasioned by setbacks. Human nature is complex, political will ebbs and flows, economic conditions fluctuate, and many factors are simply beyond our control.

Belief gives us the hope and energy to plough on despite the uncertainty, obstacles and delays. We recognise and celebrate the achievement of milestones along the way and, in doing so, we need to ensure that changes in key staff and strategies do not dilute or divert the PFO from its belief.

Engaging

In order to be lived out by all stakeholders across the organisation, the belief needs to enable people to connect and respond. We will see in this book the many ways in which people can experience the belief through the organisation.

Live the Dream

We don't want to just be the best travel
company in the world, we want to be the
best travel company for the world.

James Thornton, CEO, Intrepid Group

When I started at The Body Shop, I was really interested in *Personal Mastery*, the fourth discipline in Peter Senge's *Fifth Discipline*. As part of a learning organisation, Senge argues that personal mastery is a set of specific principles and practices that enables a person to learn, create a personal vision and view the world objectively.[90] I figured that if the person's beliefs and values align to those of the organisation then they will be more engaged, fulfilled and rewarded in their work. They will grow personally and professionally as the organisation grows.

I went across the country holding workshops in the shops after hours, asking the team what their personal values were and how the company could better live them out.

The Body Shop had a very loyal band of customers who bought their favourite products regularly and cherished the beliefs they represented. The shop staff were also passionate about the products and cared about the customers. As an important part of the customer experience, they loved to do free hand massages at the stand at the front of the shop with the creams and treat customers to a makeover with the make-up range.

However, three factors were combining to cause much angst among the shop staff. In the discussions, honesty had come out as one of the top three personal values in all but one of the shop workshops. They felt their own honesty was being compromised through a lack of honesty from the company.

Following its listing on the UK Stock Exchange, a French cosmetics industry head had come on board and started retiring a third of the products a year to introduce new products in the pursuit of sales growth and higher profit margins.

Added to this, production was being moved from the United Kingdom to South Africa causing supply shortages and difficulty in getting information on products in production and in stock, as well as delivery times. As a franchisee, The Body Shop Australia had to buy ninety per cent of its products from the international company.

Further still, the inventory system was not trusted by the shop staff when they looked up product stock amounts or deliveries on the shop's point-of-sale terminal.

The result was the shop staff couldn't tell the customer why their favourite product wasn't in the shop: it could have been retired and no longer produced, in a container on the water, in (or not in) stock in the warehouse, or being delivered to the shop. There was no reliable information from the company to tell.

Desperate not to disappoint their regular customers, they sometimes made up reasons which further comprised their honesty.

As a result of the feedback, the head of production was seconded to assist the South African factory and be a source of information, whilst stocktakes were increased to improve the accuracy of information in the inventory system.

But the retirement of products got worse as the focus on short-term profit and dividends increased and their replacements did not live out Anita's beliefs. With no refillable and less recyclable products, they were no longer saving the planet.

Self-esteem got deactivated with the introduction of anti-ageing products and photoshopped beautiful people filled marketing images. Human and animal rights got ignored with no company-led campaigns, instead preferring to support the campaigns of international development agencies such as CARE and Plan International.

Then, The Body Shop's stance against animal testing was seriously compromised when Anita agreed to sell out to French cosmetics giant L'Oréal (for which, *Ethical Consumer* magazine had given its lowest rating) having previously said, 'I hate the beauty industry, it is a monster selling unattainable dreams. It lies, it cheats, it exploits women'. Many saw Anita as selling out the beliefs of The Body Shop. Tragically, she died the following year from a brain haemorrhage, aged sixty-four.

However, the 2017 sale of The Body Shop International to Brazilian cosmetics company, Natura, offers hope for a return to a *PurposeFull* organisation with the company following its parent to be certified as a B Corporation in 2019.

Paul Polman is the poster child for *PurposeFull* organisations. As the CEO of Unilever, in 2010, he launched a radical new approach—the Unilever Sustainable Living Plan (USLP), which decoupled its growth from its environmental footprint and increased its overall social impact. Such was his focus on long-term value creation and criticism of short termism, he stopped reporting quarterly results.

Unilever's belief is that business growth should not be at the expense of people and the planet, as the true fiduciary duty of boards. This is not just in environmental sustainability, but in society's big social challenges such as inequality, unemployment and social cohesion. Without functioning communities, business can't operate.

Under Unilever's purpose 'to make sustainable living commonplace...we believe we have the opportunity—and the responsibility—to be a force for good in the world', their brands each play their own part at a scale unimaginable to not-for-profit international development agencies.

As the single most effective way of stopping child deaths, reducing the number of incidences of pneumonia by twenty-three per cent and diarrhoea by up to forty-five per cent, Lifebuoy soap has helped over one billion people around the world improve their handwashing habits, as it did when it was launched in 1894 at a time when cholera and dysentery were commonplace in Britain's slums.

Every two minutes, a child under five dies from a disease linked to unsafe water and sanitation and around 892 million people are still forced to defecate in the open. Domestos, in partnership with UNICEF, has helped over twenty-eight million people gain improved access to a toilet. With handwashing and disinfecting surfaces so important to stop the spread of infection, during COVID-19 these programs were significantly ramped up by working with governments, NGOs and communities.

Over Polman's ten-year tenure, Unilever delivered a total shareholder return of 290 per cent, and the *Financial Times* nominated him as the stand out CEO of the last decade. In reaching two billion people daily with its products over this period, Unilever has helped more than six hundred million people improve their health and hygiene, improved the livelihoods of over seven hundred thousand smallholder farmers and 1.6 million small-scale retailers, reduced its waste impact by twenty-nine per cent and now sources fifty-six per cent of its agricultural raw materials sustainably. Over half of Unilever's managers are women.

When I met the Unilever team in Myanmar, I couldn't have been more impressed with their knowledge, passion and progress on establishing these programs across the country.

This wasn't simply a company promotional exercise for them—this was them building a stronger country for their families, communities and the nation.

So, wouldn't it be life changing if Coca Cola, the world's most valuable brand outside technology, in living out its purpose 'to refresh the world', had the belief that this included the 750 million people who lack adequate access to clean drinking water and spent some of their US$4 billion annual marketing budget on advocating to governments, impact investing and supporting communities to do so.

Instead, sugar sweetened beverages (Coke, is the biggest selling) are associated with increased risk of tooth decay, obesity, type 2 diabetes and cardiovascular disease. Reminiscent of big tobacco, the company opposes the World Health Organisation's recommendation for taxes on these drinks to reduce consumption, despite evidence of falling consumption of sugar from soft drinks from the 28 countries that have implemented the tax.

The cost of income

The quest for income growth seems to be hard wired in the brains of not-for-profit management and boards because of the ongoing uncertainty over existing income with time-limited service contracts, fluctuation of fundraising receipts, government service system reforms and changing political cycles.

But the pursuit of increased revenue can also divert not-for-profit organisations from its beliefs and values.

Mission Australia was formed in 1996 by bringing together Adelaide City Mission, Hunter Mission, Perth City Mission, Sydney City Mission, Wagga Wagga City Mission and Wollongong City Mission. Brisbane City Mission followed in 1998. Understandably, I was not liked by the sector when I became the Victorian director for Mission Australia, seemingly encroaching on the territory of Melbourne City Mission which decided not to join.

Mission Australia had this and more challenges when the Commonwealth Government's new employment services tender came up. With seven hundred staff employed in the scheme and significant cash flow needed, Mission Australia came up with an innovative solution. They formed a new joint venture company with Providence USA which tendered and won a number of Job Active services, retaining about two-thirds of what Mission Australia had previously, with staff now working for the new company. This was still painful, with many staff made redundant, especially in Queensland where no services were won.

However, there was a crucial change in the new service. Instead of Centrelink staff enforcing the rules on job seekers, the responsibility was transferred to the Job Active case managers. This meant Mission Australia staff having to breach the jobseeker for not following the requirements—such as job interviews—leading to the withdrawal of their benefits, whilst Mission Australia's community services responded to the effects of the resultant poverty, homelessness, drug and alcohol misuse and mental illness.

The position was clearly untenable and to its credit Mission Australia divested its stake in the joint company and left Job Active to focus on its leading homelessness, housing, family and children and youth community services across the country.

Hip to sip

Not only has the 1.4 square kilometres of Fitzroy been home to the country's first Aboriginal legal and health services, the world's largest adventure travel company, the first youth drug and alcohol service and the world's first international volunteering for development organisation, a small tea shop that opened in Brunswick Street in 1996 ended up transforming the global tea industry.

After spending six months travelling to source homewares for a new business, Maryanne Shearer and Jan O'Connor encountered other Australian companies with very similar thoughts to their own at Frankfurt's iconic Ambiente Fair. They came home disheartened.

Whilst in New York they came across a tea-based product called Water Leaf and had subconsciously purchased many tea-related homeware samples in Europe that were now stored in their back room. On their return, they noticed there were lots of coffee shops opening up, but 'no one was doing tea'. They hit on the idea of bringing back the adventure and romanticism of tea making and tasting to Melbourne and the name, Tea Too ('Tea Two was just a little predictable'), was born three hours later.[91]

Three thousand years before, according to Chinese legend, while boiling water in the garden, a leaf from an overhanging wild tea tree drifted into Emperor Shen Nong's pot. A skilled ruler and scientist, he enjoyed drinking the infused water so much that he was compelled to research the plant further, discovering its medicinal properties.

With the belief that tea is 'wild, delightful and delicious' they set about turning one of the world's oldest beverages into something young and effervescent, attracting a new generation of tea drinkers. From tea as 'boring and for grannies', they set about creating a new 'feminine, fun and fabulous' experience.[92]

As visual merchandiser and retail architect, Maryanne and Jan were interested in the design of retail space and its effect on the consumer psyche. They set about designing the Fitzroy store to be 'welcoming, embracing and theatrical'.[93] Given the origin of tea (and because they had little money), the shop's walls were decorated with pages from Chinese newspapers and the ceiling painted pink. Forty tea blends from around the world—such a mellow mango, ruby red rosehip and fruit blush—with beautiful containers, seduced a new generation of tea drinkers.

Along with the teas, the shop sold the accoutrements that conjured up exotic places—Russian samovars, Turkish chai glasses, Moroccan tea cups and cast-iron Japanese teapots—giving the opportunity for customers to reminisce about their travel experiences.

Much like The Body Shop, the shop created passion, theatre and engagement with customers being invited to smell bowls of different teas and taste a fresh brew whilst being told the story of its origin.

T2 grew to supply three hundred cafes and restaurants across the city, before opening the T2 Tea Bar Café and Tea Emporium at Chadstone shopping centre, the largest in the southern hemisphere. Benefitting from its sourcing expertise, sustainable agricultural approach (T2 worked with Fairtrade since 2009 on the English breakfast tea blend), and global reach, in 2013, T2 was acquired by Unilever, the world's largest tea company. Seven months later, T2 opened its first London store, still with the Chinese wallpaper and with a new London Breakfast blend.

As 'a brewing force for good' and a certified B Corporation, 'every cup of T2 is an opportunity to have a positive environmental and community impact' and, with over fifty million cups of T2 sold globally annually, T2 now has one hundred per cent certified, sustainably sourced tea and tisanes and one hundred per cent certified ethically sourced tea wares and accessories. As *PurposeFull*, it makes complete business sense given that 'our brand taps into the hearts and minds of our customer. Ninety-two per cent believe that helping others defines who they are'. [94]

Back to basics

The Youth Substance Abuse Service (YSAS) was Australia's first youth specific drug and alcohol service funded by Premier

Kennett in response to the heroin epidemic in the 1990s in Melbourne, following David Pennington's report which recommended such a dedicated service.

Over the last twenty years, YSAS had built an enviable, evidence-based practice, expert youth workers, integrated quality services and outstanding outcomes for young people. I was only the third CEO and the first to come from outside the sector. In my week two, the new Coalition Victorian government announced a review into the state's drug and alcohol services, ultimately recommending its reform into place-based, consortium-delivered, mainstreamed services. Like government employment, aged care and homelessness services before it, this reform spelt trouble for specialist services that didn't fit into a one-size-fits-all model.

For a specialist state-wide service, this effectively meant YSAS would need to convince each of the twenty-six region's consortia to include them in the design and tender of the mainstream drug and alcohol services. For the health and community agencies that ran the services, this was an opportunity to get more funding, an integrated approach and, for some, to teach an arrogant and entitled YSAS a lesson.

YSAS's head of research, Andrew Bruun, had a Gary Larson cartoon on his wall. It showed a spider's web at the bottom of a playground slide. One of the waiting two spiders is saying 'if we pull this off, we'll eat like kings'. As a small PFO against the Victorian government and the state's mammoth health networks, I copied it and put it on my wall.

Over the next four years, I sat in more sector and government meetings and workshops on the service reform than I care to remember. Fortunately, the government decided to start with adult drug and alcohol services and by the time this new service model was determined and rolled out across the state, with the predicted design and funding challenges, the minister and bureaucracy had little energy and appetite left for tackling our youth services.

Given the risk, we also had to become more visible and diversify over this time. YSAS's core competency was actually working with the state's most vulnerable young people with the unshakeable belief that these at-risk young people deserved, as a basic human right, to live the lives we take for granted—of dignity, respect, supportive relationships, good health, a home, education and training, and financial independence.

So, YSAS's core business needed to be the provision of services to this cohort.

Whilst government and many health and welfare agencies saw this cohort foremost as a risk, the brilliant youth workers at YSAS, who were often indiscernible from the young people they helped, accepted them, offering non-judgemental and expert support. The drug and alcohol dependency, chronic mental health issues and antisocial behaviour typically resulted from abuse as a child and the subsequent trauma. They encountered family violence, sexual assault and alcohol and drug taking at home from an early age. It is no wonder that this becomes normalised behaviour and repeated in the next generation who make the same choices in life as they self-medicate the pain away.

One of my highlights of the year was sitting down to Christmas lunch at the residential rehabilitation service with the team and the young people remaining who had no family to safely spend the day with. The young people picked the recipes, shopped and helped the cook, Trish, put on a feast and cleaned up afterwards. They were smart and articulate and had the same aspirations for the future as their peers.

Given this core competence and the need to diversify, we formed partnerships and tendered for and won two key government services for high-risk young people: the state's only Aboriginal youth drug and alcohol residential service, Bunjilwarra, in partnership with the Victorian Aboriginal Health Service, and the integrated health service for young people in youth remand and prison, partnering with St Vincent's Hospital Melbourne and psychologist specialist firm, Caraniche.

First Nations peoples

With six out of ten Australians never having consciously met an Aboriginal person and with the premise that we can't start reconciliation without this first step, I started *Taste of Reconciliation* as an annual event which I invited senior corporate people to come and have dinner at a five-star CBD hotel to meet and ask questions of Aboriginal elders.

Three years earlier, I had joined Mission Australia who had just won a tender with the Victorian government to redevelop a derelict site in inner Melbourne into a social enterprise café to train Aboriginal young people for jobs in the hospitality industry.

The Fitzroy site had had a colourful history, housing a VD clinic after the war and then the iconic Victorian Aboriginal Health Service (VAHS), the first Indigenous health service in the country. Indeed, this suburb rivalled Redfern as the centre of Aboriginal activism in the late 1960s and 1970s after the failure of the 1967 Referendum to create real change for Aboriginal people.

African Americans had been through a similar journey. Their civil rights movement started with the Voting Rights Act in 1965 failing to legislate away racism. Aboriginal people clearly saw the parallels with their African American brothers and sisters and Australia's Black Power movement took inspiration from Malcolm X, whose autobiography showed young Kooris how to funnel their frustrations surrounding the treatment of Aboriginal people in Australian cities into constructive resistance.[95]

Unused for the past decade, the derelict building was crudely painted with the red, yellow and red stripes as the site of the unofficial Aboriginal Embassy with numerous protests starting and ending there.

Standing on the dirt floor, surrounded by rubble and gazing skyward through the vacant roof, Housing Minister Richard Wynne, VAHS CEO Jason King and I felt excited and overawed by the history and the task.

With sustainable employment the best intervention for disadvantaged young people, transitional labour market social enterprises are commercial businesses that provide training and work experience to a cohort that would not otherwise be employed in their transition to sustained mainstream employment. Crucially, from day one, it provides the environment that, for the first time, treats the trainee as a worker and not a welfare recipient. This, in itself, is often life changing.

Instead of a café with hospitality training, I wanted to aim higher. With a shortage of qualified chefs, I wanted to create a quality restaurant downstairs with trainees working with a professional team in the kitchen, plus a training kitchen upstairs, unseen by the public, to give the Indigenous young people the time and support to gain a career as chefs, rather than as lower paid and transient cooks. This also meant that the site would be a safe, one-stop-shop for the trainees with visiting trainers and support workers. I was delighted that the country's leading culinary teaching school, William Angliss Institute of TAFE, agreed to come on board.

I also wanted diners to experience Indigenous culture through the food, in the same way as my parents had done forty years before as ten-pound POMs when they went out to the local Greek and Italian restaurants for the first time.

As we had no experience running a restaurant, I needed to find a strong hospitality business partner and approached the manager of the Accor Group, which owns well-known hotels, such as Sofitel, Novotel and Mercure. He agreed to advertise the restaurant manager role internally as a secondment and development opportunity for one of their food and beverage managers, as well as providing work experience for the trainees in their hotel kitchens.

With funding from the Victorian government for the building works and equipment, the next two years of consultation with the local Aboriginal community, design, construction and fitting out were intense. In commissioning an eel trap for a hanging light from one of the two communities in Victoria permitted to make them, we inevitably offended the other, but we had no more budget left. We learnt that Aboriginal art in Victoria is not the familiar dots and circles of central and northern Australia, but lines, and we commissioned a signature piece from leading Indigenous photographer, Wayne Quilliam. Thankfully, he showed us a range of lightings of the female nude before we picked the tasteful version that sits behind the bar.

The next challenge arose under Victorian legislation, which stipulated that a company director had to hold the liquor licence, which meant a board member of Mission Australia. Not an easy sell to a PFO with a history of tackling the $14 billion of social costs of alcohol misuse in Australia,[96] including family violence, child abuse and homelessness. Thankfully, the Victoria-based director and entrepreneurial businessman, Nick Barnett, took up the challenge with the look—you better know what you are doing. I didn't, so I quickly enrolled in William Angliss's responsible serving of alcohol course, which he would need to take.

It was important that the restaurant be commercially successful to avoid draining the resources of Mission Australia (and so necessitating a new state director in the process) and ensure the closest possible work setting to a regular business. The smaller any gap, the better chance the trainee will transition successfully to mainstream employment.

I had learnt at The Body Shop that a strong commercial brand is crucial. But with six months to go to the launch, we still didn't have a name or theme for the restaurant. We convened the advisory group once again and someone mentioned a nearby laneway with a briquette factory where Aboriginal people worked and socialised, which had been colloquially known as *Charcoal Lane*, later made famous by Archie Roach.[97]

Brilliant. We had a great name and a black-and-white palette for the decor.

Unfortunately, as Daniel Flynn, the founder of thankyou, outlines below, if Australians know a business is run by a charity, they will assume it is poor quality and a higher price. Called the 'pity purchase', they buy once out of sympathy but not again.

> *Rule One: Make Great Product**
> *Rule Two: Never Break Rule One*
>
> ** Never use a good cause to sell an average product*
>
> *thankyou.*

So, following the advice from thankyou above, it was crucial that Charcoal Lane was positioned as a great dining experience first with the absence of the charity's brand in the restaurant's signage and the establishment of a dedicated website to promote the business.

To engage diners, we put a brief story on cards in the middle of the table for diners to read whilst waiting for their meals, together with more information on the website given that we needed to raise money for the training and support cost of each trainee.

We respected and continued the Aboriginal colours on the building by shining black, red and yellow through three triangle motifs in the top windows.

We wanted to avoid a patronising Aboriginal-themed restaurant and set the menu as contemporary Australian cuisine infused with native flavours. Each Indigenous ingredient has its own story, such as the Kakadu plum which has the highest natural source of vitamin C in the world and was traditionally used to treat colds, the flu and headaches.

A year later, Charcoal Lane earned a score of fourteen out of twenty in the *Good Food Guide*. Not bad, since one more point would award a coveted hat, and the team appeared in *The Age Melbourne Magazine's Top 100* that celebrated the city's most influential people.

Twelve years later, the Duke and Duchess of Sussex popped in. It's been hard to get a table since.

Back to the dimly lit Sofitel grand ballroom filled with excited guests for the Taste of Reconciliation. Although it was a venue they had frequented before, there was a decidedly nervous buzz around the room.

Despite ninety per cent of Australians feeling our relationship with Aboriginal and Torres Strait Islanders is important,[98] we can be reluctant to consciously engage with an Indigenous person for fear of saying the wrong thing or getting a guilt trip in the face of the many wrongs of the last 250 years.

There is no escaping that the European settlers have stolen the land and lives of Australia's Indigenous peoples which has led to the unconscionable suffering and the ongoing disadvantage of the First Nations people today. Almost seventy per cent of Australians accept that Aboriginal people were subject to mass killings, incarceration and forced removal from land, and their movement was restricted. However, there is a massive gap in trust with forty-six per cent Aboriginal and Torres Strait Islander people believing they have high trust towards Australians in the general community, but only twenty-seven per cent of non-Indigenous Australians reciprocate.

This is another gap we urgently need to close if we are to progress reconciliation in this country. A step in the right direction is the Victorian government's announcement in March 2021 of a Truth and Justice Commission. Named after the Wemba Wemba/Wamba Wamba word for 'truth', the Yoo-rrook Justice Commission will hold public hearings about social, economic and health disadvantage and the role colonisation and discriminatory government policy have played in fostering that disadvantage.

To ease the guests into the event, the Sofitel provided the usual five-star luxury with the menu designed by the young trainee chefs at Charcoal Lane, cooked by them with the hotel staff in the cavernous kitchen and served by them with the hotel's front of house team.

As the executives sat down, they found an Aboriginal elder sat at each table. The guests were then told by me that they would be moving tables between courses to meet other elders as well as their peers. There was a distinct sound of shifting bottoms and shuffling chairs. Always good to get people out of their comfort zone.

To set the scene, then CEO of Telstra, David Thodey AO, warmed up the corporate leaders with a stirring, from-the-heart speech on his passion for the rights of First Nations peoples and Telstra's use of digital technology to assist them. One example of which involved Machado Joseph Disease (MJD), an incurable hereditary neuro-degenerative condition which I had previously encountered at Very Special Kids. Each child of a person who carries the defective gene has a fifty per cent chance of developing the disease.

MJD starts with memory deficits, difficulty with speech and swallowing, weakness in arms and legs, clumsiness, frequent urination and involuntary eye movements, and gradually, and cruelly, leads to paralysis of the body whilst the mind remains intact. Progression to dependence occurs over five to ten years and most people are wheelchair bound and fully dependent for the activities of daily living within ten to fifteen years of the first symptoms emerging.

MJD is particularly prevalent in the Aboriginal communities in East Arnhem Land. David talked about Telstra providing computers to the MJD Foundation to build a speech bank of common phrases before sufferers lost the ability to speak. They then went on to be used for making films on bush tucker and record family histories and memories.[99]

David gave his peers a role model and the permission and inspiration to get engaged.

As the wine flowed and the delicious food served, questions like 'why aren't you black' (in reply, Wurundjeri Elder, Ron Jones, would say he was born in the daytime whilst his ancestors were born in the night) gave the opportunity for the elders to explain the history and lineage of Indigenous families.

I went on to work with David and his team at Telstra to establish their first Indigenous employment program to mainstream the recruitment, training and mentoring of Indigenous people in their divisions in a supportive and culturally safe environment.

PurposeFull organisations can play an important role in harnessing their business to support Indigenous people and businesses through an organisation-wide Reconciliation Action Plan with Reconciliation Australia, including cultural appreciation training for employees, setting employment targets, purchasing from Aboriginal businesses, recognising Sorry Day on 26 May (the anniversary of the landmark *Bringing them Home* report being tabled in the Federal parliament), engaging in a NAIDOC week event (in July) and holding an event in National Reconciliation Week (in May/June).

Diversity and inclusion

As I talked to a group of Sudanese young people in a park one day, they pointed out the unmarked police car circling. One of them had taken a video on their phone of the abusive treatment of his friend by a policeman, who then demanded his phone. He fled in fear. Clearly still petrified, having brought back the trauma of the unimaginable violence at the hands of authority that he had experienced in this home country, he pleaded with us to take his phone. They felt they were living in another police state.

Unfortunately, this was by no means an isolated case.

In the first case of its type, Flemington & Kensington Community Legal Centre and six young men took the Victoria Police to the Federal Court alleging that they were stopped, harassed and racially abused by several individual police officers between 2005 and 2009. They also stated that these incidents were part of a pattern of racial profiling that unlawfully discriminated against them in contravention of the Commonwealth Racial Discrimination Act 1975 and engaged in offensive behaviour based on racial hatred in breach of the Act.[100]

Six years after the case began, on the eve of an eight-week trial and as the Chief Commissioner was expected to give evidence, it was settled. Victoria Police acknowledged in a joint statement read out in the Federal Court that it had, in fact, received many complaints of racial discrimination.

To his credit, the Chief Commissioner in late 2013 released a three year 'Equality is not the same...' plan to eliminate racial profiling, including a review of field contact policies, a trial of 'stop and search' receipting, unconscious bias training and the setting up of stakeholder advisory groups, including the Chief Commissioner's Human Rights Strategic Advisory Committee and Young People's Portfolio Reference Group. As head of YSAS, I was a member of the latter and it was illuminating to openly talk to senior police about the issue.

We used the opportunity to take small groups of African young people and police, including a wonderful community liaison officer, Joey, on a bush retreat to role play the different perspectives, including the young people wearing police uniforms, to improve understanding, relationships and communication.

We were involved in trialling one of the measures in the plan, the piloting of stop and search receipts whereby the police officer provided a receipt that included the police officer's number and why he or she has stopped the person. The aim was to prevent arbitrary and racially discriminatory stop and searches by police, as well as assisting in tracking and documenting any racial disparities in stop and search patterns.

The upshot was that African young people were still racially profiled and stopped. Now they had a pink piece of paper to show for it. We pointed out the obvious weaknesses and thankfully, the trial was abandoned shortly after.

In the words of Leisa Hart, CEO of Disability Services Australia, 'diversity is about having a wide mix of people in the room. Inclusion is about being sure that everyone there gets treated in ways that are helpful for them, no matter what their particular sets of needs might be. Belonging is the feeling that arises if a place actually has a culture that creates genuine space and care for differences'.

ANZ's belief in having a diversity of staff for each bank branch that matches its local customer base has led to a longstanding partnership with the Brotherhood of St Laurence *Given the Chance* program to assist the company in recruiting and retaining staff with different backgrounds, including migrants and refugees.

A South Sudanese participant in the Given the Chance@ ANZ program became the top teller and exceeded referral targets because of his role as a community leader in the local Sudanese population.

Diversity and inclusion form an integral part of Australia Post's Corporate Responsibility strategy—*Everyone, Everywhere, Everyday.*[101] In working with their massive sorting and distribution centre in the south-east suburbs of Melbourne as part of a program to encourage local employment for young people of different backgrounds, I was astounded at the over one hundred country backgrounds working under one roof. At the time, the organisation itself was head up by Lebanese-born migrant, Ahmed Fahour AO.

To employ refugees and asylum seekers, the Refugee Council of Australia provides a guide for employers and PFO Refugee Talent enables organisations to hire refugees through its national database.

In most cities, there are charities that support migrants and refugees that PFOs can collect and donate household furniture and goods to help their settlement, as well as provide work experience and volunteer mentoring to achieve better education and employment outcomes.

To educate staff on the variety of religions and cultures, Liberty Financial's Our Culture and Community team hosts a series of World Expo events with external speakers that raises awareness around cultural heritage, customs and traditions which form part of the everyday lives of its staff.

To celebrate diversity in the workplace, PFOs can get involved in the annual *Taste of Harmony* event run in March by the Scanlon Foundation that encourages staff to bring in food from their background to share. Now in its twelfth year, over thirty thousand workplaces have taken part, and the website provides a handy guide to diversity and inclusion in the workplace.

Banking on purpose

The first observation made in the Final Report of the Royal Commission into Misconduct in the Banking, Superannuation and Financial Services Industry was that, in almost every case, the conduct in question was driven not only by the relevant entity's pursuit of profit but also by individuals' pursuit of gain, whether in the form of remuneration for the individual or profit for the individual's business.[102]

With many consumers doubting that banks have their best interests at heart, in its Purpose-Driven Banking Survey report, Accenture argued the case for banks to rediscover their original purpose: putting customers' interests first and helping them manage their finances more effectively, even if it means offering advice that may not immediately make money for the bank.[103]

What difference would it make if the banks were *PurposeFull* organisations?

Ten years before, I had met Mike Smith, then CEO of ANZ.

Formed in 1951 from two banks established in London in the nineteenth century, the Bank of Australasia and the Union Bank of Australia, ANZ (the Australia and New Zealand Banking Group) operates in thirty-three markets, including across the Pacific Islands.

With a purpose 'to shape a world where people and communities thrive. That is why we strive to create a balanced, sustainable economy in which everyone can take part and build a better life', two of ANZ's four target outcomes relate to improving the financial well-being of its customers and the community.

Financial literacy, as the 'ability to make informed judgements and to take effective decisions regarding the use and management of money', is central to this outcome as 'improvements in financial literacy can not only support social inclusion, but also enhance the contribution that the financial services sector makes to the nation's well-being'.[104]

The first comprehensive review of Australian adult financial literacy by ANZ in 2003 found that the lowest levels of financial literacy were associated with lower education attainment; those not working for a range of reasons or in unskilled work; those with household incomes under $20,000; and those with lower savings levels.[105]

The same year, at a conference organised by the Brotherhood of St Laurence, then ANZ CEO, John McFarlane, reiterated that 'improving savings, general education levels and financial literacy levels are perhaps more important in addressing the underbanked'.[106]

The next year, ANZ developed and launched Australia's first comprehensive adult financial education program, *MoneyMinded*, with the NSW Department of Education and Training and an advisory committee featuring nominees from the Australian Financial Counselling and Credit Reform Association (AFCCRA) and the Australian Securities and Investments Commission.

Comprising six topics, separated into seventeen workshops delivered by financial counsellors within community organisations, trained by ANZ staff, *MoneyMinded* covers planning and saving; easy payments; understanding paperwork; living with debt; everyday banking and financial products; and rights and responsibilities.

As a neutral and independent financial education program, not ANZ branded and not promoting any specific financial institution's services or products, *MoneyMinded* was initially delivered in Victoria, NSW and Queensland by the Brotherhood of St Laurence, Berry Street Victoria, Kildonan Child and Family Services, The Benevolent Society and The Smith Family.[107]

Sixteen years later, *MoneyMinded* has educated over 667,000 people[108] and has been tailored to the Asian and Pacific countries where ANZ works, including *MoneyMinded Business Basics* to provide micro-entrepreneurs overseas with the financial and business skills to start and grow their enterprises, and *MoneyBusiness* to better respond to the cultural context of Indigenous Australians, particularly those in remote communities.

The 2016 evaluation concluded that '*MoneyMinded* contributes to the improvement of individual financial well-being and plays an important role in strengthening financial inclusion in the communities where it is delivered. The behavioural changes experienced by participants include increased saving, increased use of a budget, reduced spending leaks, setting financial goals and increased planning'.[109]

The 2019 evaluation found that participants in Australia and New Zealand experienced a thirty-three per cent and 132 per cent increase in their financial well-being score, respectively.[110]

ANZ didn't stop there. It decided to tackle the lack of savings that John McFarlane mentioned at the 2003 conference and approached the Brotherhood of St Laurence.

The result, *Saver Plus*, was the first matched savings program in Australia and is arguably the largest and longest-running program of its kind in the world, with over thirty-six thousand people completing the program in sixty communities across Australia through partners and other community organisations under a Saver Plus license agreement.[111]

ANZ provides the matched funds, banking systems and various program resources. The Saver Plus National Office, housed within the Brotherhood of St Laurence, provides the administration of the program and support to community partners to assist them in implementing and delivering Saver Plus. The Australian government came on board in 2009.

Saver Plus is a free ten-month program that provides financial education to help build essential skills for managing money and becoming a regular saver. Upon completion of the program, ANZ matches savings up to $500 to put towards education costs for the participant or their children.

With nearly three-quarters of savers reporting that the total value of their savings and assets had increased since completing the program and eighty-seven per cent saving the same amount or more three to seven years afterwards, *Saver Plus* now represents a best practice example of community-business-government partnership, with each sector providing their unique expertise and resources to the mutual goal of increased financial well-being and capability for lower-income Australians.[112]

What is impressive about these initiatives is the harnessing of ANZ's core business and resources in a shared value ethos to enable economic outcomes for people in poverty whilst gaining customers.

In light of the ongoing discrimination experienced by those of faith groups, including forty-two per cent of Muslims, thirty-eight per cent Hindu and twenty-four per cent Buddhist reported by the Scanlon Foundation's Mapping Social cohesion surveys since 2006, in 2017, Australia Post, Monash University's BehaviourWorks, PwC and the Shannon Company joined the Scanlon Foundation to establish a landmark PFO—Inclusive Australia—to improve how Australians' view and appreciate the differences in others, including differences arising from varying culture, religion, sexuality, ability, gender, perspective and circumstance, in order to reduce discrimination and prejudice; improve social connectedness, belonging and well-being; and increase social harmony.

In December 2019, the PFO launched Australia's first Social Inclusion Index report which found that nearly one in four Australians had recently experienced a major form of discrimination and the same proportion have little or no contact with Indigenous or other minority groups, which is associated with higher prejudice.[113]

Despite the COVID-19 restrictions, thousands of Australians turned out to the *Black Lives Matter* protests and pro-refugee rallies across the country in 2020 shining a light on racism and discrimination in Australia.

With over three hundred cultural backgrounds and languages spoken in Australia and nearly half of us with at least one parent who has born overseas, we like to think of Australia as a highly successful melting pot of the world's cultures. We regard ourselves as the world's best practice for multiculturalism.

The reality, however, is different for many Australians with seven in ten students experiencing racism during their childhood, most of them in school.[114] One in five Australians has experienced racism in the last twelve months and a third experienced racism within their workplace or education facility.[115]

Although those who have non-European and Indigenous backgrounds make up an estimated twenty-four per cent of the Australian population, such backgrounds account for only five per cent of senior leaders.[116]

In articulating fifty daily effects of white privilege in her invisible backpack, the seminal work of Peggy McIntosh thirty years ago recognised that as her 'racial group was being made confident, comfortable, and oblivious, other groups were likely being made unconfident, uncomfortable, and alienated. Whiteness protected me from many kinds of hostility, distress, and violence, which I was being subtly trained to visit, in turn, upon people of colour'.[117]

With the white Australia policy only being dismantled by the *Migration Act 1966*, which increased access to non-European migrants, including refugees fleeing the Vietnam War, there are parallels with the struggle of Indigenous people, only having their recognition a year later with the 1967 Referendum.

PurposeFull organisations have an important role to play in enabling the diversity and inclusion of its workforce, which, in turn, enables staff to work and build relationships with their colleagues from different backgrounds to foster understanding and tolerance. It is the creation of this 'bridging capital' that is crucial to a socially cohesive society.

The first step is to recognise that we all have unconscious bias that can stop us from doing more in diversity and inclusion. We have learned stereotypes and preconceptions from our background that are automatic, unintentional and deeply ingrained within our belief system which has the ability to affect our behaviour towards gender, ethnic and cultural diversity.

Some of the common unconscious biases are:

- *Affinity bias*—the tendency to 'warm up' to people who are like yourself
- *Halo effect*—the tendency to think that everything about a person is good simply because you like them
- *Perception bias*—the tendency to believe one thing about a group of people based on stereotypes and assumptions, making it impossible to be objective about individuals
- *Confirmation bias*—the tendency to seek to confirm your pre-existing ideas and assumptions about a group of people
- *Group think*—the tendency to try too hard to fit into an existing culture, mimicking others and holding back thoughts or opinions, resulting in the loss of identity and lost creativity and innovation.[118]

I highly recommend that the PFO's management team undertake unconscious bias training so that they are aware of these biases and have the tools to address them when needed.

People with disabilities

At AVI, despite being paralysed from the waist down and in a wheelchair, the indomitable and ever cheerful Emily was the most active person in the organisation. Her role in the learning and development team saw her training the international volunteers before they left and then facilitating their in-country annual reflection workshop.

Whilst 1.2 million Australians with a disability report having difficulties using public transport,[119] accessibility for people in wheelchairs in developing countries is rarely legislated and certainly not catered for. But with her will and the boundless hospitality of locals, Emily always got to the venue and came back regaling stories of being hoisted into buses and carried over obstacles.

With one in five Australians having some form of disability and less than half of the two million working-age people with disability being employed, compared with one in eight without disability,[120] Australia ranks only twenty-first out of twenty-nine OECD countries in employment/participation of people with disability.[121]

PFOs can play an important role in providing more job opportunities to people with disabilities. As the WA government points out, it makes business sense as employees with a disability are reliable, productive, affordable, safe at work and good for business.

To assist employers, the government funded national Disability Employment Scheme has local providers that are responsible for recruiting and supporting suitable candidates as a free service.

The Australian Human Rights Commission provides a handy guide for PFOs to develop their Disability Action Plan.

Gender equality

Australia is ranked a lowly forty-fourth in the Global Gender Gap Index 2020 for the economic participation and opportunity for women, on par with Zambia and Laos, despite being atop the chart on educational attainment for women.[122]

Whilst making up just over half of the private sector workforce, women comprise only thirty-two per cent of key management positions; twenty-nine per cent of directors; seventeen per cent of CEOs; and fourteen per cent of board chairs. At this rate, Australia won't see an equal share of CEOs until the turn of the next century.

Indeed, with only five per cent of women CEOs among ASX200 companies and just one woman promoted to Chief Executive out of twenty-five appointments of Australia's largest companies in 2019 to 2020, 'gender equality in the professional world is going backwards'.[123]

This is not right and it is not acceptable. There is no excuse and it doesn't make business sense, given 'that increasing women's representation in leadership and board positions is critical to having better run, more effective companies that can respond to the diverse demands of an ever-changing business environment'.[124]

PurposeFull organisations can play a prominent role in modelling and leading gender equality.

As the government agency charged with promoting and improving gender equality in Australian workplaces, the Australian Government's Workplace Gender Equality Agency (WGEA) provides a one-stop shop for PFOs to put in place gender equality with the Gender Equality Strategy Guide and the Gender Equality Diagnostic Tool. PFOs can also apply to WGEA and join over 150 organisations that have become an Employer of Choice for Gender Equality.

McKinsey, with WGEA and the Business Council of Australia, have identified a recipe of the following practices for getting higher numbers of women into senior roles:

1. Build a strong case for change

2. Role model a commitment to diversity, including with business partners

3. Redesign roles and work to enable flexible hours and normalise uptake across levels and genders

4. Actively sponsor rising women

5. Set a clear diversity aspiration, backed up by accountability

6. Support talent through life transitions

7. Ensure the infrastructure is in place to support a more inclusive and flexible workplace

8. Challenge traditional views of merit in recruitment and evaluation

9. Invest in frontline leader capabilities to drive cultural change

10. Develop rising women and ensure experience in key roles

The Australian Gender Equality Council has a directory of consultants to assist PFOs.

Environmental sustainability

Another pioneering PFO in Fitzroy was started by café owners Jamie and Abigail Forsyth ten years after their concerns about the increasing numbers of disposable cups being used. Lined with polyethylene, they are non-recyclable.

In 2007, following unsuccessful trials of existing reusable cups, they decided to design and make their own—a barista standard reusable cup for people to enjoy better coffee on the go. Their belief in environmental sustainability led to the hope that usability, sustainable manufacturing practice and design aesthetics could drive behaviour change and make a difference to how people think about convenience culture. Today, the *KeepCup* is used in more than sixty-five countries and has become synonymous with reusable cups.

Disclosing the effects of climate change and how the organisation responds, or environmental sustainability reporting, are not mandatory in Australia, although this is being currently legally challenged and board directors may be liable already under their duty of care.

Given the climate emergency the world faces, *PurposeFull* organisations have a responsibility to minimise their ecological footprint and maximise environmental sustainability. As the Centre for Australian Ethical Research found, staff expect their organisations to take action.[125]

Originally developed as a project of The Foster Foundation and the first of its kind, PFO Greenfleet was launched in October 1997 to offer Australian motorists a tree-planting program to recapture CO_2 emissions and promote fuel-efficient technologies to reduce emissions at the source. Today, Greenfleet is Australia's largest tree planter and sells the carbon credits produced.

It is straightforward to determine the PFO's carbon emissions through free online carbon calculators and to reduce their emissions by buying renewable energy, installing solar power and energy-efficient equipment, and procuring carbon offsets.

Established in 1992 to provide for the superannuation and retirement needs of NSW public-sector employees and their families, PFO First State Super, Australia's second largest superannuation fund, made a commitment in July 2020 to transition its investment portfolio to a low-carbon economy and protect its members' retirement savings. They started by divesting from businesses that derive more than ten per cent of their revenue from thermal coal by October 2020. Rather than just setting a 2050 target, the company has set a minimum thirty per cent reduction in emissions in First State Super's listed equities portfolio by 2023, as well as advocating and supporting an economy-wide forty-five per cent reduction in greenhouse gas emissions by 2030.

Increasingly, PFOs are making the associated commitment to get to net-zero carbon emissions by 2050 at the latest. However, to stay under 1.5°C warming, the United Nations warns that the pace of progress on emissions reduction needs to accelerate five-fold. In short, total emissions must halve in this decade, halve again before 2040, and reach net zero by 2050.[126]

The commitment to reduce net emissions is gaining momentum across the globe with US$501 billion spent on decarbonisation technology in 2020, despite the economic turmoil caused by the pandemic. With over US$10 trillion funds under management, in its 2021 letter to its clients, BlackRock stated its commitment to support the goal of net-zero greenhouse gas emissions by 2050 or sooner by helping investors prepare their portfolios for a net-zero world. In doing so, it has asked companies to disclose their plans on how they intend to reshape their businesses to operate in a net-zero economy.

Similarly, in 2019, Aurecon walked away from long-standing client, Adani, and ANZ announced in November 2020 that it would engage with one hundred of its largest emitting customers to support them to establish and strengthen their transition plans by 2021.

As a global initiative bringing together the world's most influential businesses committed to one hundred per cent renewable electricity, PFO RE100 provides companies with access to peer-learning, policy support, local market insight and policy measures to achieve zero carbon electricity grids by 2040.

As a partnership between CDP, the United Nations Global Compact, World Resources Institute and the World Wide Fund for Nature, the Science Based Targets initiative (SBTi) is currently regarded as the most rigorous approach to the transition by enabling nearly a thousand companies globally to set science-based emissions reduction targets to meet the Paris Agreement.

In achieving net-zero carbon emissions, ClimateWorks Australia proposes four pillars for organisations to follow:

1. Reduce energy waste.
2. Use all electricity from renewables.

3. Implement electrification and a shift away from fossil fuels to zero- or near-zero emissions alternatives. For instance, electrification powered by renewable energy can decarbonise industrial processes such as material handling and heating.

4. Reduce non-energy emissions and offset residual emissions.[127]

In their purchasing decisions and supply chains, PFOs can have a policy to prefer, assess and monitor suppliers with demonstrated climate action and a net-zero carbon emissions commitment, including the replacement of plant and equipment for better energy efficient and electrical alternatives.

As the sixty-fourth biggest user of electricity in Australia, ALDI Australia's decision in September 2020 to use renewable electricity to power one hundred per cent of its local operations by the end of 2021, including with solar panels on its 555 stores and eight distribution centres, has prevented forty-one thousand tonnes of carbon emissions a year.

As the first Wesfarmers company, Bunnings followed suit in October 2020 with a commitment to being fully renewable powered by 2025 which will save 257,000 tonnes of CO_2. In March 2020, confectionery maker Mars, one of Australia's biggest manufacturers, shifted its six factories and two offices to renewable energy with a twenty-year power purchase deal with Victoria's biggest solar farm.

With transport being Australia's third largest source of greenhouse gas emissions with the highest rate of growth,[128] the COVID-19 pandemic's travel restrictions have demonstrated how we can work remotely and travel less to reduce our carbon emissions.

There are a number of PFOs in Australia that can assist organisations to measure and offset their carbon emissions by buying carbon credits, such as Carbon Neutral, Greenfleet, South Pole Group and Climate Friendly, that ensure the carbon offset complies with the minimum requirements of the Australian Government's National Carbon Offset Standard and is accredited under one of the internationally recognised standards, such as the Verified Carbon Standard or The Gold Standard established by the World Wildlife Fund.

Although typically more expensive than those overseas, there are a number of projects in Australia that generate their own carbon credits for sale in conservation (TreeProject and Yarra Yarra Biodiversity Corridor), tree planting (Greenfleet and the Carbon Farming Initiative), cattle management, renewables, fire management and landfill gas/carbon capture.

For PFOs that seek public recognition, the Australian Government certifies organisations, products, services, events and precincts against Climate Active's Carbon Neutral Standard. The NABERS National Administrator and Green Building Council of Australia provide certification for buildings. The Carbon Market Institute is a good place to start.

Many PFOs are involved in advocacy campaigns. For instance, Australian Parents for Climate Change is running 'Solar Our Schools' for the federal government to fully fund solar and batteries for every public and non-profit school, kindergarten and child care centre in Australia, which would create 6,870 renewable energy jobs, save schools between $12,700 and $114,000 in their energy bills per year, and save at least 1.4 million tonnes of carbon emissions per year.

Formed in 1998 as this country's representative, Climate Action Network Australia is an alliance of over seventy-five local, state, national and international environmental, development, research and advocacy groups. The PFO supports the Big Shift Campaign which calls for an end to the World Bank and other public financing of fossil fuels and a shift to investing in sustainable, renewable energy to provide energy access for all.

Named after the target level of CO_2 in parts per million, needed in the atmosphere for climate safety, 350.org has local groups in most countries and campaigns to stop new fossil fuel projects and speed up the transition to renewable energy.

PFO Climate for Change, whose purpose is to create the social climate in Australia for effective action on climate change, lists over a hundred climate advocacy organisations, including 1 Million Women founded by Australian Natalie Isaacs as a global movement for women and girls to pledge to reduce their carbon footprint. With over eight hundred thousand committing to save seven hundred billion tonnes of carbon, she is well on the way to her target.

PFO staff can get involved with their own in-house green team to find and implement ways to reduce energy, paper and waste, including office recycling. PFOs are well placed to assist, such as coming in to talk to staff about measures they can take at home with the Australian Energy Foundation, offset their personal emissions with Greenfleet and encourage staff to cycle into work by paying for an annual bike check up with Good Cycles.

Poverty and disadvantage

The Land Rover bounced over the rocky trails as we drove around the hills overlooking the majestic three-thousand-year-old rice terraces in Luzon in the Philippines, seven hours north of Manila.

On 16 July 1990, a 7.7 magnitude earthquake struck the area, producing a 125-kilometre rupture, killing 1,621 people and causing damage over an area of twenty thousand square kilometres. Because the quake had changed watercourses and loosened the earth, the area continued to suffer landslides during the annual rains, some of which tragically covered schools and even whole villages, causing more deaths.

I was there on a European Union–funded earthquake rehabilitation project that worked with the communities to rebuild their infrastructure and livelihoods.

Despite the tropical setting, malnutrition and poverty were widespread in rural villages. Vitamin A and iodine deficiency led to hideous lumps, or goitres, on people's necks; but even basic medicines would cost a month's wage.

The poorer a family, the more children they have, especially in this predominately Roman Catholic country, which puts even more pressure on the provision of food, health and education for the children.

Knowing this, men would come up from Manila and offer the father a loan, sometimes as little as US$2,000, in return for taking the child, usually a girl, to work for them and repay the loan. If the girl was lucky, she was sent to work long hours for at least six days a week in a factory. Otherwise, she entered prostitution, no matter what age. Once the costs of transportation, accommodation and exorbitant interest were added, it was impossible to repay the loan or return to her family and she became one of the millions of children kept in bonded labour.

There is nothing more evident of the inequality in our world today than the difference between the multimillion sponsorship deals with sports stars and the wages paid to the workers in developing countries to make the products they endorse.

Whilst the global manufacturing companies are a lot more careful now given the exposés of the last thirty years, there are an estimated sixteen million people globally in forced labour in the private economy, mostly in Asia, and half in debt bondage. This proportion rises above seventy per cent for adults who were forced to work in agriculture, domestic work or manufacturing.[129]

The *Modern Slavery Act 2018* requires entities based, or operating, in Australia, which have an annual consolidated revenue of more than $100 million, to report on the risks of modern slavery in their operations and supply chains, together with actions.

As testament to how *PurposeFull* organisations can achieve change on a global scale, the Minderoo Foundation founded and chaired by Fortescue Metal's Andrew (Twiggy) Forrest and his wife, Nicola, has been a world leader in this area through Walk Free, co-founded by their daughter, Grace.

Based on the UK legislation, Walk Free advocated for a Modern Slavery Act for Australia and established a global slavery index, measuring governmental policy and legislative progress, a Freedom Fund which partners with organisations to combat slavery in regions where it is most highly concentrated, an inter-faith Global Freedom network and a meeting of senior business and government leaders alongside the Bali Process on People Smuggling, Trafficking in Persons and Related Transnational Crime.

Although relatively small, Australia is no stranger to modern slavery with 841 human trafficking and slavery cases referred to the Australian Federal Police from 2004 to 2017. In 2015, 7-Eleven was found to be charging migrants up to $70,000 to help secure Australian work visas and then threatening to withdraw their visa if they didn't work long, unpaid hours.

As Australia's largest global retailer with a purpose to make a positive difference to people's lives, the Cotton On Group has been a leader in ethical sourcing with its audited *14 Rules to Trade* for their suppliers. The company has also partnered with the Australian government, Base Titanium and Business for Development to develop a scalable model for the sustainable cotton industry in Kenya when mining activities cease.

Notwithstanding the mandatory legislated reporting requirements, all *PurposeFull* organisations need to be conscious of modern slavery in their procurement decisions and supply chains.

In 2021, ALDI became the first Australian member of the Slave-Free Alliance, a social enterprise launched by antislavery charity Hope for Justice to support businesses in working towards a slave-free supply chain. ALDI conducted a Human Rights Risk Assessment and rolled out Modern Slavery Awareness Training for its employees and business partners.

Two hundred years in the making, the global Fairtrade system represents 1,226 Fairtrade-certified producer organisations in seventy-four countries with 1.65 million farmers and workers. The familiar Fairtrade Mark shows that the Fairtrade ingredients in the product have been produced by small-scale farmer organisations or plantations that meet internationally agreed Fairtrade social, economic and environmental standards.

A number of businesses have leveraged Fairtrade, such as Ben & Jerry's ice cream purchases of Fairtrade-certified sugar, vanilla, cocoa, coffee and bananas. Australian company Etiko (Greek for ethical) was the first fashion brand in the southern hemisphere to become Fairtrade certified.

We have enough resources and knowledge to enable all Australians to have what Maslow called the physiological and safety needs in life—food, shelter, clothing, education, employment, health, property and personal security.[130] But, in the face of rising wealth inequality, the incomes of the lowest twenty per cent of the population continue to decline whilst the highest earners gain at a faster rate.[131] Yes, it really is the rich getting richer and the poor getting poorer.

This inequality is readily shown in Australia's companies. At a time when wage growth remains at historical lows, the chief executives of Australia's largest one hundred listed companies received an average annual income of $5.66 million in the 2018 financial year, or sixty-six times the average full-time annual wage.

As head of one of the most important organisations in the country, the Reserve Bank governor, Dr Philip Lowe, has refused bonuses, saying, 'I can't understand the mindset that says, we have to pay you $5 million, or $10 million, or $20 million, so that you deliver value for the company'.

It is not as if paying management more assures better performance. In the United States, Morgan Stanley Capital International found that companies that awarded their chief executive officers higher pay incentive levels had below-median returns.

In 2015, the US Securities and Exchange Commission adopted a rule under the Dodd-Frank Act requiring a public company to disclose the ratio of the compensation of its chief executive officer to the median compensation of its employees. Similar requirements are in place in the United Kingdom for listed companies with over 250 employees.

In the land of the fair go, it's time for Australia to do the same. PFOs have the opportunity to lead the way by measuring and reporting their ratios in their annual reports.

Striving to achieve the ordinary

In his development of Toll from an eighteen-truck operation worth $1.5 million into a $3.8 billion international organisation with forty-five thousand employees and operations in fifty countries, Paul Little AO has always seen the potential in the businesses he has built through the potential of its people.

Paul's commitment to the support and development of employees led to the establishment of a chaplaincy program in February 2000 that provided non-denominational and interfaith pastoral care, akin to the chaplains in the police force and military.

Soon after, the founder of First Step, a bulk-billed treatment outpatient clinic for people addicted to heroin, Peter White OAM, approached Paul. First Step 'believes that chronic addiction is generally a long-term, painful adaptation to childhood abuse and neglect, and that timely and effective treatment is a matter of social justice that benefits all of society'.[132]

In 'working to keep people connected to their families, participating in society and taking control of their own lives', Peter knew how important a job is for those recovering for their self-esteem, belonging, personal development, social engagement and financial empowerment.

Paul didn't want to create a special project with targets and fanfare. He just wanted achieve the ordinary for Peter's clients. A normal job in Toll in a trusted and supported workplace that built their capacity to, in turn, give trust and support to their colleagues and to give and receive respect. As the next stage for this cohort, they called the initiative *Second Step*.

Under the guidance of the chaplain, Toll started with one part-time Second Stepper and formed a support network around them of their team leader, GP, case worker, workplace buddy and a significant other in their life.

Given that most of the clinic's clients had a criminal record, Toll started to work with post-release young people with PFO Whitelion and then with victims of domestic violence.

Toll experienced what most of us have experienced (and maybe still do so). Few young people know what they want to do in life, so Toll helped these young people to transition to other businesses, including through their network. For instance, a Second Stepper forklift driver worked in a business unit that had a monthly cooking competition inspired by MasterChef. After winning each month, he realised he had the passion and ability to cook and enrolled at night school. He went onto successfully open his own café.

In time, and with ongoing learning and improvement, the Toll team leaders knew the vacancies that would suit Second Steppers and saw that a short-term investment of their time turned into a long-term gain from the loyalty, commitment and productivity of the Second Steppers. At the same time, the team leaders became better managers, especially in developing their soft skills.

Over seventeen years, Toll achieved the ordinary for eight hundred Second Steppers in Australia, New Zealand and Singapore.

Homelessness and housing

Sitting on the Board of leading homeless agency, Hanover (now Launch Housing) for ten years, it was so frustrating to see successive governments unwilling to tackle the chronic shortage of crisis, transition, social and affordable accommodation that would have provided a responsive, housing first approach that enabled wrap-around support services and pathways out of homelessness. Instead, the system seemed to keep people in a state of homelessness (as getting a job would only move you down the list to get into public housing) until, after many years, they qualified for a place in social housing. Their reward was often appalling living conditions in areas of high unemployment with little prospect of a job.

To cut a long story short, the housing system has been under severe strain for many years, which is why a coalition of PFOs formed the *Everybody's Home* campaign to advocate for a better, fairer housing system for everyone, including government support for the five hundred thousand social and affordable homes needed by 2026. Their advocacy led to the Victorian government committing in March 2021 to build more than twelve thousand new social housing units under the $5.3 billion Big Housing Build.

Nationally, PFOs can take part in the Vinnies CEO Sleepout and participate in National Homelessness Week in August. With housing and homelessness services PFOs being state- and territory-based, PFOs can support their local PFOs in this sector by being part of events and fundraisers, as well as offering much needed employment opportunities.

Violence against women

As I strode into the Toronto head office of The Body Shop Canada, I was faced with a huge yellow flower with some petals missing. I was there to meet owner Margot Franssen who, in 1980 as a twenty-seven-year-old philosophy graduate with no business experience, signed a franchise agreement to bring the retailer to Canada. Like Graeme and Barry in Australia, she was a pioneer in spreading the company outside of the United Kingdom, with her first store in Toronto just the seventh Body Shop outlet in the world.

Over dinner that night with Margot and her partner Quig Tingley, I asked what the flower meant. They told me that they had read a shocking headline in a newspaper that reported fifty-one per cent of Canadian women had experienced violence from the age of eighteen.

At that time, violence against women was a taboo subject and in the pioneering spirit of Anita Roddick, with ninety per cent of female customers and most of their staff as women (and the previous year's campaign against poverty falling flat and actually decreasing sales), they decided to take up violence against women as the campaign for the year.

Margot explained that the flower was a daisy, a symbol of resilience as the flower grows anywhere, even in cracks in the concrete, which had half its petals remaining plus one, signifying the fifty-one per cent in the news story. The loss of the daisy's petals also represented the game 'love me, love me not', reflecting the cycle of violence then regretful behaviour from a partner.

They started by printing and handing out bookmarks with the daisy motif and campaign information, offering to donate $1 to the Canadian Women's Foundation for each bookmark returned to a shop in the month of December. There was a huge response and they decided on a full campaign with posters in shop windows the following March. Shop staff were trained in the issue and given information so they could answer questions in advance of victims coming into the shop looking for help.

Despite some threats, the staff felt they were trailblazers and change agents. Women started coming into the shop with posies of daisies to say thank you. With some of the funds raised, the company partnered with Outward Bound to pay for additional places for victims on their *women of courage* program, including self-identified staff. Company staff were also given the opportunity of seventeen paid hours per month to volunteer at local women's refuges.

With the success of the first campaign, the couple continued the cause, picking a different sub-theme each year, such a teen date violence and violence in the home. Customers and sales continued to grow.

Importantly, Margot and Quig were great marketers—they framed the issue in a way that resonated with the media, their customers and the wider Canadian public. For instance, the company's post-Christmas sales message read, 'for some women Boxing Day has a very different meaning', with the company donating $1 from each purchase to support the charities working to fight domestic assault.

Over the years, Margot became the spokesperson for violence against women and ended up chairing the Canadian Women's Foundation, before being asked by the government to co-chair the National Task Force on Sex Trafficking of Women and Girls in Canada, a prelude to co-founding and co-chairing The Canadian Centre to End Human Trafficking.

In 2002, she was made an Officer of the Order of Canada, received the Queen's Diamond and Golden Jubilee Award and the Grand Award for addressing an issue of vital concern to the United Nations.

Today, as it is in Australia, gender-based violence is widely recognised and responses are in place, including the Canadian

Government's *It's Time: Canada's Strategy to Prevent and Address Gender-Based Violence*, a whole-of-government approach that includes a range of actions to specifically address violence against Indigenous women and girls, and a new gender-based violence knowledge centre within Status of Women Canada as the focal point of the strategy.

Such is the prevalence of violence against women, it is likely that female colleagues in your organisation have experienced, or will experience, violence at the hands of male colleagues, family members or friends.

Violence against women costs Australia $21.7 billion a year and is estimated to escalate to $323 billion over the next thirty years if no further preventative action is taken.[133]

Set up in 2013 as a national leader in the primary prevention of violence against women and their children in Australia, Our Watch, a PFO with all governments as members, has identified the following national interconnected expressions of gender inequality as the drivers of violence against women:

- The condoning of violence against women
- Men's control of decision-making and limits to women's independence in public life and relationships
- Rigid gender roles and stereotyped constructions of masculinity and femininity
- Male peer relations that emphasise aggression and disrespect towards women.[134]

Such is the crisis, in 2015, the Coalition federal government proclaimed that violence against women has become a national crisis and now there are active programs in place by all State and Territory governments. PFOs can play an important role to prevent this violence.

PFO White Ribbon Australia runs a workplace accreditation program and Our Watch has a separate workplace website that includes tools and resources for PFOs, including a self-assessment tool. PFOs can also join Australia's CEO Challenge and access their workplace training.

Health

Despite our affluence, we are going backwards in our health and well-being with the rising prevalence of chronic preventable diseases such as obesity, diabetes and heart disease. Indeed, with two-thirds of Australian adults being overweight or obese,[135] we may be seeing the first modern decline in life expectancy in Australia.

As long-lasting conditions with persistent effects, chronic diseases—primarily cardiovascular diseases, cancers, chronic obstructive pulmonary disease and diabetes—are the leading cause of illness, disability and death in Australia, accounting for eighty-seven per cent of deaths, sixty-one per cent of total disease burden and thirty-seven per cent of hospitalisations.[136]

About a third of chronic disease is preventable, yet we only spend 1.3 per cent of our health budget on preventing disease.

PFOs can encourage their staff to be healthier through exercise by having walking groups at lunchtime, as well as free or subsidised yoga and Pilates classes at work.

With nearly half of us having a mental disorder in our lifetime and one in five having had a mental disorder in the last year,[137] PFOs have much to do given that ninety-one per cent of Australians believe that mental health in the workplace is important, but only fifty-two per cent of employees believe their workplace is mentally healthy and only fifty-six per cent believe their most senior leader values mental health.[138] Stigma still plays a major role with three-quarters of people feel uncomfortable telling their employer they were experiencing a mental illness.

Beyond Blue has partnered with other PFOs in the field, government and business associations to create the *Heads Up* workplace resources for employers. The Black Dog Institute also has useful Workplace Mental Health Tool Kit.

PFOs can take part in Mental Health Week, which includes World Mental Health Day on 10 October, and host an event to shine a light for those affected by suicide and mental illness in June.

Purchase for purpose

Purchasing goods and services from other PFOs leverages budgeted spending to achieve further social and environmental outcomes. PFOs can embed this by adopting a social procurement policy to buy from social benefit suppliers, including social enterprises, Indigenous businesses, Australian disability enterprises, and Fair Trade businesses, as well as minority group and women-owned businesses.

Purchasing from Indigenous businesses is made easy through membership of Supply Nation with its online business directory and events. As Australia's peak industry body for 990 PFO disability service organisations, National Disability Services (NDS) has established BuyAbility as a social procurement service for government and businesses to purchase from its national network of six hundred disability eEnterprise outlets. Since 2011, BuyAbility has facilitated over $40 million in contracts that supported the employment of over seventeen hundred people with a disability.

With over twenty thousand in Australia today,[139] social enterprises provide an excellent opportunity to support unemployed and disadvantaged people by purchasing goods and services at no additional cost, such as buying your office toilet paper from *Who Gives a Crap* and washroom soap from thankyou. PFO Social Traders has over three hundred certified social enterprises to choose from.

When compared internationally, Australia has been painfully slow to recognise the potential, produce guidance and create significant social procurement opportunities.

In 2018, the Victorian government did make a step change. It launched *Victoria's Social Procurement Framework* which embeds social procurement into the government's value for money criteria with a five to ten per cent weighting for purchasing from Victorian social enterprises, Victorian Aboriginal businesses, and other social benefit suppliers, including Victorian Australian disability enterprises.[140]

The difference is that, instead of just outlining affirmative processes, it sets targets for social procurement. For instance, under the *Level Crossing Removal Authority,* three per cent of the total contract spending goes to social enterprises, Aboriginal businesses, and direct employment of disadvantaged jobseekers in the supply chain.

Enter Knoxbrooke, a fifty-year-old PFO that provides supported employment services to people with intellectual disabilities. In 2001, it purchased the twelve-acre Yarra View Nursery site in Mt Evelyn, paving the way to securing one of Australia's largest social enterprise contracts to supply plants to the eight-kilometre Mernda rail project. Knoxbrooke currently has a pipeline of $3 million in plant orders.

Following Victoria's lead, social enterprise was integrated into the NSW Procurement Policy Framework in 2020. The other States now need to come on board to support social enterprises secure significant sales and scale with the $141 billion in goods and services procured by Australian governments annually.

To raise the profile of social enterprises, the UK provides some valuable leadership examples.

In 2016, in partnership with the UK government, Social Enterprises UK launched the Buy Social Corporate Challenge with a group of twenty high-profile businesses, including PwC and Lendlease, to collectively spend £1 billion with social enterprises. Three years later and £65.2 million has been spent with social enterprises, creating 637 jobs. Importantly, one hundred per cent of the corporate partners believed that the purchased goods and services were at the same or better quality as existing suppliers.[141]

Animal welfare

'Elephants sell' was the mantra at Intrepid Travel. Everybody wanted to ride elephants on their popular Chiang Mai adventure with the front cover of the Thailand brochure displaying a joyful traveller atop a resplendent elephant.

Dating back to the 1500s, as warm-blooded armoured-tanks, Indian elephants in Thailand were captured to fight in battles against the Burmese, Malays and the Khmer to protect the kingdom, earning their place as the national symbol and playing a starring role in cultural festivals to this day. In lieu of machinery, elephants have also been used extensively in farming and commercial logging.

An elephant requires an area of at least one hundred square kilometres to ensure sufficient food. With Thailand's forest cover shrinking from ninety per cent to thirty-two per cent, numbers have declined from over one hundred thousand domesticated elephants at the start of the twentieth century to between three thousand and five thousand now, with all but a thousand in captivity. As a result, the elephant officially became an endangered species in Thailand in 1986.

Elephants are not built to carry weight on their backs and in order to be ridden, elephants must first go through a process known as *Phajaan* ('the crush') in which they are bound with ropes, confined in tight wooden structures, starved, and beaten repeatedly with bull hooks, nails and hammers until their will is crushed.

The banning of elephants for logging in 1989 led to jobless elephants and their mahouts ending up on the streets, wandering across farmlands or taking shelter in dangerous spots like highway underpasses. To survive, the mahouts took their elephants to tourist spots, roaming the streets with baskets of fruit for the tourists to buy and feed the animal in return for performing tricks. On 17 June 2010, elephant protection laws were passed making these acts illegal.

However, a doubling of tourism to Thailand from 15.9 million to 32.6 million visitors between 2010 and 2016, led to a thirty per cent rise (1,688 to 2,198) in elephants poached from the wild and held in captivity for tourist activities, replicating the money-making human orphanage business model.

It started with a query from a traveller in 2010, who expressed their discomfort to their local Intrepid guide about the treatment of the elephant on their ride. As a PFO with responsible travel at its heart, the word soon got up to management which then partnered with World Animal Protection to commission a study into captive elephant venues. The research found that, of the 220 sites offering rides by 2,923 elephants at tourist venues investigated in Thailand, Sri Lanka, Nepal, India, Laos and Cambodia, seventy-seven per cent were found to be treated appallingly, including being taken young from the wild, separated from their familial groups, broken again and again using sharp hooks and other tools, chained up at night and denied good nutrition.[142]

The study's author noted that any elephant tourism, no matter how well-intentioned, drives a market where abuse is inevitable.

As a result, in a world first, Intrepid Travel, from January 2014, no longer offered elephant rides on any of its trips. Since then, some 160 travel companies have committed to stop selling tickets to, or promoting venues offering, elephant rides and shows. In 2016, TripAdvisor announced that it would end the sale of tickets for wildlife experiences where tourists come into direct contact with wild animals, including elephant riding.

The Intrepid Foundation matches their traveller's donations to the World Animal Protection and partners with Friends of the Asian Elephant in Thailand, a conservation project that helps rehabilitate elephants used for tourism.

Organisational culture

A deep, values-based culture—based on underlying beliefs, compelling purpose and lived out behaviours—is what, in my view, defines PFOs.

However, like plumbers who have leaky pipes at home, in my experience, not-for-profits who care and support people in need do not always behave the same way towards their own employees. Over the years, I've seen managers promoted from their operational roles with poor interpersonal skills who then micromanage and disempower their team, as well as the expectation of devotion and self-sacrifice in the name of the cause taken for granted, accompanied by thankless long working hours.

Could it be that the overriding care and concern for the constituents leaves little for its own staff?

If business tends to be transactional, charities are relational. Although short-term outputs are important for contractual compliance and stock market reporting, ultimately, PFOs must take a long-term view and build ongoing relationships with government, staff, supporters, clients and many other stakeholder constituents if they are to attain their reason for being and retain their social licence to operate.

These relationships have to be built on behaviours that live out the values of the PFO. These behaviours, in turn, determine the culture. However, all too often the values, like the vision and mission, are workshopped by the executive team as generic, nondescript human traits that do not capture the essential ethos of the belief and purpose. For instance, integrity is claimed by over half of the Fortune 100 companies as a core value.[143]

Who wouldn't want 'we act with purpose and respect' as a core value? After all, we all want a culture where we are all treated with respect. Even better when this value is explained as 'we act with the highest ethical standards' from an iconic company with 170 years of helping millions of Australians.

Unfortunately, this value didn't extend to the thousands of dead superannuation customers who were charged for life insurance by AMP, despite knowing that there was no longer a life to insure. Nor did it apply to the Australian Securities and Investments Commission, which AMP's head of financial advice admitted to losing count of the number of times the company misled the corporate regulator.

AMP's living superannuation members didn't fare any better with some getting worse returns than they would have if they had put their money in an interest-bearing account due to underperformance and fee gouging. The shareholders of AMP didn't feel particularly respected when its chief executive received a pay raise of $1.76 million at the same time as unveiling a loss of almost $2.5 billion. A year later though, the shareholders, led by PFO Australian Council of Superannuation Investors, took a stand on the AMP Board's failure to appropriately handle sexual harassment complaints affecting senior managers, including the elevation of one to head up AMP Capital despite a previous sexual harassment allegation against him, necessitating the AMP chairman and former head of Commonwealth Bank, David Murray AO, to resign and leave the company.

This is why the PFO's values statement must reflect the behaviours that it deems critical in living out its belief and furthering its purpose. These behaviours need to be articulated and embedded across the organisation and lived out at all levels every day.

With the organisation's leaders being watched, it is particularly important that the board and management are self-aware of, and accountable for, their behaviour, including setting a culture where their colleagues can positively challenge behaviours that they see do not come up to expectations.

Even before they join the organisation, in position descriptions, applications, interviews and psychometric testing, candidates need to demonstrate how they have lived out the organisation's valued behaviours. Reward and recognition are then key to sharing and reinforcing behaviours, including with inductions, staff awards and performance reviews.

The behaviours that I subscribe to in PFOs are as follows.

Selflessness

Beneath the imposing bronze statue of the Leeds United great, Billy Bremner, at their Elland Road ground is an inscription which reads, 'side before self, every time'. He epitomised the selfless, hard-working, committed and determined attitude that rose Leeds to become the most feared team in Europe. This selflessness ethos is alive and well nearly fifty years later with players, coaching staff and management volunteering to take a wage deferral during the COVID-19 pandemic to ensure that the club could continue to pay all its 272 full-time staff and the majority of casual staff.

In what we call developing countries, I've found a deep and abiding community cohesion based on the unquestioned support for others. The Zulu name for this in South Africa is *ubuntu*, *unhu* in Zimbabwe, *Ujamaa* in Tanzania and *uMunthu* in Malawi. In Melanesia and Papua New Guinea, it is *wontok*, or literally 'one talk'. In the Philippines, it is *kapwa*.

It means, *I am because we are*. Then President Bill Clinton summed it up at Nelson Mandela's memorial to mean 'we are all bound together in ways that are invisible to the eye; that there is a oneness to humanity; that we achieve ourselves by sharing ourselves with others, and caring for those around us'.

PFOs are a community—an ecosystem encompassing all of its stakeholders. Its beliefs enable people to come together with the sense of ownership and belonging, whilst the purpose enables them to work together to achieve the aims of the organisation.

In order to foster a culture of selflessness and interdependence where everyone is working for the whole, there is an African proverb—*Go fast, go alone. Go far, go together.* In this culture, it is a joy to see credit freely given and achievements celebrated by the whole organisation. In turn, this builds relationships of mutual trust and respect, enables personal growth, professional development and a conducive environment for agility and innovation.

It also aligns with the groundbreaking approach of servant leadership developed by Robert K. Greenleaf forty years ago, as the servant leader's motivation as a servant first.[144] To be attentive to the needs of their people, including their own growth, the servant leader questions how the organisation can serve better to reach its purpose and seeks new ways to do so.

However, a note of caution here. Left unchecked, selflessness can become martyrdom leading to an unquestioning devotion to the cause, as well as the diversion of people from their own essential work.

Humbition

The all-boys school common room for years 11 and 12 was not for the faint-hearted. A haven from the thousand junior boys and teachers, a new-found freedom mixed with large doses of testosterone meant little study was ever done. Our prized possession was a record player (yes, it was that long ago) and I only remember one record—*Come on Eileen* by Dexy's Midnight Runners, played loud on repeat.

The master in charge of these thrusting young roosters was a stocky, bald, wise man in his sixties. We didn't know it at the time, but he was dying from cancer. He sat us down one day and implored us to remember the one value which should define us. Above all else, he said, we should be humble. It seemed so odd to me at the time. It appeared so weak given the arrogance we possessed that nothing was going to get in the way of us conquering the world.

Today, humility is recognised as an essential trait for effective leadership.[145]

The world's most successful sports team, the All Blacks put humility at the centre. They are never too big to do the small things that need to be done, like sweeping out the sheds at the end of the game.[146] So, do all the staff, no matter how senior, wash out their mugs at work? Do they all clean the lunch table? Do they tidy up the room after a meeting?

Jim Collins in *Good to Great* outlines that level 5 leaders possess a powerful mixture of personal humility and indomitable will. They are incredibly ambitious, but their ambition is first and foremost for the cause, for the organisation and its purpose, not themselves.[147]

Fowler similarly emphasises humility whilst maintaining an 'inner self confidence that is not dependent on possessing power, but, in contrast, is expressed in a willingness to share it'.[148]

This combination is termed *humbition*.

Don't drink the Kool-Aid

In competing with another organisation for a government tender, I decided not to emphasise the long-standing heritage of my organisation, whilst my competitor spruiked their shorter anniversary, adding it to their logo and promotional materials to the chagrin of my team. I figured, successfully, that the government would want an organisation that worked alongside them in partnership with support to achieve their outcomes, not an organisation that put itself ahead of them.

PFOs, especially those with a high level of marketing, can be prone to believing their own rhetoric, or drinking its own Kool-Aid, and be cocooned in its own bubble, unquestioning of the organisation. It can be cult-like in its beliefs and lose perspective of the changing world around it (like Arthur Andersen), including the expectations of its funders and supporters.

With fierce competition for players and fans, sports administrators have had to learn from other sports, such as the coach of the Australian men's cricket team, Justin Langer AM, who makes a point of picking the brains of his counterparts in other sports, be it the Socceroos, Hockeyroos or AFL coaches.

I make a point of having a coffee each week before work with someone outside of my organisation, including from other PFOs, government, government-owned agencies, consultants, entrepreneurs, peak bodies and business.

Encouraging managers to meet up with their counterparts in other PFOs will allow them to learn from others and build a network, particularly those that have direct colleagues, such as the marketing, finance, IT and human resources managers.

I also recommend joining another PFO's board, subcommittee or project group to experience different cultures and challenges and have the opportunity to learn from others. As a chief financial officer, for instance, I've had the privilege of sitting on the finance committees for PFOs Oxfam Australia and Hanover and learnt much about their risks, challenges and opportunities.

Passion

For me, passion is what separates PFOs from for-profit organisations. It flows from the belief in a better future and the purpose to get there. It is the glint in the eye when describing your work to others. It is the animation in advocacy. It is the energy and drive to influence others of our belief and purpose through our work. It is the resilience to deal with the complexity and setbacks.

If you or your colleagues are not inspired and passionate for what you do as a PFO then I suggest you make way for someone that does. Go and work for more money in a for-profit business. Sorry to be so direct, but I feel strongly about this. Passion is the glue that holds us together as a team or community. It is the burning platform which pushes us to strive for better outcomes for the individuals, families, communities and environment that we support.

Challenge and be challenged

As a young Andersen Android grunt, I would work away diligently checking the financial accounts to their source and took great pride in finding errors or unjustified amounts that I would raise as proposed audit adjustments. At the end of the audit, I would sit back and admire the list of these adjustments, neatly summarised on the yellow audit paper, as the hard-won achievement of my toil.

On the last day of the audit, the partner would visit, go through the list and have lunch with the client. Invariably, he (sadly, there were no women partners in my day) would return smiling to say that the adjustments had been passed. That is, not accepted. In effect, ignored. No reason was given and it was seen as impertinent to ask. Deflated and disillusioned, I would question why I was there.

This is not unusual. In many organisations I've worked in and known, it was a CLM (career limiting move) to challenge those in power and authority.

I know that nobody likes bad news, let alone being contradicted, but as a manager I've made it a point to encourage being challenged by, and challenging, others. This relates to all stakeholders of the organisation, be they colleagues, board members, suppliers or investors.

When I joined the Brotherhood of St Laurence as chief financial officer, the recurrent annual operating deficits meant that the organisation had only eighteen months of cash remaining. As you would expect, I quickly went through every cost line in an effort to stem the losses.

Cleaning did not escape the review, which was carried out daily by a husband-and-wife couple across a number of sites. Deciding that I could get a better rate and make savings, I proceeded to put in place a tender process.

Thereupon, I was politely stopped in corridors and firmly told that this course of action was ill advised. After all, they were part of the Brotherhood family. I prickled at the challenge to my authority, but decided to put the process on hold.

As they started the office cleaning at 5 p.m. each day, I got to know Helen and Viv well. Cleaning was just a sideline. They were, in actual fact, the Brotherhood's grapevine, its informal knowledge management system. They knew everything that was going on in the organisation and a constant source of wisdom and support to many, including me. I dropped the tender.

In agreeing with Brené Brown's definition of a leader as 'anyone who takes responsibility for finding the potential in people and processes, and who has the courage to develop that potential',[149] we have to be able to challenge each other to get the best out of ourselves. This is what Brené calls rumbling with vulnerability.

Challenging each other on behaviour is critical to holding everyone to account for living out the behaviours and culture set by the organisation. But, being nice people who tend to avoid conflict, how much do we challenge others, and, being in our comfort zones, how much do we welcome feedback and challenging from others?

No one has all the answers and we are not always right. We all rely on the expertise, knowledge and commitment of those around us to do our jobs. If we are not challenged, we fail to get the benefit of the wisdom of others or fail to make the best decision.

It takes courage to be vulnerable and ask for and accept feedback. It needs a trusting environment to be able to be honest and have, at times, a difficult conversation. I've found that corporates can have assertive (and sometimes aggressive), command and control behaviours in an authoritative hierarchy. There is always pressure on getting things done and delivering results, driven by directives in short-term cycles with stretch output targets. With this culture, it is more difficult to challenge those in authority and talk 'truth to power'.

On the other hand, not-for-profits can 'kill with kindness'. As nice people, we don't want to upset anyone and so don't confront and challenge bad behaviours or poor performance. This aversion to conflict means we don't give honest feedback and bottle up frustration.

Unfortunately, this means that passive-aggressive behaviour exists in both types of organisation.

Because of the deeper sense of ownership and the emotional engagement in *PurposeFull* organisations, as well as the range of stakeholders, relationships need to be the foundation of the culture to enable honest and direct feedback to be given without offence. In her bestseller, Kim Scott describes this as *Radical Candor*—a combination of Care Personally and Challenge Directly.[150]

Working for a PFO is a vocation, not just a job. As like-minded people that are attracted to the belief and committed to the purpose, there is a readiness to share oneself and a frame of reference to help build relationships. Just as the underlying belief is personal and unites people in and around the PFO, the genuine care and concern for people through building mutual respect and trust is deeply personal and rewarding.

Decisiveness

As PFOs have a culture of ownership and consultation, the resultant 'paralysis by analysis' can lead to a lack of decision-making, or, worse still, consensus decision-making.

On joining YSAS, I asked why the organisation had seven internal committees based out of its head office, given it had not more than thirty people working there. I was told that the organisation had recently commissioned a new committee to review the number of committees and had ended up adding another committee!

Consensus can lead to settling for the lowest common denominator to avoid conflict. A judgemental or blame culture may also exist which prevents people making decisions where they see themselves as being put at risk. Instead, through trusting and open discussion, alignment can be found around a common goal, objective or interest.

Staff should be empowered to make decisions under their position descriptions, work plans and targets (unpacked from the Annual Plan), committee terms of reference, project briefs and the organisation's Delegations of Authority.

Perspective

I remember with much affection the volunteer ladies that ran the Brotherhood's opportunity shops. They were a force to be reckoned with. The best shops subsisted on donations dropped off at the shop, rather than rely on donations through the seven hundred bins across the state, which could yield as low as five per cent suitable quality for the shops. When you had to drop of the clothes and look the ladies in the eye, you weren't going to give them rubbish to sell.

The volunteers received, sorted, priced and displayed the goods in the shops, as well as serving the customers. This not only led to big differences in the quality, price, presentation and service between shops, many a heated discussion ensued as the volunteers disagreed with the price set, what and how the items should be displayed.

Faced with the shop fiefdoms, the Brotherhood's retail manager had achieved little success in putting in procedures to get consistent pricing, merchandising, customer service and stock practices. We had to find a way of challenging each volunteer to appreciate the importance of this approach. Firstly, with the support of board member Graeme Wise of The Body Shop, we got their brilliant retail manager, Tracey Horton, to show the volunteers why consistent stock presentation and appreciative customer service were important to their brand and profitability.

Secondly, the volunteers had never been shown what their shop profits funded. The Brotherhood's then-executive director, Bishop Michael Challen, took them to see a service that relied on these funds. They met and connected with mothers from low-income migrant families about the challenges in raising their children and the Brotherhood's pilot program that provided structured education for the mothers to give their kids at home.

Stock presentation, customer service and competitive pricing were never really an issue again as the volunteers saw, with pride, that better merchandising, stock turnover and pricing raised more much-needed funds for the mothers.

Engagement of staff and stakeholders

The good news is that a 2018 survey by Futerra found that ninety-six per cent of consumers believe that actions such as ethical buying and recycling can make a difference and eighty-eight per cent of consumers want brands to help. But the survey also finds that forty-three per cent of consumers believe that brands make it harder for them to have an effect and twenty-nine per cent say that they don't know what role brands play.

One issue is the way companies, governments and not-for-profits portray and promote themselves as the heroes of change and, in doing so, relegate their stakeholders to mere spectators.

In order to maximise their impact and enable its people to grow personally in contributing to a better world, PFOs have both the opportunity and responsibility to actively engage and involve their staff, members, customers, clients, investors, funders, supporters, government and other stakeholders.

When Spotlight's customers donated their used sewing machines to the Stitch in Time campaign, they became part of another woman's life on the other side of the world. When The Body Shop customers sent a postcard to ban battery hens, they became part of a movement for change. When the Officeworks staff mentor students in Years 9–11 with The Smith Family's *iTrack* program to provide advice and help them explore post-school options, they enter the hopes and dreams of children like their own.

Events

The challenge for the annual *febfast* campaign was to get people from around the country to do what most would consider to be un-Australian—giving up alcohol. The founder, as we will hear later, in acknowledging the challenge, wisely chose the shortest month of the year. After a summer's holiday of over indulging, we can all repent by taking a pause for a cause by giving up alcohol, sugar, caffeine, TV, junk food, selfies, swearing, meat or inactivity.

For the Very Special Kids' annual Piggy Bank Appeal, the nearby Bupa head office started a twenty-four-hour Treadmill

Challenge for their staff to get involved and be sponsored with funds matched by the company. The challenge was so successful that it became an event in a marquee on the VSK grounds with The Fitness Generation, Fenix Fitness Clubs, ALH Group, Bupa, Commonwealth Bank, Essendon Football Club, Toyota and ASG.

There is no shortage of events across the country where PFOs can get their staff and stakeholders involved, from painting nails with ygap's Polished Man, to shaving heads with the Leukemia Foundation's World's Greatest Shave, to taking part in the Australia's Biggest Morning Tea, to abseiling down forty stories for Scoop Australia, to golfing, running, walking, swimming and cycling as a team.

Workplace Giving

Entertainment retailer JB Hi-Fi reported saving $8 million per annum on staff recruitment and training because of the positive impact of its workplace giving initiative. Established in 2008, eighty per cent of its twelve thousand employees donate to nine charity partners through regular payroll donations and generating $15 million to date. The company found that through the workplace giving scheme ninety-one per cent of staff felt proud to be a JB Hi-Fi employee; seventy-six per cent thought that workplace giving made JB Hi-Fi a better company to work for; and sixty-five per cent of workplace giving employees felt more actively engaged in their work.

Employers can encourage their staff to make pre-tax deductions from payroll to a set number of charities decided by the staff and matching the donation amount up to a limit. This is the most effective and efficient way for employees to give.

However, with less than five per cent of employees that are offered Workplace Giving taking advantage of it,[151] the scheme and the selected not-for-profits need to be well aligned to the PFO's beliefs and purpose as part of a wider engagement approach.

Donate goods

My first prime time TV appearance came on a Sunday as I was called by the Brotherhood's donated goods manager to say that the truck driver had found that one of the iconic green bins on his rounds had been broken into. In the fifteen minutes I took to get there, I found myself staring at cameras from channel 7, 9, 10 and the ABC. My quote made the evening news and my kids were chuffed at seeing their Dad exclaim indignantly that it was 'unconscionable to steal from the poor'. It must have been a very slow news day.

Instead of donating goods into the clothing bins (which is costly), PFOs can encourage their staff to collect and donate goods directly to the local opportunity shop or the PFO, such as household items to help refugees settle into public housing or sanitary supplies for those experiencing homelessness.

I took up donated goods again when I joined World Vision just after the devastating 2004 Boxing Day Asian tsunami to head up their gifts in kind program. I looked forward to working with Australian and international companies to source and harness their products and services to support the poorest communities around the globe.

So, it came as a bit of a surprise to find myself knee deep in expensive lingerie in a packed warehouse stacked high with donations of company products from toothbrushes to teddy bears to lace teddies.

In killing at least 225,000 people across a dozen countries, including twenty-six Australians, we all watched in horror as the waves surged over once packed beach resorts and people clung to road signs as the torrent threatened to wash them away.

The outpouring of generosity was unprecedented with Australians desperately wanting to do whatever they could, including sending their unused stock to our warehouse. I was thankful a few weeks later to be sent to the recovery program in

Indonesian to work with international companies to donate their products and services, including a million dollars' worth of oil from Caltex. I will never forget the hour-and-half long helicopter ride from Banda Aceh down to Meulaboh. Looking down, apart from the odd concrete slab, there was nothing left of the villages along the 238-kilometre coastline. We sat in silence for the whole time, unable to relay the horror of what we saw.

The company's own products and services can be really valuable to PFOs. I was forever grateful to Sydney-based pharmaceuticals company Novartis and generic drug manufacturer Alphapharm for their support to establish a mobile clinic run by Dili hospital for communities south of Dili in Timor-Leste. Having seen expired and dubious drugs being used in Africa, as a first step, I asked Novartis to send one of their pharmacists to review the list of drugs being used. He found many to be inappropriate and kindly stayed to produce a standard list of generic drugs out of patent with the hospital staff, including what was needed for the mobile clinic.

Next, I needed a reputable generics manufacturer company to donate the drugs needed by the mobile clinic and turned to the largest producer in Australia at the time, Alphapharm. They kindly agreed to donate and ship the required generics on a quarterly basis.

Volunteering

I would get a call at least weekly from companies when I was at Very Special Kids to come and volunteer. Could you take a group of five or ten and put on lunch? If I had a quick drying paint, I could have had daily shifts painting the fences around the property.

Nearly four in five Australian companies provide at least one paid day a year to their staff to volunteer in their community or for not-for-profits as part of their corporate social responsibility,[152] but only seventeen per cent of corporates achieve their volunteer days target.

There are valuable benefits to PFOs from their staff volunteering with US research finding that eighty-nine per cent of corporate volunteers reported increased job satisfaction, eighty-seven per cent reported greater pride in the company and seventy-six per cent said they developed core work skills.[153]

Accordingly, there is a great opportunity for *PurposeFull* organisations to harness volunteering to engage their employees and stakeholders in the community to live out its beliefs and purpose, as well as enable personal and professional development.

However, the resultant sheer number of volunteers to place has meant that not-for-profits are inundated by requests, leading to two-thirds of them not engaging due to limited resources and opportunities.[154]

As Accenture notes, 'The voluntary sector is facing new challenges to accommodate the anticipated growth in the number of volunteers. Businesses will need to help the voluntary sector absorb this support in a way that drives positive social outcomes. They will also have to be vigilant to ensure their own programmes respond to the needs of the voluntary sector without creating additional work and costs.'

Whilst, as the UN Secretary-General notes, volunteering is 'misconstrued and undervalued', companies will not harness the transformative power of volunteering for their staff and their organisation. They will have little return on their investment, especially by staff not utilising their skills with partner organisations aligned to the business's beliefs, values and purpose. At the same time, not-for-profits will not benefit from desperately needed skills.

PurposeFull organisations can strengthen their employee volunteering by investing in internal capacity to develop long-term partnerships with not-for-profits that harness the expertise of their staff to build capacity, not just pack boxes or paint fences. I also believe that the not-for-profit should be paid an agreed contribution to offset the additional work and cost needed to administer volunteers.

Volunteering Australia has launched a Volunteering Resource Hub with evidence-based and current best practice resources, tools, research and information to support effective volunteer management. In addition, a number of PFOs exist to place corporate volunteers, such as Communiteer and Vollie, as well as, Seek Volunteer and GoVolunteer.

Not-for-profits also need to be smarter. Volunteers often get left with human resources, who are already under resourced, to consider compiling assignments and putting adverts out. At the same time, organisationally, volunteers are seen as peripheral and, at times, what has to be begrudgingly accepted with a corporate partnership.

All not-for-profits lack sufficient skills and time needed to undertake all their activities, especially governance, so building in the requisite volunteering into annual plans and projects up front is essential.

Demonstrate Impact

Impact needs to be brought to the heart of our society and take its place at the center of our economic system.

Sir Ronald Cohen[155]

It's a baking hot day and all I can see around me is a sea of different shades of brown—dirt on the road, encasing the car, blanketed over bushes and covering the leaves on the trees— thinking whether there is a range of African names for the beige dust just as the Inuit people have for snow.

With an eight-month-long dry season, little grows out here. We speed along the rutted road with a majestic plume of dust following on the way to an audit job. Out of nowhere, long bands of white material appear, and I can see the tops of plants sticking up above the fence line.

As we get nearer, I can see they are rows of white, red, purple and yellow flowers. Surreal as it is against the backdrop of the barren terrain, this is a farm growing chrysanthemums for the cut flower market in Europe during their winter. It's one of the UK government's international development programs run by the Commonwealth Development Corporation (CDC), which started life in 1948 to assist British colonies in the development of agriculture with a mission to 'do good without losing money'.

As the world's first development financial institution, the CDC has been at the forefront of supporting companies that help poor countries grow and today has a portfolio of six billion pounds as part of United Kingdom's aid that has helped lift millions of people out of poverty by creating jobs.

With the country's main cash crop, peanuts, earning, well, peanuts, the business generated much needed jobs, taxes, exports and foreign currency for the country, and my first introduction to how development can achieve long-term social and economic impact.

The defining difference of *PurposeFull* organisations is that, in delivering their products and services and engaging their stakeholders, they go well beyond short-term outputs to achieving the long-term outcomes that harness their belief, live out their purpose, and demonstrate the social and environmental impact.

The challenge is though, as the Centre for Social Impact quite rightly notes, 'much of what is measured is reporting activity as opposed to outcomes', let alone longitudinal impact.

With only twelve per cent of executives reporting a high level of confidence in their organisation's information on social and environmental impacts,[156] and less than half of Australia's not-for-profits saying they measure progress towards their mission/impact, there is a recognition that the capacity to collect, analyse and use data to guide activities and pursue their mission is very ordinary.[157]

PFOs can argue that this is because their financiers—be they shareholders, governments, donors, members, philanthropists, trusts and foundations—only require the justification of outputs and there are insufficient resources to systematically measure outcomes and impact, or their reputation is at risk if the reported results don't come up to expectations.

Ultimately, however, the lack of systematic outcome and impact measurement and reporting means that funding may not be allocated effectively to achieve the best impact, resulting in, as we have seen, a lack of progress on social and environmental challenges. This needs to change if organisations are to restore the trust and confidence of Australians and show the progress to achieving their purpose.

In the not-for-profit sector, this leaves a vacuum for donor advisory companies to gather data from the regulatory filings with the ACNC of charities to compare their 'performance'. For instance, Charity Navigator 'believes that there are two dimensions of a charity's operations that an intelligent giver needs to consider when selecting a charity to support—financial health and accountability and transparency'.

This approach is so not intelligent. It is dumb. Surely, any supporter would want to know what outcomes the PFO achieves to fulfil its purpose, not its administration cost ratio or working capital ratio.

The absence of systematic outcome and impact measurement also omits a key driver of continuous quality or service improvement, seriously hampers the organisation's ability to demonstrate effectiveness to its stakeholders— including motivating staff and supporters—and fails to produce the evidence needed for effective advocacy.

As the Salvation Army Australia Eastern Territory's Impact Report notes, 'Impact is not as easy to measure as the number of meals we offer daily or the beds we provide every night. It is far more complex'.

The challenge for government-funded services is that contracts require numeric outputs to be achieved with no requirement or resourcing available for routinely measuring outcomes, let alone impact. There is also little flexibility in the contracted outputs for changes or new outputs proposed by the PFO that could improve outcomes.

Accordingly, output-based contracts can be frustrating for PFOs that want to be accountable and funded for the quality of their services and the outcomes they achieve for their constituents in achieving their purposes, especially when their government contract manager has little corporate history and content knowledge, and government departments work in silos.

Political cycles often don't help either.

In 2008, as a board member of Hanover (now Launch Housing), a leading homelessness services agency, we were excited to hear that the local federal minister had visited the agency's main crisis accommodation centre. He, along with all his ministerial colleagues, had been told by then-Prime Minister Kevin Rudd to go out and visit homelessness services as the PM announced the goal of halving the number of homeless by 2020 as a once-in-a-generation opportunity to drastically reduce homelessness in Australia.[158]

With two out of three people seeking emergency accommodation every night being turned away, suddenly homelessness was in the spotlight. We really hoped that this would herald a new national coordinated approach and new funding to tackle this intransigent, wicked issue.

We were all delighted to read the depth of the analysis and the comprehensive proposed response in the subsequent white paper, as a clear blueprint of action with additional funding, and reassured that 'by taking action now, the government is confident that we can reduce homelessness by 2020'. Less than two years later, *The Australian* reported that the Rudd government had conceded that the homeless crisis has worsened.

However, recent government inquiries arising from years of advocacy and tragic stories of harm and injustice have had a deep focus and provide the opportunity to redesign the service system with the requisite funding levels, such as the Royal Commissions into Institutional Responses to Child Abuse; Aged Care Quality and Safety; Victoria's Mental Health System and into Violence, Abuse, Neglect; and Exploitation of People with Disability.

It is vital that PFOs record and report outcomes and impact in order to demonstrate efficacy; improve services; motivate staff, customers and stakeholders; harness impact investment; solicit prospective supporters and customers (forty-one per cent of Australians would donate more if they knew how their money would be spent);[159] and influence better policy and systems.

Whilst there is no generally accepted and used methodology for measuring impact, there are a number of methodologies used, such as triple bottom line, Global Reporting Initiative, Social Return on Investment, London Benchmarking Group and the Integrated Reporting Initiative.

At the same time, apart from the Commonwealth and State/Territory governments *Closing the Gap* targets, there is no agreed and accepted set of national measurable goals for improving social outcomes in Australia that is supported by governments, not-for-profits, business, philanthropy and the populous. This means that there is no coordinated national scorecard that PFOs can report their contribution against.

A valiant attempt recently has been the Community Council for Australia's *The Australia We Want* which was workshopped by sixty community leaders and comprises four domains and metrics based on existing published measures:

1. Just, fair, safe—incarceration rates, income distribution, feeling safe

2. Inclusive, equality of opportunity, united, authentic—suicide rates, educational attainment, transparency, employment access, housing access

3. Creative, confident, courageous, optimistic—environmental sustainability, confidence

4. Generous, kind, compassionate—giving, volunteering, international development assistance

In the 2019 report, Australia improved from -3 to -1 with only one State going backwards—New South Wales—with the highest level of income inequality in Australia, an increasing suicide rate, increasing CO_2 emissions and a high level of housing unaffordability.[160]

Recently, Alliance Social Enterprises teamed up with Simetrica, which built the UK Social Value Bank, to establish the Australian Social Value Bank (ASVB), which uses a set of sixty-two social values to determine a well-being valuation.

Recently, New Zealand followed Bhutan in turning to a Happiness Index, a marker that focuses on the well-being of its citizens and prosperity of local communities rather than the nation's gross domestic product as a different approach for government decision-making that focuses on improving mental health, reducing child poverty, addressing the inequalities faced by indigenous Māori and Pacific Island people, thriving in a digital age, and transitioning to a low-emission, sustainable economy. Measured by Statistics NZ, the framework aligns to the OECD's Better Life Index and the United Nations Development Programme's Human Development Index.

It is time Australia did the same.

Australia has a proud tradition of PFO advocacy groups, sector peak bodies, research institutions and think tanks that partner internationally and produce and leverage evidence-based research to influence policy decision makers and galvanise public support.

For instance, the Obesity Evidence Hub reported that a levy on sugar-sweetened beverages would help to reduce Australia's obesity epidemic and the flow-on increase in chronic disease burden, in line with World Health Organisation recommendations and the thirty countries that have done so, including Mexico and the United Kingdom.

Founded by urban planning and building companies Urbis and Mirvac with local governments and not-for-profits, PFO

Social Impact Measurement Network Australia supports over a thousand members to improve their measurement practices, including recognition with annual awards. The 2016 Excellence in Social Impact Measurement award went to The Smith Family for its longitudinal measurement of school attendance, school completion and post-school engagement in employment, education and training for the over thirty thousand school children supported each year through its flagship *Learning for Life* program.

Growing the evidence base is crucial in the quest for policy and system change, including PFOs measuring and reporting their outcomes and impact, such as through the methods below. More metrics are available on an online database of thirty thousand social impact measurement metrics at the Global Value Exchange.

Sustainable Development Goals

Under the United Nation's *Agenda 2030*, agreed by 193 Member States on September 2015, the Sustainable Development Goals (SDGs) represent the world's only endorsed global plan for our species and planet, comprising seventeen goals, 169 targets and 232 indicators. There is no Plan B.

Initiated by then UN Secretary-General Kofi Annan to mobilise the private sector around the world for the SDGs, in 2000, the UN Global Compact is the world's largest corporate sustainability initiative with nearly fifteen thousand participants and other stakeholders in over 170 countries.

Companies sign up to ten principles that, at a minimum, meet fundamental responsibilities in the areas of human rights, labour, environment and anti-corruption; and they must demonstrate that they incorporate them into strategies, policies and procedures, so establishing a culture of integrity.

With eighty-four per cent of business leaders saying they are taking action on SDGs, only sixty-one per cent are developing products or services that contribute to the SDGs, and with only forty-six per cent embedding them into business, the UN Secretary-General launched SDG Ambition in January 2020 as an 'accelerator initiative that aims to challenge and support participating companies of the UN Global Compact in setting ambitious corporate targets and accelerating integration of the 17 Sustainable Development Goals (SDGs) into core business management. SDG Ambition enables companies to move beyond incremental progress and step-up transformative change—unlocking business value, building business resilience, and enabling long-term growth'.

With 140 businesses, not-for-profit and academic members, the Global Compact Network Australia (GCNA) is the body enacting the UN Global Compact in Australia and produces a handy guide to the SDGs for business.

COVID-19 has made the SDGs even more relevant as they provide an 'internationally agreed framework, which also works at national, regional, and local levels, alongside and reinforcing existing plans and commitments. They enable the Government to work cross-departmentally and with stakeholders to create programmes and policies that are coherent with the needs of our economy, society, and environment both domestically and internationally'.

The take up by business is increasing with thirty-seven per cent and eighteen per cent of the ASX150 companies mentioning and disclosing integration with their business strategy, respectively, in their reports,[161] and sixty of the ASX200 companies.[162]

With over a hundred allies, the World Benchmarking Alliance (WBA) supports the private sector to measure and compare its impact to the SDGs through a set of benchmarks covering food and agriculture, climate and energy, digital inclusion and gender equality and empowerment.

The SDG Compass also provides guidance for companies on how they can align their strategies, as well as, measure and manage their contribution to the realisation of the SDGs.

PFOs can register their projects with the Australian SDG website, such as Bank Australia's Conservation Reserve that supports SDGs 13 and 15—Climate Action and Life on Land. In 2008, the bank purchased the first of three conservation properties, in order to act on customer concerns about climate action and protecting threatened animal and plant species. The reserve has since grown to 927 hectares and the bank has invested over $2.5 million over ten years, planting nearly one hundred thousand trees and working with community groups, bank customers and staff to rehabilitate the reserve, protecting thirteen threatened species and biodiverse Australian habitats.

Other examples are PFO Australian Ethical Investments which lists its $4 billion of investments with sustainable impact examples against the SDGs and T2, which focuses on five of the SDGs: *SDG1 No Poverty* by ensuring all of its products are ethically sourced; *SDG5 Gender Equality* with over half of its leadership positions and over three-quarters of its global workforce filled by women; *SDG 12 Responsible Consumption and Production* by converting all of its packaging and consumables to be either reusable, recyclable or compostable, as well as reducing its waste output; *SDG13 Climate Action* by reducing its carbon footprint, including one hundred per cent offsetting of net emissions; and *SDG15 Life on Land* by ensuring its entire range of tea and herbal and fruit infusions are from one hundred per cent sustainably certified ingredients.[163]

International methodologies

Over the years, a number of international reporting and certification systems have been started from the United States and Europe. None have widespread acceptance at this time, but in 2020, five committed to working together on a joint vision

- the Climate Disclosure Standards, CDP, Global Reporting Initiative, International Integrated Report and Sustainability Accounting Standards. Those most prominent are shown below.

Business for Societal Impact (B4SI), formerly the London Benchmarking Group

Established in 1994 by six companies and coordinated by Corporate Citizenship, the B4SI is a common standard for measuring community investment. Now being used by 180 companies globally, including in Australia by ANZ, Myer, Foxtel, Australia Post and the Geelong Cats, the framework has recently expanded to include *Business Innovation for Impact* and *Procurement for Social Impact.*

Global Reporting Initiative (GRI)

Through their Sustainability Reporting Standards, GRI helps businesses and governments worldwide understand and communicate their impact on critical sustainability issues such as climate change, human rights, governance and social well-being. Of the 142 members, eleven are Australian, including Westpac and Stockland.

Social Value International (SVI)

With members in forty countries, including Australia, Social Value International works to embed core principles for social value measurement and analysis, to refine and share practice through the SVI Framework and Social Value Principles. Staff are trained as accredited practitioners and the organisations are certified a level 1 (commit), 2 (implement) or 3 (maximise).

Sustainability Accounting Standards (SASB)

With seventy-seven standards, the SASB enables businesses around the world to identify, manage and communicate financially material sustainability information to their investors. Australian members of the SASB Alliance include Cbus Superannuation.

Integrated Reporting (IR)

As a global coalition of regulators, investors, companies, standard setters, the accounting profession, academia and NGOs, the International Integrated Reporting Council has recently developed and trialled the International Integrated Reporting Framework with 140 businesses and investors from twenty-six countries to 'promote a more cohesive and efficient approach to corporate reporting that draws on different reporting standards and communicates the full range of factors that materially affect the ability of an organization to create value over time'.[164]

IRIS+

Managed by the Global Impact Investing Network, the IRIS+ system is the generally accepted system for impact investors to measure, manage and optimise their impact. It supports the practice of impact investing and promotes transparency, credibility and accountability in the use of impact data for decision-making across the impact investment industry.

The Impact-Weighted Accounts Initiative

As a joint initiative of The Global Steering Group for Impact Investment and the Impact Management Project, this project is backed by the father of impact investing, Sir Ronald Cohen, and seeks to create financial statements that transparently capture external impacts in a way that drives investor and managerial decision-making through the addition of line items on a financial statement to produce impact-weighted accounts. These items reflect a company's positive and negative impacts on employees, customers, the environment and the broader society.[165] In this way, there will be *generally accepted impact principles* that sit alongside generally accepted accounting standards.

The Impact Weighted Accounts Initiative already has measured the environmental impact of thirty-five hundred companies. For instance, PepsiCo's estimated annual environmental cost of $1.8 billion was half that of its rival, Coca-Cola, despite twice the revenue, due primarily to its lower net water usage.[166]

Stakeholder Capitalism Metrics

In September 2020, in collaboration with the International Business Council, the World Economic Forum published a core set of 21 Stakeholder Capitalism Metrics and disclosures to align company mainstream reporting on performance against environmental, social and governance (ESG) indicators and track their contributions towards the SDGs on a consistent basis.

Social Return on Investment (SRoI)

Led in this country by Social Ventures Australia, SRoI is a form of stakeholder-driven evaluation blended with a cost-benefit analysis tailored to social purposes. It tells the story of how change is being created, places a monetary value on that change and compares it with the costs of inputs required to achieve it.[167] The SRoI gives the social return for every $1 invested and is typically used to demonstrate value to government, donors or investors.

SRoI can be measured retrospectively based on outcomes achieved (evaluative) or predicting the social value if the targeted outcomes are met (forecast).

Food Connect Brisbane (FCB) provides households in Brisbane with ethically grown, fresh produce direct from local farmers and producers through a unique 'City Cousin' distribution system, whereby food boxes are delivered to a home or community centre and then locals pick up their box. Undertaken for its investors, FCB reported a SRoI of $16.83 for every dollar invested.[168]

For its supporters, the Mirabel Foundation, which assists fifteen hundred children who have been orphaned or abandoned due to parental illicit drug use and are now in the care of extended family, reported a SRoI of $6.60 of social and economic value created.[169]

B Corporation certification

Started in the United States in 2006, the latest attempt to recognise and support PFOs is B Corporation certification for 'businesses that meet the highest standards of verified social and environmental performance, public transparency, and legal accountability to balance profit and purpose'. B (for 'Beneficial') Corps go through a set impact assessment questionnaire and are rated by B Lab, which in turn can be compared to the over three thousand certified B Corps in more than sixty countries.

More accessible than global measurement systems, especially for PFOs that are not large multinationals, applicants must score eighty or more out of two hundred under the B Impact Assessment that measures the PFO's social and environmental performance, along with recommendations on ways to improve its impact. Included in the resources is an SDG Action Manager to assist B Corps set goals, track progress and stay motivated on their actions towards the SDGs.

In addition, companies must sign the B Corp Declaration of Interdependence which commits the business to be a force for good in the world, as well as give legal protection to directors and officers to consider the interests of all stakeholders, which may require the company to change its articles of incorporation.

In Australia, there are now over two hundred certified B Corps and many more in the pipeline.

Environmental, social, and governance (ESG)

Led in Australia by the Australian Council of Superannuation Investors (ACSI), the measurement and reporting of environmental, social, and governance (ESG) has been gaining momentum with investors eager to find companies with values that match their own.

The Financial Services Council and ACSI have issued an *ESG Reporting Guide for Australian Companies,*[170] with guidance on reporting on environment management policies and systems (e.g., biodiversity impact management), environmental incidents, environmental footprint); climate change (carbon emissions, risk mitigation); human capital management (workplace/occupational health and safety, labour and human rights); stakeholder accountability (tax, corporate conduct); and corporate governance.

Whilst the 2019 edition of the ASX Corporate Governance Council's Corporate Governance Principles and Recommendations encourage improvements to the disclosure of ESG risks, including that a 'listed entity should disclose whether it has any material exposure to environmental or social risks and, if it does, how it manages or intends to manage those risks',[171] there is no generally accepted and enforceable ESG measurement standard, with PwC reporting in 2020 that forty-two per cent of ASX listed companies had insufficient reporting on ESG and significant variation in the disclosures of the remaining corporates.[172]

However, as PwC notes, over the past few years, organisations have come under mounting pressure to share with stakeholders their ESG strategy and measures.

Theory of change or program logic

The most generally accepted methodology for connecting processes to be able to articulate and measure each stage is a theory of change or program logic, which can be carried out on an organisational, program or project level.

In this model:

- *Inputs* are the resources needed for the activities to occur, including people, money, equipment.
- *Activities* are the specific interventions that will take place, for instance the number of training sessions.
- *Outputs* are the results of the activities, such as ten training sessions undertaken or one hundred participants trained.
- *Outcomes* can, in turn, be divided into short-, medium- and long-term outcomes depending on the period available. They represent the result of the outputs and their effect, such as the measured educational attainment or skills acquired in this training example, as well as getting into work or a promotion.
- *Impact* is the holy grail as the closest measure to fulfilling the PFO's purpose as the social or environmental change envisioned, such as the trainee's career path progression and the associated wealth and well-being benefits.

This model needs to be compiled from right to left, starting with the impact.

An excellent example is Centre for Social Impact's examination of the current Australian veteran support system which used a theory of change to propose an improved system to contribute to better health and well-being outcomes for veterans and their families.[173] Another exemplar is World Vision Australia's Youth Livelihood and Empowerment Theory of Change.[174]

Two excellent free guides can be found online at UK's National Philanthropy Centre—*Theory of Change in Ten Steps*[175] and *Understanding Impact*.[176]

Environmental impact

With ninety-four per cent of businesses saying the Australian government's approach is insufficient to meet Australia's 2030 Paris commitment[177] and its growing commitments to a net carbon emissions target by 2050 or before, the private and not-for-profit sectors in Australia are not as active as they should be.

The Science Based Targets initiative (SBTi) provides companies with the framework to set targets in line with what the latest climate science deems necessary to meet the goals of the Paris Agreement, which are then independently validated. In September 2020, the Woolworths Group became Australia's first retailer and second ASX200 company to have its emission reduction targets endorsed by the SBTi.

To assist, there are a number of specialist PFOs that have, as their purpose, the measurement and offset of carbon emissions, such as Carbon Neutral that supports organisations across Australia to minimise their impact on the environment by working with them to measure, reduce and offset greenhouse gas emissions.

Not-for-profits can join the Climate Action Network for support, a worldwide network of over thirteen hundred NGOs in more than 130 countries, working to promote government and individual action to limit human-induced climate change to ecologically sustainable levels.

Work for Change

When the truth is replaced by silence,
the silence is a lie.

Yevgeny Yevtushenko

I mentioned earlier that I had the privilege of working on the Lutheran World Federation's emergency program during the war in the former Yugoslavia. One of the maps given out at the weekly security briefing is framed on my wall and shows in red circles the many conflict zones across the country—Croatian versus Serbian, Serbian versus Muslim, Croatian versus Muslim, and even Muslim versus Muslim in the Bihac enclave in North West Bosnia.

The besieged enclave around the town of Srebrenica sits in a circle in the far east of Bosnia-Herzegovina on the map. Nineteen months later, more than eight thousand Bosnian Muslims, mainly men and boys under the protection of the United Nations Dutch peacekeepers, would be massacred by the Bosnia Serb Army under the command of Ratko Mladić in the worst case of genocide since the Second World War. Nine years on, the International Criminal Tribunal for the former Yugoslavia ruled unanimously that the massacre of the enclave's male inhabitants constituted genocide, alongside the forcible transfer and abuse of at least twenty-five thousand Bosniak women, children and the elderly. Mladić was sentenced to life imprisonment. Four years later, the UN Secretary-General admitted in his report that 'we made serious errors of judgement, rooted in a philosophy of impartiality' and that 'the tragedy of Srebrenica will haunt our history forever'.

One of our projects involved supporting farmers near the front line inland from Zadar, a beautiful city on Croatia's majestic Dalmatian coast. Although at that time there was limited movement in the front lines, there was regular sniper fire and shelling from each side. For the residents, especially those held in camps and conscripted into the army, their greatest fear was that they would not be able to return to their homes and so lose their land and their livelihood.

The project helped the farmers rebuild a room in their house so they could return and tend their fields at night, being less visible to the snipers.

As we drove up to one of the farms we were welcomed by a husband and wife with joy and open arms. They insisted that we sit down with them first to have lunch. Laid out with much pride on the table outside were their tomatoes, bread and prosciutto. I can't imagine they had much more than this to eat themselves.

As we got to work identifying the fertilizer and crop seeds they needed, the Serbian army shells were flying over our heads and we could hear their dull thud towards Zadar.

We finished mid-afternoon to give us time to get back to Zagreb along the coast road. On the drive back, we came across the result of one of the shells. Body parts of children, men and women were strewn across a road junction and neighbouring fields.

Nobody spoke on the way back. Grief and anger filled the car. Expecting that this would be a major news story, I made a point of watching the Croatian news the next day and reading the local newspapers.

Nothing.

OK, I said, it may be just another day in what has been so many days of killings during the war, so why would it get reported locally. So, I listened to the BBC.

Nothing.

I sobbed. The kind that shakes your whole body.

I wept over the sheer evil of the war and the needless loss of life. I cried that these lives had been lost unnoticed and neglected by the world. There would be no recognition of these killings, nor angry calls from eminent people to end them.

In my own tiny act of recognition, I printed a version of the quote above and pinned it to my wall. This piece of paper has travelled with me to every workplace since.

My fiancé, Linda, spent her time volunteering for a local charity that took testimonies from rape camp victims. In a particularly vile method of ethnic violence, Bosnian Serb forces set up rape camps where women were subjected to being repeatedly raped and only released when pregnant.[178] She helped translate the unimaginable practices and terrors into English so the charity could present them to the United Nations to advocate for rape to be treated as a war crime.

It took another fourteen years and, on 19 June 2008, the United Nations Security Council adopted resolution 1820 which determined that 'rape and other forms of sexual violence can constitute war crimes, crimes against humanity or a constitutive act with respect to genocide'.

In order to live out their beliefs and realise their purpose, the greatest impact of all *PurposeFull* organisations is to influence change in international and national laws, regulations, policies and systems to better achieve the rights of people and the sustainability of our planet, rather than just provide products, programs and services that respond to the downstream effects. Without systematic change, we will only continue to run the same programs tackling the rising social and environmental symptoms rather than preventing them.

Advocacy is not new. Ten days after gazetting a monthly mining licence fee of thirty shillings, forty miners rallied opposing government policies of oppression including the licence fee. The first of many, including the Battle of Eureka Stockade, the protests culminated in the passing of the Electoral Act 1856, which mandated suffrage for male colonists in the lower house in the Victorian parliament.

Women's suffrage would take longer, with the colony of South Australia allowing women to vote and stand for election in 1894, second in the world after New Zealand a year earlier. Northern Territory and Western Australia followed and the Commonwealth Franchise Act 1902 enabled women to vote at federal elections and stand for election to the Australian Parliament, making the newly federated country of Australia the first in the modern world to do so.

In 2010, *Aid/Watch Incorporated v Commissioner of Taxation* confirmed that policy advocacy by charities, which is undertaken to further a charitable purpose, is itself charitable. This decision was subsequently legislated in the Charities Act 2013.

In 2019 alone, there were five big wins for advocacy:

1. Disability groups succeeded in calling for a royal commission to properly address the violence and abuse of people with disabilities.

2. After the successful 2018 campaign to decriminalise abortion in Queensland, NSW Pro-Choice Alliance and other advocates in New South Wales achieved the removal of abortion from the NSW Crimes Act.

3. With around sixty-two thousand people under the age of sixty-five living in residential aged care in Australia in

2018, advocacy from the Summer Foundation and other PFOs included the issues in the scope of the aged-care royal commission which resulted in the federal government announcing $4.7 million funding and the establishment of a joint agency taskforce to ensure no people under forty-five and sixty-five are living in aged care by 2022 and 2025, respectively.

4. Following the death of Tanya Day by a brain haemorrhage sustained from a head injury while in police custody for public drunkenness, more than eighty community groups successfully advocated for the Victorian government to abolish the offence of public drunkenness and replace it with a health-based response.

5. The advocacy work of groups such as Impact Investing Australia resulted in the federal government creating the Social Impact Investing Taskforce.

But despite starting off as passionate movements demanding better rights and responding to gaps in service systems, PFOs, as government service providers, have been accused of self-silencing for fear of risking their financial security, charity status or attracting political retribution. Proposed changes to the Australian Charities and Not-for-Profits Commission Act 2013 go further. In the words of Senator Zed Seselja, then Assistant Minister for Finance, Charities and Electoral Matters, they are designed to deter activist organisations masquerading as charities, such as from public protesting or breaking into businesses to film human or animal abuse. As the Community Council of Australia notes, charities could be deregistered for blocking a footpath, trespassing on private property, not moving on when legally being instructed to do so, and damaging any property.

As Emmeline Pankhurst said of the Suffragette protests 'we are here not because we are law breakers; we are here in our efforts to become law-makers'.

At the same time, the private sector can be reluctant to take a strong stance on social or environmental issues for fear of alienating their hard-won customer base.

Despite the challenges of each sector and the enormity of the issues, I've met some amazing entrepreneurs and intrapreneurs that create positive and lasting change by harnessing stakeholders from all sectors to advocate together for a common belief and goal.

With government

From the richest place in the world 150 years ago to the most disadvantaged area in the state, I showed up to present on social enterprise to the Go Goldfields Alliance. With intergenerational poverty, young children at risk, poor health, domestic violence, and a general lack of aspiration, the council had coordinated a business case that identified in 'overcoming generational poverty all possible cross departmental and support mechanisms are in place at all stages of child and young adult development. This includes the stages of health in pregnancy, early parenting, pre-school, primary and secondary education, employment/career planning and post-compulsory education. In order to provide adequate support, a long-term whole-of-community, whole-of-government approach is warranted to provide optimal development and learning support for our up-coming generations'.[179]

As well as the new way of working, the Alliance believed that the work needed to focus on achieving desired community outcomes rather than on just service provision, and identified:

- A reduction in the incidence of notifications to Child Protection Services;

- Improved communication and literacy skills, opportunities and positive life experiences for children and their families;

- Improved community connectedness for children, youth and families;

- Improving youth connection to appropriate training and education to achieve employment outcomes; and

- Increased breastfeeding rates.[180]

With support from the State government, flexible funding, departmental engagement, and with the belief that 'our community needs to work together, to challenge and change any system that impedes our goal', the Alliance's hundred local experts in five working groups were set to 'challenge ourselves to be dynamic, to continuously collaborate, to maximise the benefits of co-design, to be accountable and to ensure long-term sustainability in our work'.

The presentation was an amazing experience. The passion, drive and insights of the group were second to none and we ended up spending the afternoon modelling a range of social enterprises for young people in the area.

With services managed by individual government departments who tend not to work well with each other, it is no wonder that PFOs themselves are operating in thematic silos with a lack of coordination at the local level.

The Go Goldfields Alliance has showed that systematic change is possible by governments through the co-design of community services with the local community, local coordination of service delivery by providers, accountability to the community based on outcomes, continuous improvements in services and systems, and the measurement and reporting of outcomes.

Having experienced the deeply unfair labyrinth of disability services for two of his sons with cerebral palsy, and, as Chairman of Yooralla, Bruce Bonyhady AM saw that successful outcomes for children with developmental disabilities depended largely on their postcode or family's financial standing. His belief in justice for people with disabilities and his passion for a better system led him to a conversation with then Deputy Prime Minister Brian Howe AO.

With Bruce's extensive career as an economist and econometrician in both the private and public sectors, including in the funds management and insurance industries with ANZ Investments, BT Funds Management and the National Mutual Life Association, the lightbulb moment came when they decided to approach the issue not as a welfare problem but as an insurance risk.

He went back to the Woodhouse report which had been commissioned by the Whitlam government and pulled it off the shelf, had a look at it, and started thinking about an insurance scheme that could address some of the disability sector's issues. Bruce joined the Disability Investment Group in 2008, set up by Bill Shorten, then parliamentary secretary for Disabilities and Children's Services, along with the CEO of Australian Super, Ian Silk, and John Walsh, Bill Moss AM, Professor Allan Fels AO and Mary-Ann O'Loughlin AM, and current AVI Chair Kathleen Townsend. A year later, the group produced its seminal report, *The Way Forward*, with its principal recommendation for a feasibility study into a national disability insurance scheme for Australia.[181]

Disability pioneer Professor Rhonda Galbally AC set about wider support by establishing the National Disability and Carer Alliance in 2009 comprising three peak PFOs— National Disability Services (specialist disability service providers); Australian Federation of Disability Organisations (organisations representing people with disability), and Carers Australia (families and carers).

I have never heard Bill Shorten so genuinely passionate as when he spoke to a group of business people about the rights of Australians with disabilities, and I'm sure he was a driving force behind the scenes. As Rhonda notes, 'He characterised it as an outrage, a real abrogation of human rights, and it was sort of like a non-welfare approach to it, and also a waste: he characterised it as wasteful of people's potential'.

In 2011, the Productivity Commission took this on board and in response to finding that the 'current disability support system is underfunded, unfair, fragmented, and inefficient, and gives people with a disability little choice and no certainty of access to appropriate supports', it recommended 'a new national scheme—the National Disability Insurance Scheme (NDIS) that provides insurance cover for all Australians in the event of significant disability. Funding of the scheme should be a core function of government (just like Medicare)'.[182]

The same year, the Alliance launched the *Every Australian Counts* campaign, amassing hundreds of thousands of supporters from its community and beyond in the now familiar red T shirts.

Two years later in July 2013, the NDIS started trials in a small number of locations before being rolled out across the country in 2016.

It has been a long journey for people with disabilities. From ostracisation as sinners, the possessed and degenerates (handicap comes from having to beg 'cap in hand'); to living and dying in poorhouses as 'impotent poor' in the 1600s to 1800s; to being locked up in institutions in the 1800s and 1900s; to resettlement in the community in the 1970s but with little social inclusion, poor quality disability services and high unemployment; to the global recognition of the rights of people with disabilities in 2008; to full operation of the NDIS in 2020 supporting nearly four hundred thousand people and fifteen thousand providers living out the 'respect for inherent dignity, individual autonomy including the freedom to make one's own choices, and independence of persons.[183]

With the NDIS having major implementation issues, including the growth in service gaps that providers cannot meet; insufficient and inflexible prices leading to the financial position of many providers becoming more precarious (less than half made a profit of three per cent or more in 2019);[184]

the government's introduction of 'independent assessments' causing distress; high administrative burden; and policy inconsistency from the NDIA,[185] Bruce and the *Every Australian Counts* campaign continue to passionately advocate for a better NDIS.

With companies

With a focus on small government and the free market, corporates in the United States have a history of being active in politics. In recent times, major company chief executives have taken on an activist approach on human rights and environmental sustainability as a result of government moves to undermine them, whilst using their corporate's values to justify their advocacy.[186]

With Bank of America's CEO Brian Moynihan noting, 'Our jobs as CEOs now include driving what we think is right',[187] he took a stand against a North Carolina law requiring people to use the bathrooms corresponding with the gender on their birth certificates, which became a referendum on transgender rights, alongside PayPal's CEO who cancelled the company's plans for a new global operations centre in Charlotte.

Meanwhile, blue chip corporate CEOs in Australia have been less vocal. That is, until a plucky Irishman poked his head above the parapet.

Excitedly announcing plans for the first direct flight from Australia to the United Kingdom at a business breakfast event in Perth, Qantas CEO Alan Joyce AC was given a surprise dessert in the form of a lemon meringue pie thrown by Western Australian farmer and Christian, Tony Overheu.

Weeks before, openly gay Joyce had used the announcement of the company's annual financial results to passionately advocate for marriage equality, saying that Australia had fallen behind on progressive issues and now lagged behind twenty-two countries in legislating for same-sex marriage: 'The sooner the better we can get this passed and send a message to the rest of the world'.

When developing the *StarKids* program, I met Alan, then CEO of JetStar. Known as shy and nerdy who used his passion and talent for numbers to model seat utilisation and schedule flights at Ireland's national carrier, I saw a steely resolve and a deep sense of social justice.

Corporate activism in Australia came of age during the marriage equality debate. As well as the 851 corporations who signed up, it was amazing to see the 'Yes' posters in virtually every shop and office window. With eighty per cent of Australians voting, the result was a resounding sixty-two per cent in favour of changing the law to allow same-sex couples to marry.

Despite the conservative politicians, think tanks and business commentators that still decry the corporate meddling[188] of CEOs going beyond their authority and told to stick to their wealth generation knitting, there is now global acceptance of corporate responsibility encompassing the social, economic and environment challenges faced on local, national and international levels.

The 2020 Edelman Trust Barometer survey reports that ninety-two per cent of respondents say that it is important for their employer's CEOs to speak out on issues such as climate change, income inequality, the impact of automation and diversity. Seventy-three per cent believe a company can both increase profits and improve conditions in the communities in which it operates.[189]

As John Denton AO, the first Australian to lead the International Chamber of Commerce, the world's largest business organisation representing forty-five million businesses across a hundred countries, noted in response to commentators decrying companies for going outside their shareholder remit and not sticking to their knitting: 'This is our knitting. Business doesn't operate in a bubble. Business operates in the environment and it operates in a community and it has a legitimate interest in these things. There is an expectation by employees that, in the absence of leadership from the political class, the leaders of business should stand up'.

In recent times, corporate CEOs have publicly highlighted another fundamental human rights issue and led the way in responding.

Sam Mostyn AO has one of the world's longest LinkedIn entries. As well as a captain of industry as chair of Citibank and board member of Transurban and Mirvac, she is the president of AVI, chairs the Foundation for Young Australians, Australia's National Research Organisation for Women's Safety and Ausfilm, and is on the board of the Sydney Swans, Climate Council and the Centre for Policy Development. In 2020, Sam was appointed president of PFO CEO Women, which educates and influences all levels of Australian business and government on the importance of gender balance.

As the first female commissioner of the AFL, Sam has been a powerful and vocal advocate for gender equity in sport, leading to the recent introduction and success of the AFLW, the women's league of the Australian Football League.

As one of the ten most influential women board directors, Sam has also campaigned over many years for gender equality at the corporate board table. For the first time in 2020, the number of women directors of the top two hundred companies on the Australian stock exchange exceeded thirty per cent.

This may sound promising, but progress is slow and many would say even flatlining. There are only ten female CEOs in the ASX200 and from a total of fifty CEO appointments over the last two years, only three appointees were women.[190] Only twelve of these companies have fifty per cent or more of the board as women, a hundred companies have failed to reach thirty per cent, thirty-four companies still have only one female director and six companies still have none. Less than ten percent have female board chairs.[191]

Australia's longest serving Sex Discrimination Commissioner, Elizabeth Broderick, has made sure that male CEO advocates are not left out by founding the Male Champions of Change which activates peer groups of influential male leaders, supports them to step up beside women, and drives the adoption of actions across the private sector and government.

With collective action

With a purpose 'to build trust in society and solve important problems' and 'in an increasingly complex world to help intricate systems function, adapt and evolve so they can benefit communities and society', PwC Australia saw the opportunity to view and tackle homelessness and housing as both economic and social challenges that aligned to their skill set and desperately required system analysis and change.

With a multi-year commitment of $1.5 million in seventy-five thousand chargeable pro-bono hours, in 2018, PwC created the *Constellation Project* with Australian Red Cross, the Centre for Social Impact and Mission Australia.

Chaired by Shamal Dass, Head of Philanthropy at JB Were, the project accelerates practicable solutions to end homelessness by bringing together corporates, governments, academia, philanthropists and not-for-profits, as well as the voice of lived experience and First Nations.

The first co-design workshop with fifty people was the first time this range of stakeholders had come together and the group committed to the belief of ending homelessness within a generation, launching three work streams:

- *More Homes* to increase the supply of safe, affordable, accessible, appropriate and secure housing for people in Australia on very low to moderate incomes.

- *Better Journeys* to prevent entry into homelessness and accelerating journeys out.

- *Leading Together* across sectors to change policy and practice.

A year later, the project had developed a network of 1,155 people across 320 organisations, including government departments, and produced four emerging solutions for the housing supply:

1. a housing capital aggregator to enable large scale institutional investment in affordable housing

2. removing barriers for the implementation of mandatory inclusionary zoning

3. a replicable aged-care model and business case for First Nations communities

4. federal and state co-funding model to enable public capital to flow and operate more efficiently[192]

The project's outcomes are a testament to the benefits of co-design and co-working across sectors.

The CEO of Save the Children Australia, Paul Ronalds, notes that organisations in his sector are 'increasingly involved in activities that seek to strengthen civil society, improve the legal and institutional underpinnings of the rule of law, strengthen the role of the media and other sources of independent information, increase human rights education, promote grassroots demand for good governance, fight corruption, and even promote political development'.[193]

As my boss at World Vision Australia, Paul was passionate about the imperative to achieve positive change in policies and systems as the greatest impact the organisation could make through evidence-based advocacy, rather than simply just managing projects or programs.

As a system change often means governmental changes to laws and regulations, it is hard for individual PFOs to risk advocating to government for fear of damaging the relationship with its funder, regulator or customers. The peak body that represents them is a safer option and can be highly effective in gathering evidence from members, researching and reporting, meeting with government, and running public campaigns.

At the risk of getting shot by both sides, the life of the head of the peak or industry body is not for the fainthearted. They must constantly walk the tightrope of actively and strongly advocating for members whilst working constructively for change with government. Often accused of not being hard enough on government in the view of the members versus alienating ministers and government officials by being seen as too adversarial, they must be seen to be balanced and evidence informed in their approach.

One of the best operators I've seen is Sam Biondo, the head of the Victorian Alcohol and Drug Association. The stone in his shoe is the over three hundred Victorians dying annually from prescription drug overdoses, double that of deaths from illicit drug taking and more than the State's road toll, and yet there was little awareness or action. For Sam, 'It was a story that needed to be told and the system held accountable for the deaths'.

With annual opioid dispensing increasing by seventy-eight per cent from 2006–2013,[194] the highest increase in deaths were due to addictive opioid painkillers such as oxycodone, codeine and fentanyl.

Afraid of Australia following the epidemic rates of over fourteen thousand annual opioid prescription deaths in the

United States at the time, Sam and his team used the coronial data to call repeatedly for a comprehensive strategy to reduce the deaths at a national and state level, with the same importance as the road toll.

In 2016, a total of 1,808 drug-induced deaths were registered nationally,[195] the highest number in the last twenty years. Sam got the interest of the state's health minister, who set up an expert advisory committee to consult and consider responses. Known major issues were the overprescribing by doctors and doctor shopping, whereby a patient could go to a number of doctors to get prescriptions without the other doctors knowing.

In response, in 2018, the government committed $30 million to implement the country's first comprehensive real-time prescription monitoring system. After successful trials in Western Victoria, *SafeScript* was made mandatory from April 2020 for doctors to check prior to writing or dispensing a prescription for high-risk medicine, including opioids. This system effectively allowed both monitoring of client usage by doctors and pharmacists as much as it allowed the authorities to also monitor the health professionals.

Accompanying the new system, a dedicated SafeScript Training Hub provided updates on training and resources, and SafeScript GP Clinical Advisors enabled peer-to-peer mentoring to GPs to discuss clinical issues relating to client complexity arising from high-risk prescription medications identified through SafeScript. A public awareness campaign on the addictive nature and harms of prescription medicines, *Stay on the Safe Side*, was also rolled out on free-to-air television, radio and social media.

The change in the government system that Sam fought for over the years has and will save lives. Although the stone may be smaller now, it is still there, nagging away. He is now looking to the data to show how the drug and alcohol service system has reduced the harm to those abusing prescription medicines. Then the next story will be told.

Another form of collective action is to form a consortium of PFOs in a coordinated and well-marketed campaign. A recent example is *The Home Stretch*, a partnership of over a hundred PFOs across Australia in family and child, drug and alcohol, heath, housing and homelessness, youth, education and Indigenous services, together with leading philanthropic foundations. It advocates:

> As the largest parent of all, we are seeking all state and territory governments to provide an option, whereby the provision of care can be extended to any young person needing or seeking this, until 21 years, much like what is happening in any other family setting in Australia. We believe that giving young people in state care the extended care option, will provide them with the platform to make the right start in life and enjoy a better long term life outcome.

Current government policies require the child protection system to begin preparing a young person to leave care as early as fifteen years old, before leaving their care placement during their sixteenth or seventeenth year. In comparison, children residing at home in the wider community with one or both parents are remaining at home longer, with almost fifty per cent of young people aged eighteen to twenty-four having never left the family home.

As a cohort of young people that have gone through the trauma of sexual abuse, family violence and breakdown, leading to serious mental health issues and chronic drug and alcohol self-medication, over a third were homeless in the first year of leaving care, nearly half of boys were involved in the juvenile justice system and nearly a third were unemployed.[196] The campaign demonstrates that where care is extended until the age of twenty-one, education participation doubles and homelessness rates are halved.

Tasmania led the way in early 2018 with both major political parties agreeing to extend support to out of home care to twenty-one, followed by South Australia and West Australia. In April 2019, the Victorian Government launched a trial for 250 young people for continued care up to the age of twenty-one, together with a transition to independence program called Better Futures. The Home Stretch is now calling for a national approach to ensure all States and Territories are on board.

Sometimes, a global network is needed to create change.

Seven years after publishing her first Harry Potter book, Joanne K. Rowling CH OBE saw a black-and-white photograph in a newspaper. It showed a small boy, locked in a caged bed in a residential institution. With an agonised expression, his hands clutched what appeared to be chicken wire containing him. Ashamed of her reflexive refusal to look, she forced herself to turn back to the picture and read the article. It told of a nightmarish institution where children as young as six were caged most of the day and night. The article would be a turning point in her life.

Many people have visited the estimated eight million children in orphanages on their travels, naturally drawn to what appears to be vulnerable children in a caring place with food, shelter and education. But what they do not know is that over eighty per cent have a living parent who could take care of them given the right support. Similarly, UNICEF reports that seventy-seven per cent of children in orphanages in Cambodia in 2009 had at least one living parent. In Sri Lanka that number was ninety per cent in 2007.

Orphanages have in fact become a lucrative business in developing countries, attracting generous funding and donations and leading to the trafficking of children to fill them.

Between 2005 and 2015, the number of orphanages increased by sixty per cent in Cambodia to 406 with 16,579 children, with half concentrated in the tourist destinations of

Phnom Penh and Siem Reap. The Cambodian Ministry of Social Affairs notes that thirty-eight per cent have never been inspected by the Ministry, twelve per cent are not registered with any branch of the government, and twenty-one per cent of the institutions do not have a Memorandum of Understanding with the government.[197]

With Baroness Emma Nicholson, J. K. Rowling set up Lumos after the spell she created in Harry Potter to bring light to dark and frightening places. As a *PurposeFull* organisation, Lumos is dedicated to working towards ending the systematic institutionalisation of children worldwide and demonstrating it is less expensive and more successful to close orphanages and, instead, redirect their funds towards community-based solutions that support children in their homes where they belong.

Following on from Lumos, *ReThink Orphanages* was created in 2013 by Better Care Network and Save the Children UK to stop volunteering in orphanages through tourism. This PFO has been particularly successful in Australia with individuals and organisations from international aid and development, child protection, tourism, philanthropic, education and faith-based communities.

According to UNICEF, Australians are among the top financial supporters of orphanages in many south-east Asian countries, including Cambodia, propping up the industry through volunteers, donations and tourist visits, arranged by Australian travel agencies, 'voluntourism' companies, charities, churches, universities or high schools.

The scale is huge with over half of all church attendees in Australia contributing funding to institutional care overseas, 245 registered charities directly funding or sending volunteers, and 565 Australian charities involved with or operating residential care institutions overseas. In 2018, *ReThink* reported that over half of Australian universities advertised orphanage placements.[198]

Many of the children found in orphanages come from poor backgrounds and are handed over by their families on the promise of receiving an education, being well-cared for and well-fed. However, in 2017, Guardian Australia reported that a nine-year-old who sang and danced for tourists at an orphanage in Cambodia was being starved and that she and the other children hunted and ate mice in order to survive. The orphanage's director beat and raped her repeatedly over the course of several years. She was forced to toil in his rice paddies and farms without pay. Clothes and toys donated to her would be taken to the market, sold and used to line the director's pockets.

As children, especially younger children, placed in institutional care are more likely to experience poor health, developmental delay and emotional attachment disorders,[199] ReThink was formed to stop support to orphanages, including funding, donations, tourist visits, volunteering and missionary work.

Enter Western Australian Senator Linda Reynolds. During a visit to Cambodia with Save the Children in January 2016, she 'became aware of an issue—voluntourism. Thousands of Australians support the trafficking and institutionalisation of vulnerable children in so-called orphanages, often in slavery like conditions'.

In 2018, the advocacy of ReThink Orphanages and Senator Reynolds resulted in Australia becoming the first country in the world to recognise orphanage trafficking as a form of modern-day slavery in its Modern Slavery legislation.

Australia's business groups are also active.

In its *A plan for a stronger Australia*, the country's largest business group, the Business Council of Australia, includes advocacy for a Productivity Commission inquiry into entrenched disadvantage, an increase in the single rate of Newstart for those who have been on the payment for a long time and a price signal that places a value on technologies that produce lower emissions.[200] Meanwhile, the Australian Industry Group has published a practical plan for rapidly transforming the energy management market that supports Australian industry with the Energy Efficiency Council.

With digital movements

Georgie, my daughter, excitedly showed me a video everyone at school was talking about. Aiming for five hundred thousand views, Jason Russell's *Kony 2012* video on 5 March 2012 reached the target in three hours and went onto to register one hundred million views and 1.4 million likes in six days. *Time* magazine named it the most viral video ever and $20 million was donated to the cause.

Social media has enabled the widespread engagement of people across the world around a cause. In the midst of the twenty-five billion views of cat videos on YouTube, every PFO dreams of striking gold with a video that goes viral and delivers instant supporters and donations.

With the Howard government winning a majority in the Senate, Australia's first mass digital movement was founded in 2005 by Jeremy Heimans, David Madden and Amanda Tattersall with a board that included John Hewson AM, Evan Thornley and Bill Shorten (then National Secretary of the Australian Workers' Union). *GetUp!* encouraged visitors to email Coalition senators that read 'I'm sending you this message because I want you to know that I'm watching. Now that you have absolute power in the Senate, it is only people like me who can hold you accountable. And we will'.

Get Up! urged supporters to tell a friend who would then turn into a recruiter and bring their own, similarly minded, contacts into the community. In this way, the PFO became a group of 'connected connectors', sharing a worldview, networked to one another and influential in their reach. Identifying and cultivating the right connected connectors explains *Get Up!*'s success.[201] Today, it is a movement of over a million people that sign up to petitions and volunteer for advocacy events.

Serial lobbyist Heimans then went onto found the world's largest and most powerful online activist network, Avaaz (meaning "voice" in several European, Middle Eastern and Asian languages), which has over fifty million members speaking fifteen languages in 194 countries. Heimans recent book with Henry Timms, *New Power*, is a must read for any PFO wanting to establish or grow a digital movement.[202]

I first met the founder of the world's largest digital movement when he was twenty-three years old. Hugh Evans had already spent time with a family in the sums of Manila, attended a school in the foothills of the Himalayas, worked with HIV/AIDS orphans in South African as World Vision's inaugural youth ambassador, participated in The Hague International Model United Nations, co-founded youth international development PFO Oaktree, awarded a Junior Chamber Internationals' Outstanding Young Persons of the World and been Young Australian of the Year.

Two years later, Evans started the *Global Poverty Project*, which was involved in Australia's version of the *Make Poverty History* campaign that led to a commitment from Kevin Rudd to double Australia's foreign aid budget if elected, before developing the initiative into Global Citizen that aims to build a movement of one hundred million action-taking Global Citizens to end extreme poverty by 2030.

To date, followers have taken over twenty-four million actions by signing a petition online, sending an email, tweeting, taking a quiz or watching a video. In return, they get reward points that can be redeemed for concert tickets, including the annual Global Citizen music festival with the likes of Queen, Pharrell Williams and Alicia Keys.

In 2017, then chair of the Global Partnership for Education, Julia Gillard AC, used Global Citizen to call for US$3 billion in funding to provide 870 million children with access to education. Nearly three hundred thousand followers responded by sending emails and social media message to world leaders and corporations leading to US$2.3 billion being raised.

In 2020, the world saw the power of Global Citizen's digital movement with the *One World: Together at Home* concert with Lady Gaga and a host of music stars which raised US$127 million and featured communities impacted by COVID-19 across the world, together with conversations and tributes to the political leaders, scientists, health care professionals, and other essential service workers on the frontlines.

With experiences

The cheap and relatively pure heroin that flooded the streets of Australia's capitals in the 1990s caused many deaths and led Premier Jeff Kennett to implement the recommendations of David Penington's 1997 *Turning the Tide* report,[203] including Australia's first specialist youth drug and alcohol service, the Youth Substance Abuse Service (YSAS). Thirteen years later, I went to work for YSAS.

Despite then Prime Minister Bob Hawke's breaking down in tears on camera about his daughter's heroin addiction, youth drug and alcohol misuse is not typically the subject of nice conversation around the dinner table. Add to this the common perception that young people have themselves to blame, how could YSAS publicly advocate and fundraise?

Enter one Fiona Healy. At a barbecue with friends in late 2006, Fiona came up with a plan to atone for the silly season. The idea was to give up alcohol for the year's shortest month and donate funds raised from the challenge to combat youth substance abuse. Fiona and a friend raised $910 at the first *febfast* in February 2007.

Fiona was camped in an office at the back of YSAS trying to run febfast on her own. We both saw the potential of investing in the marketing, technology and partnerships to enable the campaign to grow. Former marketing manager at Lonely Planet, Howard Ralley, came on board and febfast grew into one of Australia's top ten campaigns, engaging twenty thousand Australians in awareness of youth recovery from dependence on alcohol and other drugs and raising over $1 million annually.

Nothing beats supporters and decision makers getting immersed in the cause whilst raising funds.

Another inspirational woman to do so is Lyn Swinburne AM. Diagnosed with breast cancer when her children were eight and six years old, she experienced how poor the clinicians were at listening and understanding her and her family's needs, not just the disease. So, she set out to change the doctor-patient relationship across the country. With a grant from the National Breast Cancer Foundation, she organised for 350 fellow women from across Australia to meet in Canberra to workshop solutions and produce a report for the medical world and government.

But she was worried. How would a report capture attention and actually lead to action when so many reports ended up in out trays and bookshelves. On top of this, how could she raise the funds needed to carry on the advocacy?

As she was flying into Canberra for the conference, she noticed the green lawns of Parliament House and suddenly visualised ten thousand pink silhouetted heads of women planted there, representing those that are diagnosed with breast cancer annually. What a picture and what an impact. Messages could be written on the silhouette and they could be sold to raise funds to help build a network of women.

Lyn knew an art teacher from Melbourne Grammar and the silhouette of the pink lady was born. A chance encounter with former Nylex CEO, Sir Peter Derham, got the plastic material cut, made and transported to Canberra, followed by permission from the leaders of the Senate and House of Representatives with the help of businessman and philanthropist, Sir Lawrence Muir.

The silhouettes were sold for $20 or $100 and with the help of local scouts twenty-five hundred white silhouettes were planted around the ten thousand pink ones to remember those that had died from breast cancer over the last year. It looked beautiful, poignant and brought home the impact. Politicians came over to see the spectacle and read the messages. The money raised was enough to start a new PFO. As truly grassroots advocacy, the Field of Women came to define the new Breast Cancer Network Australia (BCNA).

Meanwhile, Lyn had played in the same netball competition as Lesley Gillespie and taught her daughter. Lesley had heard on the grapevine that Lyn had breast cancer and had resigned from teaching and started BCNA. With her husband, Roger, she went to a talk with Barry Jones AC. As it happened, Lyn was the warm-up act and talked passionately about what she was doing and they approached Lyn afterwards to see if she needed any office space in their new offices.

So began a twenty-year partnership with the founders of Bakers Delight which has raised over $18 million for the BCNA through the annual pink buns campaign.

In 2006, financial planner, Bernard Fehon, was on the organising committee for the Vinnies annual gala dinner, targeting CEOs and business owners that would have the most money to bid on the auction items secured for the event. But he felt uncomfortable having a feast to raise money for those who couldn't afford their next meal. With his kids doing a Sleepout for Vinnies at their school, he came up with a *CEO Sleepout* instead.

With no allowance for their status, the CEOs spent a cold winter night with only cardboard between them and the concrete. Since then, the event has raised over $30 million and inspired similar events in the United Kingdom, South Africa, United

States, Taiwan and New Zealand. Even during COVID-19 when CEOs were spared the cold floor and invited to sleep in their cars, backyard or couch, over fifteen hundred CEOs fundraised in excess of the $5 million target. As well as the cash, Vinnies have amassed the best black book of influencers and decision makers in the land.

Social enterprises are a great way to engage supporters, especially where their quality product or service attracts customers first who then get to know the PFO and cause.

At YSAS, it was not possible to engage prospective supporters in the services with vulnerable at-risk young people going through their treatment and rehabilitation. With employment the best intervention for these young people, giving them dignity, belonging, esteem and financial independence, leaving a Department of Human Services meeting one day, I walked past an unloved café and had an idea.

With the rise of Melbourne's hipster café scene, the shop appeared to be left behind. Specials were scrawled on the window, a hunk of roast beef sat ageing on the counter and a few leftover pies withered in the warmer. Over the next two months, I walked the same way to and from the meetings without seeing a customer. Running a restaurant in the evening, the Japanese couple were not only exhausted, they were losing serious money.

With the government putting in place a social procurement policy, I knew that a social enterprise café would be a preferred catering supplier to the two thousand public servants next door, and a refit and rebranding would attract coffee and lunch customers from the competing cafés in the vicinity.

Legendary chef, Andrew McConnell, who had helped me with Charcoal Lane, asked his restaurant designers, Projects of Imagination, to lend a hand. Looking through cards with Paul Kelly song titles, 'Ways and Means' was chosen (I was out voted on 'Leaps and Bounds').

Donated Terrazzo tiles, wooden ceiling and tables, and a state-of-the-art coffee machine later, the café proudly took its rightful place in the world's coffee capital.

Making their own way on public transport, young people in the last stages of recovery came to work as trainees to give them the start of a CV. As they and their families had typically been welfare recipients all their lives, Ways and Means, by treating them as an employee, gave them a profoundly different perspective and they came back excited to want to work and plan for study or a job.

At the same time, the café provided a new and different way for the ministers and public servant colleagues to see the young people—with skill and hope—as well as YSAS in a new light. It was a proud moment when one of these young people was made head barista. And even better when he served the head of the government department that funded YSAS his daily flat white.

Partner with Purpose

Fight for the thing that you care about, but do it in a way that will lead others to join you.

Ruth Bader Ginsburg

I was petrified one Tuesday morning at World Vision. It was the first time a business had presented at the weekly devotions, let alone a Jewish family business.

Three months earlier in a cramped small room in a village in North Uganda stood six sweating Australians and a translator around a young woman sitting at a table sewing a dress.

We learnt that she had been a child bride in the Lord's Resistance Army (LRA). Joseph Kony (of the viral video fame mentioned earlier) formed the LRA in northern Uganda in 1987 to overthrow the government of President Yoweri Museveni. An estimated thirty thousand children were abducted from their homes, drugged and forced to fight, along with thousands of young girls who were trafficked and forced into sexual slavery.[204]

She told the harrowing story of being raped, falling pregnant and having a baby. Returning to her village, she had been ostracised by her family and the community, and so had to flee to the city.

One of the group asked her age.

'Twenty', she said.

I then asked the age of the baby.

'Ten', she replied.

Silence.

Tears followed as we did the maths.

She was raped at ten years old.

My relationship with the Spotlight Group had started some two years earlier after I had visited a large refugee camp in Northern Uganda and noticed a women's sewing enterprise. The camp was home to some twenty thousand refugees and had turned into a town with a main street and shops. In the middle sat eight immaculately dressed women at tables with donated sewing machines making beautiful clothes to sell in the camp.

World Vision had programs in the area to support the refugees escape the camp and transition back to their villages or start their own businesses in urban areas. When I visited, the training consisted of bicycle and vehicle repair courses for men. Sending sewing machines would be an opportunity to train the women and give them the opportunity to start their own businesses.

Spotlight is Australia's biggest retailer of sewing machines through over a hundred stores across the country, but sales struggle because sewers come to cherish their machines and the level of technical change is low.

I pitched a program which I called *Stitch in Time* for Spotlight's customers to donate their working sewing machines to World Vison in return for a discount voucher to buy a new machine, together with Spotlight staff volunteering to test the machines before being shipped to Uganda.

It worked. Over two thousand sewing machines were donated, checked and shipped to women in North Uganda and other World Vision programs, whilst Spotlight's sewing machine sales rose.

Spotlight went further with staff visiting the program to train the women before coming back to tell their story to the staff at their annual conference. Whilst there, they worked together on a design for a tote bag to be made for Spotlight to purchase and sell in their stores. They even successfully lobbied for the local electricity supply to be extended to the new sewing business hub so that faster electric sewing machines could be used.

The 2020 Edelman Trust Barometer notes that 'one of the most consistently low scores for NGOs, business and government is on partnership, with each institution not seen as a good partner to the others. For three out of four of the institutions—not-for-profits, business and government—Australians feel that partnering with the other two could be a trust-building opportunity'.[205]

The good news is that *PurposeFull* makes it easier for organisations to identify and build collaborations, partnerships and alliances through the common ground that it enables, whether it is joining an association for fair trade, a network reducing carbon emissions, or a group for combatting modern slavery.

Between corporates and not-for-profits

Partnering between companies and charities is challenging. For-profits and not-for-profits live in different countries (if not continents)—each with their own time zone, language and customs. The private sector operates on shorter timeframes, commercial terminology and business cycles, the combination of which can be incomprehensible, pushy and threatening to not-for-profits. The resultant urgency, strict deadlines and deliverables can be foreign to a charity partner.

At the same time, the not-for-profit sector can be seen as slow, cumbersome, uncoordinated, bureaucratic, emotive and brand-first to the for-profit partner. Or, as one prominent businessman said to me – *full of logos and egos*.

The only way forward is to take a trip to and spend time in the other country to experience, understand, accept and build relationships with the partner's people and their culture. Partnering between corporates and charities is a lot like international development.

Intrepid Travel constantly needs to develop sustainable, experience-rich travel products for small groups to stay ahead of the competition. Meanwhile, AVI has been building skills for livelihoods and inclusive economic growth for over sixty years across eighty-nine developing countries. We chose Myanmar as, at the time, a growing tourism market and development program, which had offices of both organisations in Yangon.

Intrepid brought the market knowledge of what tourists would buy in Myanmar and AVI contributed the community development and cultural awareness. We worked across both AVI and Intrepid Melbourne and Yangon teams to develop the Sustainable Tourism Hub which focused on harnessing the existing knowledge and systems in the country, rather than bringing in our own.

It would have been straightforward to facilitate microcredit, but the businesses would not have gained a credit history with a bank for subsequent loans as their businesses grew. It took us eighteen months to work with the banks, which had not historically loaned to small business, to get the businesses access to loans and advice from Myanmar's third-largest bank. The businesses had product development support from Intrepid, pro bono support for their business cases from the local EY firm, free local legal help and socially responsible tourism training from the International Labour Organisation. To date, ten predominantly women's businesses have been established and included in Intrepid's Myanmar offering.

It is understandable that not-for-profits can be reluctant to engage with corporates. The amount of time needed to work with the company is seen as disproportional to the benefit received, there is an ongoing uncontrollable associated reputation risk from the company's actions, their ability to advocate against the private sector could be compromised, and there is an unwillingness to give access to its supporter database.[206]

In finding a better way to forge partnerships between business and PFOs, in 2011, Porter and Kramer argued for a reinvention of capitalism by 'companies taking the lead on bringing business and society back together' through *shared value*.[207] They defined shared value as 'creating economic value in a way that also creates value for society by addressing its needs and challenges'.

The Shared Value Project defines shared value as 'policies and practices that enhance the competitiveness of companies while improving social and environmental conditions in the regions where they operate. It is a business strategy focused on companies creating measurable economic benefit by identifying and addressing social problems that intersect with their business'. Because it harnesses the company's core business to achieve social and environmental change, shared value presents the opportunity to garner widespread support from the private sector and be more sustainable than its predecessors. It sits at the operational heart of the business, not in a resource constrained marketing or human resources budget. It can provide valuable professional and soft skills development for staff, as well as build the brand and reputation of the company.

As a recent example, Coles and the Heart Foundation teamed up to launch a new health initiative, the Coles Health Hub, to provide information and solutions to help Australians reach their health goals. The Hub features tasty, heart-healthy, exclusive recipes from the Heart Foundation, together with Coles' recipes to support healthy eating and build happier lives.

With useful tips and information that cover nutrition, exercise, health and well-being, customers can learn about the goodness of whole grains for heart health, the difference between good and bad fats, ways to start exercising alone or with their family, and how to cook healthier family meals at home.

To support this health initiative, News Corp Australia's Sunday mastheads feature a new weekly double-page spread called *#RejuveNation*, supported by an integrated editorial, print and digital campaign that runs across News Corp Australia channels.

As Oxfam and other not-for-profits have, quite rightly, exposed corporate irresponsibility and harm, not-for-profits have understandably been wary and sceptical of partnering with business. However, the sector should not ignore the considerable knowledge, expertise, networks and scale of corporates. After all, giving by small, medium and large businesses reached $17.5 billion between 2015 and 2016 and community partnerships accounted for sixty-nine per cent of the total value of large business giving of $6.2 billion.[208]

Between not-for-profits

In the chilly hall of the Noble Park community centre, I stood in front of representatives from over forty PFOs and government departments providing services across the gamut of State health and social services—primary and allied health, mental health, drug and alcohol, housing, homelessness, family and children, domestic violence, youth and out-of-home care.

A former McKinsey consultant, CEO of Foundation for Young Australians, and chair of the Commonwealth Advisory Committee on Homelessness, Mary Wooldridge knew much about Victoria's complex and siloed array of health and human services when she was elected to represent Doncaster in 2006 and became shadow minister for Mental Health, Drug Abuse, Community Services and Environment and Climate Change.

When the coalition won the 2010 State election, Mary became the minister for Mental Health, Women's Affairs and Community Services and wasted no time in issuing a case for change[209] 'to address the complex and interrelated nature of individual and family problems and entrenched disadvantage' and appointed former top public servant in the Howard Government and brilliant strategist, Peter Shergold AC, to lead her Service Sector Reform project.

There was much excitement and anticipation in the room packed full of sector CEOs for the first consultation. Like many a sports team supporter at the first game of the season, anticipation, passion and hope overrode the disappointment of past experiences. Called courageous, brave and ambitious, for the first time the government spoke of co-designing a system that would genuinely place people at the centre of a coordinated, sustainable and quality service system.

With health and human services being provided by contracted agencies to each individual family member, often without any knowledge of the other, they could easily accumulate over fifty interventions a week. The resultant revolving door of case workers was time-consuming and confusing, achieving little sustainable change. The growing complexity and interrelatedness of their circumstances and needs meant that this siloed approach was costly and ineffective.

For better outcomes for the people we supported, we all wanted to see 'placed-based, people-centred, integrated services'. Indeed, it has been a lifelong aspiration for all sector CEOs that I have met that goes to the heart of the people in need to receive appropriate, coordinated and timely services that address their needs.

What gave us hope was that Mary Wooldridge realised that the government, which created the service system, had to fundamentally change and that it needed the cooperation and support of the sector. No minister had attempted this reform then (or since).

Important projects need good branding, and the workshop started with the presentation of the new Services Connect logo and its dramatic change from the traditional conservative blue theme of departmental documents. Now a more vibrant and urgent bright orange would lead the way. With new Services Connect lanyards and pens at the ready, we eagerly enlisted.

In that community centre, for the first time, providers discussed and compared their service offerings. Their various service locations, specified cohort, entitlement criteria, assessment methods and referral points. It was a revelation to all.

With the Liberals losing the 2014 Victorian election, unfortunately, the project became another victim of changing political cycles and lost momentum, ceasing in 2016.

Not-for-profits are fiercely competitive—far more so than business in my experience. This often comes as a complete surprise to corporate people entering or working with charities. Not unsurprisingly then, partnerships with not-for-profits within their sector are not as common as they should be.

A safer bet is to work between sectors, such as when, in 2019, supported by pro-bono legal and business advice from Herbert Smith Freehills and PwC, four of Australia's top charities, CanTeen, Starlight Children's Foundation, National Breast Cancer Foundation and UNICEF Australia came together to establish an independent not-for-profit social enterprise, Rippling, to deliver an innovative, cost-efficient approach to fundraising. With ever more competition, falling individual donations and rising costs, the charities have combined their expertise and resources to scale up their fundraising, achieve cost-savings economies of scale, and trial new methods and ways of raising funds.

Business to business

Jay Coen Gilbert was celebrating New Year's Day in 2005 at his colleague and friend Bart Houlahan's house when he broke the news that, after they sold their basketball-apparel company to American Sporting Goods, he was going to start an organisation that would allow companies to apply for a designation that would publicly hold them accountable for the ways they benefitted workers, communities, the environment and customers.

Jay believed that shareholder primacy, where share price and dividends go before everything else, created toxic short-termism and is fundamentally flawed. His organisation would create a movement to shift the way businesses are run.

After researching business for social good, he created the *PurposeFull* organisation *B Lab* (the B is for 'benefit'), which certifies companies as *B Corporations* that meet its standards of verified social and environmental performance, public transparency, and legal accountability to balance profit and purpose.

Fifteen years later and there are currently over twenty-five thousand certified B Corporations in more than fifty countries. In the past five years, certified B Corporations in Australia and New Zealand have grown seven-fold—from thirty-three in 2014 to 269 in 2019 with a further thirty-five thousand businesses across sixty industries having started the process.

B Corporations have engaged with each other in non-aligned sectors such as insurance and banking, as well as joint campaigning on social and environmental issues such as climate change.

With seventy thousand mainly US businesses, Jay is currently executive co-chair of Imperative 21, a business-led network that believes the imperative of the twenty-first century is to reset our economic system so that its purpose is to create shared well-being on a healthy planet.

Co-founded by Australian technology company Atlassian, another global initiative is Pledge 1%, a movement that encourages and empowers over one thousand companies in one hundred countries of all sizes and stages to donate one per cent of their staff time, product, profit, and/or equity to a cause based on the company's long-term growth and business model.

With government

The arrival of Julie Bishop as the minister for Foreign Affairs in 2013 brought two major pivots to the Australian Government's foreign aid policy which continue today—the engagement of the private sector in development and the empowerment of women and girls in our region.

With a billion lifted out of poverty through economic growth, principally in India and China, she 'aligned the goal of poverty reduction with the pursuit of regional economic growth' and with it there 'must be a major role for the private sector in the development sphere'.

As a result, the Department of Foreign Affairs and Trade was tasked with engaging with Australia's corporates in partnering on the aid program. The resultant Business Partnerships Platform has led to thirty-three business-NFP partnerships investing over $40 million, including Mastercard partnering with the Vietnam Bank for Social Policies and the Asia Foundation to develop and roll out a mobile banking platform to improve access to digital financial services in Vietnam for low income customers.

With the use of private-sector financing, transfer of risk to the private sector, efficiencies arising from private-sector innovation, and the whole-of-life benefits achieved by bundling maintenance services into the contract, public-private partnerships (PPPs) have been attractive for governments to partner with business to fund and deliver costly infrastructure, such as toll roads.

PwC notes that 'the additional rigour which the investors and lenders apply to the risk assessment and monitoring of a project is perhaps the single biggest factor that explains the superior cost and time performance of PPPs over traditional procurements, after contracts are signed'.[210]

With community

At the time, it was known as the second worse place on the planet, behind Dafur in Western Sudan. I am standing in a field with two thousand newly displaced refugees on the outskirts of Goma who had fled killing and rape in their villages over the past two weeks. Thanks to the Guardian pharmacies 'Guardian Angel' program, I had brought blankets knitted by kindly aunts and grandmothers thirteen thousand kilometres away to give some comfort to the destitute children and warmth to the babies.

Three months before, I was sitting with the knitters as they packed out ABC's Ultimo studio. They were devotees of PFO Wrap With Love, a network of thousands of volunteers, who knit, crochet and weave in knitting groups or at home to make twenty-five by twenty-five centimetre squares and send them onto sewers to make them into multicoloured wraps. Since 1992, over twenty-five thousand volunteers have spent seventy-seven million hours making over half a million wraps for people in over seventy-five countries to protect them against the cold.

Just across the Rwandan border on the banks of Lake Kivu in eastern Democratic Republic of the Congo (DRC), Goma sits uncomfortably on the lava flows from the active Mount Nyiragongo; a volcano that lies just north in the beautiful Virunga National Park, home to the endangered mountain gorillas that Dian Fossey studied and made famous by the 1988 film, *Gorillas in the Mist.*

The size of Western Europe, the country is rich in diamonds, gold, copper, coltan, cobalt and zinc. This so-called 'resource curse' has led to the mass exploitation and enslavement by European colonialists, most notably King Leopold's Belgium, made famous in Joseph Conrad's *Heart of Darkness*, and then Mobutu Sese Seko's harsh thirty-two-year totalitarian regime which included the hanging of the prime minister and three cabinet ministers in front of fifty thousand spectators along with the embezzlement of up to $15 billion.

In 1994, Rwandan Hutu militia forces fled Rwanda into Eastern DRC during the genocide following the ascension of the Tutsi-led government and then used the Hutu refugee camps as bases to attack ethnic Tutsis in the area and into Rwanda. The Rwandan forces attacked the camps in 1996, before the Hutu militia forces joined forces with the DRC army to fight against the Tutsis militia who were now joined by Ugandan troops, in what would become known as the First African War. A year later, the Tutsis coalition marched into Kinshasa, ousting Mobutu and its leader, Laurent Kabila, declared as president.

A year later, however, Kabila's former allies in Uganda and Rwanda had turned against him and backed a new rebellion in the same eastern region which led to another five years of war, this time with Angola, Namibia, and Zimbabwe joining Kabila, along with a variety of local Congolese warlords. Over five million have died in the conflict, mostly from disease and starvation, and countless millions displaced.

I arrived four years after Kabila's son had taken over following the assassination of his father and two attempted coups. Not only were the Rwandan- and Ugandan-backed militia still launching raids on villages, raping women and children and burning their houses, Congolese army militias were doing the same.

As the most dangerous place on earth to be a woman, rape has been used as a weapon of war by all sides for the last ten years and was endemic, with the belief that sex with prepubescent girls gave strength in battle.[211]

Since their 2002 report *War Within the War,*[212] PFO Human Rights Watch was been raising the issue internationally by documenting rape, working with women's rights activists to organise advocacy efforts, lobbying judicial officials on cases, and urging journalists to cover the issue. After their meeting with Kabila, the military announced a zero-tolerance policy for sexual violence and other abuses, leading to rape trials and the conviction of army officers.

In 2009, then US Secretary of State Hillary Clinton visited, saying 'in 11 days of travel across Africa, I saw humanity at its worst—and at its best. In Goma last week, I saw both'. On meeting the rape victims, she said that 'the United States will stand with these brave people' and pledged US$17 million in aid for victims of sexual violence.

We were greeted by a band of green bereted, machine gun toting young rangers as we drove up to the ranger station in the Virunga National Park. The day before, one of their colleagues had been shot and killed by one of the militia groups that lived in the forest, logging and poaching illegally, especially for elephants, to fund their activities. Understandably, they were a bit jittery.

Despite being outnumbered and outgunned, I've never met more dedicated, positive and passionate people who have an unshakeable belief in conserving the park and its animals. Since then, another 150 rangers have sadly lost their lives at Virunga.

But one PFO believes that it can prevent these deaths.

In 2003, Australian park ranger Sean Willmore sat around the fire at an international conference one evening, hearing the stories of his fellow ranger delegates. To his surprise, a

Zimbabwean ranger revealed his head scar from a machete where he had been attacked by poachers. One by one, others followed suit showing their wounds. Sean decided there and then to sell his car and mortgage his house to travel around world to film their stories.

Coming back broke, Bryce Courtenay AM saw his story on the ABC's *7.30 Report* and sent a cheque, followed by other donors. Sean wanted to donate the money to the ranger's families but couldn't find a dedicated charity. Sitting next to him on a plane was a specialist in setting up charities and The Thin Green Line was born which 'protects nature's protectors' by bringing equipment and training to rangers, together with support to the families of those killed, including paying for their kids to go through school. Sean had become the ranger for rangers.

Seeing the constant flow of women and children walking into Goma from the village raids, we came across a long queue of hungry children in tattered clothes, most with no shoes. They had come into what I later realised was a school, after seeing a group of children sitting outside on benches looking at a blackboard perched on some bricks. At the end of the line was a teacher, who was checking for any obvious signs of disease and taking their names. Behind him, the shelves were empty.

On the drive back to the office, we were overawed by the sheer need and hardship around us. A young boy approached the car as we got out, holding an impressive model of a car made out of what appeared to be bits of a soft drink can. I asked him if he could make a model of our car. He came back the next day with an amazing replica, including rubber tyres, World Vision logo on the door and painted number plate. Since then, I've kept the model to remind me of the considerable, and often surprising, resilience and skill of people in adversity in developing countries.

Back in Australia, I went around the companies that supplied schoolbooks and stationery and managed to get regular donations shipped out to the school.

Unfortunately, the violence around Goma has continued to flare up over the years with little deterrence from the presence of UN peacekeepers. In October 2008, the Tutsi militia, under former Congolese Army General Laurent Nkunda, captured the territory around Goma and displaced another quarter of a million people with widespread destruction, looting and rape. Angry that the United Nations had done nothing to prevent the advance, Goma locals pelted the UN building with rocks and Molotov cocktails.

Distressed at this turn of events and frustrated with the lack of coverage in Australia, I contacted the Congolese Community of Victoria to discuss what could be done. We agreed to hold a 'Concert for the Congo' at Federation Square to showcase the wonderful Congolese music and musicians and get the news out, sponsored by my then-organisation, Mission Australia with the Victorian Multicultural Commission and Caritas, which was actively involved in campaigning to end the violence. On 12 December 2008, the crowd braved torrential summer rain to watch the awesome Musiki Manjaro.

From Britain's suffragettes in Holloway Prison embroidering slogans onto handkerchiefs, *Craftivism* (a term coined by Betsy Greer in 2003)—using craft for political and activist purposes—is gaining ground as a popular and effective way to call for social change. With Knitters for Knockers, women across the country have knitted thousands of cotton prostheses for breast cancer survivors that have had a mastectomy.

Knitting Nannas is an international 'disorganisation' where people come together to sit, knit, plot, have a yarn and a cuppa to 'ensure that our land, air and water are preserved for our children and grandchildren'. With trees, lamp posts and bicycles covered in brightly coloured woollies popping up at random, the highly secretive yarn-bombing, or guerrilla knitting, is a global phenomenon, including to protest the proposed demolition of trees or buildings, such as the historic St George's Terrace in Parramatta.

Multi-sector

As noted in the last chapter, collective action for a specific community outcome can provide the foundation for an effective multi-sector partnership.

Speaking at the 2016 Homelessness Conference, former Adelaide Thinker in Residence, Rosanne Haggerty, issued a challenge to solve homelessness for the five hundred people sleeping rough in inner city Adelaide through collective action.

The result was the Adelaide Zero Project with a coalition of forty not-for-profits, government agencies, businesses and service providers for Adelaide to become the first city outside North America to implement an approach that has seen a number of communities achieve Functional Zero homelessness where the number of people experiencing homelessness on any given night is no greater than housing placement availability.

The project has created a real-time names list, common assessment tool and an online dashboard with monthly data. Three years later, it is housed nearly six hundred people with those actively homeless falling to less than two hundred, including just over a hundred sleeping rough.

Ten rules for sustainable partnerships for purpose

1. Find the purpose fit

When I walked into the meeting with senior management of Jetstar, I only had one shot at the pitch. As a new airline, I knew that they had no charity partner and they wanted to deepen their brand from being seen only for cut price fares.

I was conscious that, starting in 1991, the parent company Qantas' *Change for Good* partnership with UNICEF had raised $25 million and invaluable profiling and supporter acquisition for the agency.

With both of us in the 2006 Leadership Victoria Williamson Community Leadership Program, Jetstar's then-head of Human Resources, Rohan Garnett, and I saw a fit between the two organisations as the interest of staff and passengers in the communities and culture in the destinations that Jetstar flew to, such as Vietnam and Cambodia.

Jetstar's low fares enabled more Australians to travel overseas, but it was also important to get them excited and wanting to travel to experience a wonderful and different place and people. Jetstar wanted to appeal to our hardwired curiosity to explore.

World Vision also wanted to introduce Australians to these communities to build their awareness and cultural understanding, especially as resilient and enterprising people that just needed a hand up, not a hand out. This was an important part of World Vision's pivot from showing the issues associated with communities it supported, (such as kids playing in polluted water), to the promotion of the outcomes achieved from its interventions (kids drinking clean water from new hand pumps).

Together, we developed *StarKids* with donation envelopes on flights as well as positive stories of children and their communities in the destination countries in the in-flight magazine and videos. For the staff, representatives from the air crew were selected to visit the communities and write up their experiences for World Vision and Jetstar communications.

Thirteen years later and $11 million has been raised for World Vision projects.

To anchor the partnership and have a reference point that underpins decision-making, the identification and matching of the underlying beliefs, values and purpose is essential from the start.

2. Engage emotionally

PurposeFull organisations have a secret weapon in any partnership. When judiciously applied, it can cement a lifelong commitment and passion for the organisation and the partnership.

Subject to safeguarding the dignity and respect of the people served, the PFO has the opportunity to show the partner its services and talk to clients to understand their challenges and the life-changing outcomes that can be achieved.

At Hanover, the homelessness service PFO, the residents painted portraits of themselves and others, and put them up as an exhibition. Each portrait told a very special story.

A tour of the hospice at Very Special Kids, where children with neurodegenerative conditions were cared for at the end of their lives, couldn't help but be heartbreaking and unforgettable. With families being torn apart by the tragic decline and loss of their loved one, the PFO exists to work with family members individually and as a unit to keep them together, including separate Dads, Mums and siblings' programs. This was the message of hope that led to many close partnerships with corporates and their staff, including Bupa and the Commonwealth Bank.

3. Build relationships

The most enduring and successful partnerships are built on mutual respect and trust through the building of relationships. In our transactional, busy lives we need to make time to get to know our counterparts, find out what makes them tick and display the behaviours we want to see in the relationship—honesty, openness, accountability, responsiveness and understanding. Only then will the partnership be more than just a short-lived deal for the convenience of the partners.

These relationships are held between various positions in the partners, starting with the most senior, who agree on the fundamentals of the arrangement as the reference point for its operationalisation with staff across the organisations.

4. Match the value

As we went into the Jetstar head office room and exchanged business cards, I noticed that the orange colour on both logos was exactly the same. Holding up the cards, I exclaimed 'we have a match already!'.

Inevitably there is a power differential between prospective partners, usually in favour of the business by providing money in compensation for the charity's service and reputation. This is OK, but it is not a partnership. It is a commercial arrangement.

I've found this especially so with corporate social responsibility and sponsorship initiatives, with the company's human resources or marketing driving the PFO to maximise the return for their spend.

A sustainable partnership needs to minimise, if not eliminate, this differential.

It is important to demonstrate there is significant value to each partner and not a one-sided arrangement, such as with a program logic outlined in the last chapter. With *StarKids*, Jetstar had access to over 220,000 Australians as child sponsors with World Vision through their newsletters and website, most of whom would be potential passengers, the content generation needed for Jetstar's communications and facilitating crew visits to World Vision programs.

5. Set the objectives

To avoid uncertainty, conflict and disappointment, it is important to determine and agree to the objectives of the partnership up front in as much clarity as possible, including the measurement of specific targets. This process also reveals what each partner truly values in the partnership.

Jetstar committed to raising $1 million annually for World Vision, which also measured the acquisition of donors coming though the staff engagement and in-flight giving and communications. World Vision also surveyed its brand awareness.

Increases in passenger numbers, especially to the destinations profiled in *StarKids*, were important to Jetstar, as well as the crew visits and their stories contributing to its staff well-being measures and the leveraging off a trusted brand to strengthen their own brand.

6. Agree on the arrangement

Whilst it is important to have the partnership arrangement agreed in writing, I've seen thick contracts issued by the company's lawyers that ensure the company owns the intellectual property and disclaims their liability, which effectively places all the risk on the not-for-profit without the reward.

Yes, this makes commercial sense to the business, but it is not a partnership agreement. Such an agreement should have equal provision for the ownership of the assets produced and any liabilities arising, as well as stipulating the basis on which the partnership has been formed, objectives and values to be adhered to, and the responsibilities and approvals required, including spokespeople and media.

7. Be responsive

The biggest complaint I get from corporates is the slow and bureaucratic response from not-for-profits, especially the larger agencies. Whilst this may be due to constrained staff time availability, too many times, not-for-profits add the partnership work that needs to be done to the existing already full day jobs of its staff.

I have to say that this was the case at World Vision for *StarKids*. It took an enormous effort to get all the departments needed—partnerships, marketing, public relations, finance, legal, programs and the office of the CEO—to work together to look like a seamless organisation to Jetstar.

Any partnership needs to be properly planned and project managed by all the partners. With the Myanmar Sustainable Tourism Hub partnership with Intrepid Travel, we used their agile planning approach using Atlassian's Trello to coordinate the planning and execution across Intrepid and AVI offices in Melbourne and Yangon such that it was visible at all times.

8. Leverage the partnership

On a hot day in the middle of the Melbourne Zoo, a highly excited women came rushing up to then-Victorian Premier John Brumby AO, desperately wanting an autograph. She stood expectantly in front of him with a black pen in hand proudly offering her cleavage. With discretion the better part of valour, John took the pen, deftly sidestepped and signed her back.

In a partnership between Zoos Victoria, Mission Australia and the RACV, we were at the Family Day at the Zoo, a free annual event for refugees and migrants. Zoos Victoria, which knew it could do better attracting visitors from different backgrounds and outer suburbs, provided free admission.

Mission Australia worked with this cohort across Victoria through its family and employment services and sought to increase their social participation and mobility. Most of the refugees and migrants had no concept of a zoo and had limited travel outside their suburb so the government's public transport agency provided free travel cards, maps and advice to families so they could navigate the system with RACV staff volunteering at the train and tram stations to assist families with their journey.

Rather than a special occasion, we wanted the families to have the experience that any other family would have and be confident to come back. The only exception was an inconspicuous launch of the event mid-morning by the premier. Zoo staff were amazed to see so many people from different backgrounds. The picnicking families on the main lawn looked like lunch time at the United Nations.

9. Celebrate achievements

Not-for-profits can feel guilty about spending valuable time and money in looking back, acknowledging and celebrating the outcomes of the partnership. So, it helped at Mission Australia that celebration was one of the organisation's core values.

Whether it is an anniversary, milestone reached or simply a beneficiary's story, regular get-togethers between the partners staff are essential to maintain the commitment, passion and connection with the purpose, as well as continue to build relationships.

10. Review and adjust

The partnership will inevitably evolve over time, especially with changes in key staff, strategic direction, operational plans and the availability of resources. Regular review points need to be part of the partnership's plan with a formal review process annually that is ideally externally facilitated. The review is another way to build relationships, reaffirm the commitment, celebrate achievements and plan for the future.

Evolve (or Else)

We will never have such slow change as we are experiencing now.

Andy Penn, CEO Telstra[213]

One day in 2012 I got a call from the founder of the 'IT for social justice' PFO, Infoxchange, Andrew Mahar AM, to ask me to meet with Luke Wright and Loretta Curtin who had a great idea for a social enterprise which they called Good Cycles.

With the doubling of workers cycling into work over the previous decade to thirty thousand daily,[214] their idea was for mobile bicycle servicing. With office blocks now having bike parks to encourage their workers to commute by bicycle, their concept was for bike mechanics to come and service the cycles on set days while their owners worked upstairs.

Luke and Loretta had also identified the need for more bike mechanics in the industry and Good Cycles would employ young disadvantaged jobseekers as trainees to work alongside the qualified mechanics, together with providing work experience at partner bike shops.

With co-founder of Intrepid Travel, Darrell Wade, providing the initial donation as the angel investor and PwC setting up the PFO in record time, the four of us met on the top floor of PwC. With a majestic view and silver service, we had gathered an impressive group comprising a prominent PFO board member, senior legal adviser and eminent people in the mobility sector to establish a Board for Good Cycles. After all, we wanted to start out with good governance.

After a lecture on how the board members would be personally liable for a range of risks and the many reporting requirements that management would need to provide to the board for good governance, Luke and Loretta suddenly found themselves losing their possessions and being captured in board servitude, rather than in the excitement and passion of getting Good Cycles going.

So, taking a step back, for the next year, we went back to a management committee, this time on folding chairs over sushi and beers at the back of the training space.

The next challenge was to get twenty businesses with bike parks to commit to regular servicing days and engage their staff to pay for the service or, even better, the company contributing under its environmental sustainability and staff well-being programs.

Despite tapping into our corporate contacts, we failed to get sufficient commitments.

So, with the support of free retail space from the Victorian government's property developer, VicUrban, and the Westpac Foundation, a Good Cycles shop was established which provided another income source, opportunity to employ the trainees and cheaper parts for the servicing business.

With no other bike shops in the area, income improved, although losses were made in the slow cold months when, for some reason, bike commuters preferred their transport to be dry and heated. This meant Good Cycles could take on a manager with experience in the cycle industry and grow the business.

Every now and again, amazingly talented people come from business onto the radar of PFOs, wanting to use their skills to make a difference and taking a pay cut for the privilege.

Jaison Hoernel is one of these special people. As a natural entrepreneur and influencer, he is an unstoppable force. He had established St Kilda Cycles, designed bike products and consulted internationally in bike share schemes. From replacing the need for $50,000 car park places at train stations to connecting transport nodes and reducing inner city traffic, he knew that Good Cycles could create a step change in bike-based mobility and sustainability.

To their credit, Luke and Loretta gave the space and support needed for Jaison to come in as the general manager, despite being horrified at times by the un-Good Cycles-like language in communications to supporters and Jaison's state of perpetual motion.

Two important acquisitions followed that led the PFO to be financially viable and provide more salaried traineeships for disadvantaged young people. Good Cycles won the maintenance contract for the blue bikes in the State government's Bike Share scheme managed by RACV and then took over Bicycle Training Australia (BTA). The bike shop was relocated nearby after VicUrban left the building thanks to support from Lendlease, which gave room for the training. Jaison then worked with the City of Melbourne and funders to trial a pop-up shop in a container on the harbour esplanade.

Given that the hardest work for such social enterprises is the transition of disadvantaged people into sustainable mainstream employment, support from Social Venture Partners enabled the design of a program logic. Steve Shepherd, from youth coaching company Two Point Zero, provided the skills training framework and funding from Gandel Philanthropy recruited a transitions coordinator to work with business to identify their needs and support the transition in the workplace.

Then, one day on his way home from work, Jaison noticed a yellow bike sticking up from beneath a large tarpaulin near his train station. Going closer to investigate, he had inadvertently stumbled on hundreds of hidden *obikes* which were about to invade the city and turn his world upside down.

Like the blue bikes in Melbourne and the red Santander cycles in London, cities around the world have put in government-funded bike share schemes to enable another form of mobility for residents and visitors. But the expensive infrastructure with its payment and docking stations in interspersed locations around the city proved to be its Achilles' heel.

In 2014, five students from the Peking University's cycling club came up with a way that liberated bikes from their stations by scanning a QR code on the bikes with a smart phone, which then charged the rider per period used and which could be left anywhere to be picked up again. Starting with Beijing university campuses, they called the company 'ofo' because the word looked like someone riding a bicycle.

The result was a wave of tech start-ups with billions of dollars raised by forty bike-sharing companies. Cities around the world were inundated with competing fluorescent orange, canary yellow, ocean blue, scarlet red and other brightly coloured shared bikes. At the time, more than two million bikes were available for sharing from fifteen companies in Beijing alone.

Without any State regulations or local by-laws specifically preventing them, suddenly thousands of yellow obikes filled the streets of Melbourne, followed by orange Mobikes in Sydney. Riders just downloaded the app, found a bike, rode away and left it standing and locked up with the app when finished. Available, convenient and cheap.

The problem was that, at the time, the Victorian government's contract for its bike scheme, from which Good Cycles derived a third of its income and half its traineeships, was up and it was considering whether to continue the program and its funding in light of the new—and at no cost to them—bike share offerings.

At an emergency Good Cycles board meeting, we considered everything from exposing the safety issues in the press to starting our own bike share service.

Then, reminiscent of the unexpected bacteria inflicting the aliens in the War of the Worlds, social media turned on the invaders. Compromising photos of yellow bikes in trees and on railway tracks started appearing on Instagram, Twitter, Facebook and Snapchat. Film of hundreds of obikes being fished out of the Yarra river went viral and appeared on the primetime nightly news. The tide of public opinion changed. The share bikes were now seen as a blight on the world's most liveable city. With $3,000 fines for each littering bike announced by the State's Environmental Protection Agency, obike quietly left Melbourne, followed by exits from Munich, Amsterdam, Taiwan, Austria, Malaysia, Switzerland and Singapore.

Like all good PFO CEOs, Jaison rode the wave and embraced the change, partnering with Mobike to win the bike share scheme for the Gold Coast Commonwealth Games.

Five years later, the bike share world war has left few survivors and little remains of the global phenomena or the billions of dollars invested. Meanwhile, biding their time, the global car share companies have now swooped in with Uber's Jump electric bikes and scooters, and Lyft's takeover of Ford's GoBike and Citi Bike in the United States.

In Australia, Newcastle-based and family-owned PFO BYKKO 'wants to change the way people move' and operates electric bike shares in university campuses, apartment blocks, resorts and environmentally friendly developments. Brisbane still has a dock-based bike share scheme, CityCycle, with an app to show the availability of bikes on each station, and Lime's scooters are in Brisbane and Sydney. Jump is trialling in Melbourne and Sydney. Their partner? Yes, you guessed it— Good Cycles!

With the bike share threat over, Jaison really got on his bike. Known as bike-based street services, he designed and implemented a commercial model for providing inner city services by bicycle, from washing advertising boards to collecting recycling from restaurants. At the time of writing, he is looking to set up a 'last mile' delivery service with impact investment, similar to Zedify in the United Kingdom.

Back to the future

The establishment of purpose-driven organisations by business is not new. The first consumer cooperatives arose in coal mining towns in England in response to the high grocery prices charged by the mine owners in the Industrial Revolution who also owned the store. Named after the first, these 'Rochdale' cooperatives played an integral role in the lives of communities in mining districts, metropolitan areas and rural regions of Australia from 1859, such as the Hunter Valley, the Illawarra region and the Lithgow Valley in NSW, Wonthaggi in Victoria and Collie in Western Australia.

The cooperative's values of self-help, self-responsibility, democracy, equality, equity and solidarity led to the model being used to provide finance for members. Credit unions and mutuals were born so that customers became owners. Australia's State and Territory public servants were the first to take up this model, with the South Australia and ACT associations the founders of what today is Beyond Bank.

Robert Keogh, CEO of Beyond Bank, explains that 'it also goes beyond benefitting just the customer; it benefits their community as well. It's about recognising the mutual dependence all three have with each other. They are interdependent. If customers and their community are benefitting, then the bank will benefit also. This means the business can continue to deliver more and hence the circle of mutuality continues.

Communicating a clear purpose not only has implications for improving an organisation's financial health and competitiveness through a customer lens, but employees find greater meaning in their work and better offer their energy and dedication to the business. They grow rather than stagnate. They do more—and they do it better'.[215]

Designed in partnership with a group of former teachers, Beyond Bank harnesses its expertise in providing the Beyond Money financial education program to primary school-aged children to teach them about earning, saving and spending in alignment with the Australian school curriculum.

Similarly, started in 1957, the CSIRO Co-operative Credit Society has grown and evolved, joining together seventy-two credit unions and co-operatives to become Australia's first customer-owned bank—Bank Australia.

Today, Australia's customer-owned banks, comprising thirty-five credit unions, thirty-one mutual banks and one building society, collectively are Australia's fifth biggest deposit holder after the big four banks, with over $100 billion in deposits and over a thousand branches around the country.

As testament to their purpose to improve the economic and social well-being of all their members who are also their customers, according to the latest Roy Morgan research, the mutual banks have a much higher customer satisfaction average of eighty-nine per cent, compared to the big four banks rating of seventy-seven per cent.

The biggest risk

Facilitating an organisational risk workshop for a leading social services PFO, I asked each manager to describe the key risks to the organisation. I went around the table and, one by one, each manager listed the risks from their perspective. By the last manager, we had a good mix on the whiteboard—fraud, client death, staff injury, loss of government contracts and a crisis of public confidence.

Keen to wrap up and start scoring the risks, I came to the last in line, the chief executive. Starting as a social worker, over a decade he had risen to services manager and then to lead the agency. Calm and grounded, he was not known for needless displays of passion or excitement. He sat back in his chair and said something that I will never forget: 'The biggest risk is that we don't take risks'.

On closer examination, his methodology was to invest the PFO's hard-earned fundraising income into the 1) systematic research of the characteristics and needs of its clients; 2) design and implementation of pilot projects that enabled enhanced outcomes for his cohort over and above its core services; and 3) ongoing evaluation data that demonstrated effective delivery results and improved the program.

Over the last twenty years, I've seen literally hundreds of such trials and pilots come and go. All these projects and programs had passionate advocates and demonstrated tangible outcomes for people in need but never attained ongoing financing, whether through fees, government funding or other support.

So, here are six key steps to maximise the chances of ongoing success:

1. The need is ongoing, hasn't been adequately addressed and will always be important to government to resolve, as identified in government policy.
2. Governments are engaged throughout, including in formal review and evaluation processes.
3. The agency owns the issue by publishing the research and evaluation data, and becomes the go-to, trusted agency to government and media.

4. The design of the new project or program is founded on demonstrated practice from past experience and so leverages the evidence and reputation of the PFO.

5. The delivery is well executed and produces excellent demonstrated outcomes, minimising any risk to government.

6. The PFO has the capacity and local knowledge to scale up or replicate the project or program in other areas.

This may look like augmentation or enhancement of the PFO's services, but in my experience, to government, it represents the incremental type of service innovation that they seek. To the PFO, it can offer sustainable growth.

Given the level of uncertainty and change PFOs experience with short-term funding contracts, fundraising competition, government political cycles, rising levels and complexity of needs, it is no wonder that the Study of Australian Leadership carried out by the University of Melbourne found that 'public sector organisations were more likely than private sector organisations to have reported high levels on both types of innovation'.[216] The same result was reported by CommBank's Innovation Index which ranked the not-for-profit sector higher than any other Australian industry.[217]

Meanwhile, there is ongoing criticism that Australian businesses are backward, risk averse and happy with mediocrity. In 2020, CSIRO and the University of Queensland reported only nine per cent of Australian innovations were market-leading and only about half of companies had released a new product in the past three years. It said Australia was a nation of adopters but not creators. At the same time, the Australian Institute of Company Directors reported that nearly three quarters of company directors continue to see a risk-adverse decision-making culture on Australian boards.[218]

With an estimated US$5-7 trillion needed to achieve the Sustainable Development Goals and the rapidly growing impact investment market worth less than half, the chasm that exists between the demand and supply of investible social ventures is a global call to action for more evidence-based, innovative solutions to our social and environmental challenges.

Scaling up

I was highly suspicious of Michael Perusco when he walked into the interview room at the Brotherhood of St Laurence. As a fellow alumni from Arthur Andersen, I couldn't believe there was another Andersen Android that would want to work for less money and status. It was his longest ever interview as I repeatedly questioned his motives.

In the true tradition of the Brotherhood, Michael has never been afraid to develop new program models that, when trialled and successful, challenge and attempt to change the system to improve people's lives.

His next stop was heading up Sacred Heart Mission, whose clientele comprises aged people experiencing chronic physical and mental health issues and homelessness. Since being victims of trauma in their childhood, they have bounced around social services all their lives. With at least eight different case workers, they have a full-time job being chronically homeless. The service system makes their homelessness bearable and, like *Million Dollar Murray* in the United States,[219] they have cost the taxpayer a small fortune over their lifetimes.

Rather than just doing the best for these people to ease their burden and help them survive, Michael had the courage to challenge the welfare world and devise a way to get them out of chronic homelessness and the welfare system itself.

He set up a trial program called Journey to Social Inclusion (J2SI) that, with donor support, set up one case worker per four clients to coordinate their care and act as the significant other in their life, a key role that wants them to succeed and raises their expectations of resolving their health issues and gaining economic participation.

In J2SI, Michael placed an emphasis on monitoring and evaluation, including a randomised control trial, to ensure timely and rigorous evidence was produced to influence his network of donors, politicians and senior bureaucrats.

The program, which is now government funded and the heart of a social impact bond, has succeeded in not just getting people out of the chronic homelessness system, it has changed perceptions of this cohort by government and services providers. Now with Berry Street, he is currently doing the same for young traumatised people to get them out of the out-of-home care system.

As part of its third way approach, the incoming Tony Blair government set up the Social Investment Task Force (SITF) in 2000 to 'look at ways to create wealth and promote enterprise to support economic regeneration and community cohesion'. Chaired by the head of the United Kingdom's largest capital venture firm, Sir Ronald Cohen, it led to range of significant social impact investment initiatives in the United Kingdom, including the Big Society Bank (with unclaimed monies from banks and building societies), Bridges Ventures Fund (investing in businesses in deprived areas) and Social Finance UK, which launched the first social impact investment instrument, a Social Impact Bond (SIB), in 2010 to improve the rate of recidivism of short-term prisoners.

This instrument is unique because it spreads the risk across the investors (who provide the capital but only earn a return if the social outcomes are achieved), government (which guarantees the capital but only pays the return if the social outcomes are met) and the PFO (which runs the program and delivers the outcomes).

Since then, sixty Social Impact Bonds have been launched in fifteen countries, raising more than $200 million in investment to address social challenges.

In Australia, the New South Wales government has led with three Social Benefit Bonds (SBBs), including a $7 million, seven-year Newpin SBB run by Uniting to deliver its program to enable children in out-of-home care to be restored to their families and prevent at-risk children from entering care. The bond was a resounding success, returning 391 children to the care of their families with an overall restoration rate of sixty-one per cent and delivering an annual financial return of ten per cent to investors.

Tasked with improving housing affordability in Australia, in March 2019, the National Housing Finance and Investment Corporation issued its first $315 million fixed rate, ten-year social housing bond. It was oversubscribed by almost a billion dollars.

The same approach has seen the establishment of Development Impact Bonds (DIBs) with a funder paying the return rather than a developing country government. The first, in June 2014, saw Instiglio, Children's Investment Fund Foundation, Educate Girls, IDinsight and UBS Optimus Foundation partner to reduce the gender gap in education in rural India by getting girls into school and learning.

In 2016, in a global first, Monash University raised $218 million through a climate bond to part finance their five-year Capital Development Plan with new low-carbon teaching facilities and solar panels, followed by $66 million and $116 million raised in 2017 and 2018.

With a global market size of up to US$2.1 trillion, the global impact investment market is doubling each year,[220] and still growing despite COVID-19, it is estimated that the market is meeting only about ten per cent of the demand.[221] At the end of 2019, the value of Australian impact investment products was $19.9 billion with 111 Impact investment products widely on offer to Australian investors, a fifth of the potential demand.[222]

To date, the largest and most successful impact investment in Australia was the $22.5 million raised by forty-one social investors for the purchase of 678 former ABC Learning centres by Good Start with a consortium comprising Social Ventures Australia, the Benevolent Society, Mission Australia and The Brotherhood of St Laurence, led by former co-founder and executive director of Macquarie Group's private equity and CEO of Social Ventures Australia, Michael Traill AM.[223]

In 2017, HESTA invested $19 million from its Social Impact Investment Trust in a village designed to recreate real life experiences for those living with dementia in partnership with a PFO aged-care provider, Glenview, Social Ventures Australia and the Commonwealth government. The site in the Tasmanian suburb of Glenorchy has fifteen demographically tailored homes set within a small-town context complete with streets, a supermarket, cinema, café, beauty salon and gardens.

The factors for most PFOs in considering impact investment that needs to generate a return to investors are:

- risk profile of the PFO's board
- the cost of developing the project to the prospectus needed to attract the investors
- the period and form of the investment, such as debt and/ or equity
- availability of investors
- the risk that the project does not realise the required return
- cheaper and less risky capital may be accessible, given the current low interest rates, for instance bank lending against an asset owned by the PFO
- risk of government or other income generated by the investment

The allocation of up to five per cent of their $260 million capital to impact investments was one of the reasons that I joined the Board of the Lord Mayor's Charitable Foundation (LMCF). This has seen first mover investments in innovative digital products, such as Hire Up, a digital platform enabling people with disabilities to organise their own carers to build their social, employment or educational opportunities.

However, Michael Traill AM notes that 'the shortage of social impact investment opportunities with transparent measurement of social outcomes and financial performance is a major barrier to further growth'.[224] I can appreciate the challenge of the financial and time investment needed by PFOs to produce the business case needed by investors, as well as the additional risk they acquire, which is why there is a lack of supply of impact investment ready initiatives.

Some trusts and foundations, such as LMCF, can fund this development and Impact Investment Australia manages the Australian government's Impact Investment Ready Growth Grant to develop the capacity of PFOs to seek impact investment.

If we are to realise the potential of impact investment, PFOs, especially with the social and environmental intrapreneurs within them, need much more funding and support to model and scale up to be impact investment ready. PFOs rarely have this capacity in-house and can harness other PFOs, such as Social Ventures Australia and Social Enterprise Finance Australia.

The UK government solved this dilemma by putting £400 million lying in unclaimed bank accounts, with a further £200 million from the United Kingdom's four major banks, into Big Society Capital (BSC), the world's first social investment bank. Since its inception, the BSC has provided nearly £2 billion financing to charities and social enterprises, through fund managers and social banks, in order to build the infrastructure of a thriving impact sector that brings investment to social organisations that have previously depended exclusively on gifts and grants.[225]

The United States government similarly established a US$1 billion fund for impact investing and in 2020 Prudential's impact investing fund hit US$1 billion.

The Australian Securities and Investments Commission administers $1.1 billion of lost money yet to be claimed from bank accounts, shares, investments and life insurance policies. A one per cent allocation from the Future Fund for impact investing would yield another $1.6 billion. As we recover from COVID-19, this would enable a boost to the capacity of PFOs to deliver much needed social and economic impact.

Change is hard without government leadership. In 2019, the Morrison government established the Social Impact Investing Taskforce comprising an expert panel to develop a strategy for how impact investment can provide additional solutions to address entrenched disadvantage, achieve measurable social impact and facilitate private capital investment in the impact investment market.

In its interim report, the taskforce recommended four key action areas for the government to develop a mature and sustainable social impact investing market in Australia:

1. Measure and incentivise social impact by supporting the widespread use of accurate methods for measuring, reporting and evaluating social impact.

2. Foster the growth of social impact investing opportunities, in particular, supporting social enterprises to build capacity to attract investment and win social procurement contracts, and streamlined payment-by-results programs such as outcomes funds and social impact bonds.

3. Support capital to flow to social impact investments by reducing the barriers individuals and organisations face when investing in social impact investments.

4. Enable a well-functioning market by ensuring the underlying structures are in place to support an efficient and effective social impact investing market that delivers a broad public benefit.[226]

Responding to COVID-19

Who would have thought that the supermarket aisles of Australia would be the scene of conflict broadcasted around the world with the fights over the panic buying of toilet paper being beamed around the globe? With #toiletpapergate and #toiletpapercrisis top trending on social media, rolls were being flogged for hundreds of dollars online and listeners were calling into radio stations to win packs of triple-ply. The Northern Territory News even printed a special eight-page lift out—of blank pages—to use as toilet paper. I'm sorry to say I even put our office stockpile under lock and key, lest the temptation of my colleagues be too great.

But, for three Australians, COVID-19 proved to be godsend.

Eight years before, Simon Griffiths was sitting on a toilet in a draughty warehouse videoed live to thousands of people. He refused to move until he and his co-founders, Jehan and Danny, had raised enough pre-orders to start production. Fifty hours of staying awake and one cold and aching bottom later, they had crowdfunded over $50,000 and Who Gives A Crap was off and running.

During his six years at university studying engineering and economics, Simon worked with a variety of not-for-profits in developing countries and became aware that, while there were heaps of organisations doing incredible work, there was a consistent problem—a lack of sustainable funding. As a result, their scalability was limited and a lot of time was wasted trying to source funding.

With 2.3 billion people not having access to a toilet, the lack of basic sanitation causes disease and death, including one child dying every two minutes from diarrhoeal diseases caused by poor water and sanitation—the biggest killer for children under five.

He had come across bottled water company Ethos water (later acquired by Starbucks), started by a McKinsey consultant after working in communities in South Africa, to fund programs to increase access to clean water. Walking into a bathroom one day, Simon noticed a six pack of toilet rolls and the name came into his head. He knew he could have fun with the product among the more serious brands, utilise sustainable paper and harness the profits to build toilets.

Their first production run sold out quickly with people showing their colourful arty toilet rolls around the world on social media going viral. With the goal for everyone to have access to a toilet by 2050, they have expanded their range to include tissues and kitchen roll.

With the hoarding of toilet rolls during COVID-19, Who Gives a Crap made a record profit and donation of $5.85 million to sanitation PFOs, including Water Aid and becoming its largest donor.

The COVID-19 pandemic has been the ultimate adaptive challenge for all organisations around the world, whilst presenting unique opportunities for some PFOs. As T2 co-founder, Maryanne Shearer, noted 'COVID-19 is an opportunity to recalibrate' and 'reconnect with what they love and the money will flow'.

I first met Craig Fitzgerald, the head of international operations of Aspen Medical in Fiji after the PFO had been selected by the Fiji government to develop, finance, upgrade, operate and maintain Lautoka Hospital, the country's second largest health facility, as a public-private partnership with the Fiji National Provident Fund.

Given the precarious state of health services I had seen over the years in lower income countries, I thought at the time that this was a brave move. Having been established in 2003 by two friends with military backgrounds, I soon learned that Aspen Medical relished parachuting into a health crisis anywhere around the world at the request of governments at a scale no other organisation could attempt.

This belief has created a loyal band of workers who also value the opportunity to go to challenging situations, such as into Sierra Leone and Liberia to set up and work in the Ebola treatment centres.

So, it's no wonder then that Aspen Medical was speed dialled by the Australian government to tackle COVID-19. Their clinicians screened and tested the Ruby Princess crew members stranded at Port Kembla, set up 140 respiratory clinics across Australia in six weeks, built and operated a fifty-one-bed facility in Canberra in forty-four days, and (not without controversy) sent in replacement staff to manage the COVID-19 stricken aged-care facilities, Newmarch House and St Basil's Home for the Aged in Sydney and Melbourne, respectively, before being contracted to give COVID-19 vaccinations in aged-care homes.

As a *PurposeFull* organisation, Craig makes the point that, although corporate social responsibility (CSR) is welcome, 'it is not going to move the dial' to effect the change needed.

Faced with the suspension of international flights with airlines across the globe parking their planes due to the pandemic, the Intrepid Travel team took their small group adventure ethos and developed a suite of itineraries for their travellers to see their own country. They say it much better than I can:

> Created by locals, for locals—Intrepid Retreats are a brand-new way to discover incredible places just a few hours away from home. We've taken the best bits of an Intrepid adventure—the insider info and guidance of a local, support for local communities, memorable stays, and experiences you can't have on your own— all rolled up into a short getaway near you. Welcome to a whole new way to explore your own backyard.

With masks first being made mandatory in Melbourne in July 2020, PFOs from around the country stepped up. With a purpose to make and provide handmade items to those suffering from distress, health crisis or disadvantage and the communities that support them, the Toowoomba Women's Shed based Sewing for Charity Australia got its three thousand volunteers making masks. With twenty-five hundred volunteers nationally, Masks for Aussies has supplied more than one hundred thousand free masks during the pandemic, and refugee fashion social enterprise The Social Studio sold out of the five thousand masks they made in the first week.

Supporting refugees, migrants and people seeking asylum, social enterprises SisterWorks and Second Stitch also made and sold out of their masks, as did the Alperstein Designs range of face masks using offcut fabrics featuring stunning Aboriginal artworks.

In contrast, in the same month, Australian activewear brand, Lorna Jane, was fined $39,960 for allegedly claiming that its new line of antivirus activewear, LJ Shield, prevents and protects against infectious diseases, implying it is effective against COVID-19.

Going digital

After I came to YSAS, I started getting worried calls from friends and past colleagues. After noticing a funny smell on their son's clothes, a small packet of weed under the bed, or hearing of a bong being passed around a party that their daughter went to, they were filled with dread that their precious one was only a short step to dying horribly in a laneway from a heroin overdose.

Their fear was real and all I could do was talk to them about the necessary and normal risk-taking behaviour needed to develop teenage brains and that a supportive, non-judgemental environment around them, particularly family and friends, was key to ensuring they came out the other side unscathed.

At the same time, young people would call YSAS each week worried about their drug and alcohol consumption, whilst many others did not know who to turn to in order to get reliable information and wouldn't go to a drug and alcohol service to do so.

We know that when it comes to health, prevention is better than cure. But, with tight government budgets, limited resources are focused on the most in need, with less than two per cent of total health expenditure going towards prevention.[227] Australia's youth drug and alcohol services are no exception. The limited day and residential rehabilitation places available need to be reserved for chronic cases.

With the support of the Youth Action Groups and the funds raised by febfast, we developed an easily accessible online self-assessment platform with its own branding and website called YoDAA (Youth Drugs and Alcohol Advice) with quizzes and advice videos from YSAS' youth workers depending on the outcome of the assessment.

The use of technology has grown exponentially during the pandemic. McKinsey reported in May 2020 that 'we have vaulted five years forward in consumer and business digital adoption in a matter of around eight weeks of COVID-19'. The same month, based on its deliveries data, Australia Post reported an eighty per cent increase in online shopping compared to the same time last year with 5.2 million Australian households shopping online.[228] Click-and-Collect has now entered our common vocabulary.

With the shift to online shopping and a fifty per cent increase in readership for the company's digital catalogue, Coles ceased its paper catalogue, replaced by *coles&co*, a digital, personalised alternative that offers shoppers specials along with exclusive content to inspire customers with new products, tips and recipes, and saving $42 million in the process.

With the first lockdown in Melbourne, PFO Tourism Victoria created the website *Click for Vic* to offer a 'selection of the many restaurants, cafes, bars, producers, growers, and artisans offering you a slice of the good life delivered straight to your door', resulting in more than 159,000 visits in its first week.

PFOs have been at the forefront of pivoting during COVID-19 to a digital offering, whether it is the elephant cam at Tooronga Zoo, Sydney Dance Company's Virtual Studio or a virtual tour of the National Gallery of Australia.

No longer being able to hold their annual public Million Paws Walk event in May 2020, instead the RSPCA held the *Million Paws Walk: Walk This May* with over ten thousand participants walking their pets in their own backyards, tagging their photos and raising over $700,000.

With only three per cent of international volunteering for development relating to environmental sustainability, I pitched my organisation, AVI, to host the annual global conference of the sector's peak body, the International Forum for Volunteering for Development, in October 2020 in the Pacific with the theme of volunteering for climate action.

As the flagship event for members, I was keen to go ahead despite the lack of international travel during COVID-19 with an experience as close as possible to the real thing. I approached the four companies that, until COVID-19, were in the little-known virtual conference centre business. The result was a Pacific-themed virtual lobby, an auditorium for the presentations, world café virtual booths for the members to show their work with videos, downloadable documents and an avatar to talk to; and a networking Bula lounge to meet and email delegates. Studios in Melbourne and Suva (by Fiji TV) allowed live commentary and Q&A with pre-recorded presentation sessions.

Over twice as many delegates were able to attend than the usual face-to-face conference and future events will incorporate virtual sessions.

The growth of blockchain as a more secure way of transferring data and payments is another opportunity to innovate and grow, with Tokens for Humanity the first blockchain-powered charity to be recognised by the ACNC. In April 2021, it announced another Australian first with the sale of sixty-four non-fungible token (NFT) artwork collectibles to raise funds.

Diversifying income

A world's first at the time, Very Special Kids (VSK) is a PFO in the inner-city suburbs of Melbourne founded by two families whose children died of leukemia in 1985. VSK aims to care for children with terminal neurodegenerative conditions in a hospice and to keep the family from disintegrating through this traumatic experience through a family therapy service.

Its first Director, Sister Margaret Noone's relationship with the chairman of Tattersalls resulted in funding for the development of the site and high-profile conscripts to the board and the VSK Foundation. Tattersalls' marketing company came up with the idea of plastic pink piggy banks on counters at Tatts venues to collect donations with personalised supersized versions on trailers that visit the venues. Penelope and her colleagues were born and the annual piggy bank appeal raises over $1 million annually to fund the organisation.

VSK recognised they were totally reliant on this appeal income and I came in 2003 with relationships with the Commonwealth and State health departments to seek government funding for its services. I failed. Why would government fund a venture that had so much support? It took two subsequent CEOs and ten years of advocacy for VSK to achieve this outcome.

Whether it is relatively new PFOs seeking or growing government funding, or heavily government-funded PFOs seeking other income sources, every PFO I know is looking to diversify its income base to improve its financial sustainability in this environment of increasing competition, change and uncertainty.

Before we look at different income generating activities, let's go and ask a hedgehog for directions.

In his seminal work, *Good to Great*, Jim Collins outlines the Hedgehog Concept[229] with great companies achieving the intersection between:

- What are you deeply passionate about;

- What can you be the best in the world at; and

- What drives your economic engine.

This model equally applies to PFOs. Passion comes from our purpose and beliefs, the economic engine represents our sales, funding and fundraising, and PFOs have leading evidence-based practice in their services, if not world-class.

Business has mastered the creation and marketing of new products and services that are incrementally differentiated from their core or base product/service. Just look at the cereal aisle in your supermarket. So, the first place to start is building on your existing products or services.

Start a commercial business

There is nothing to stop PFOs commercialising their knowledge, systems, experience or intellectual property and starting commercial businesses to generate net profits to fund its work, including as a wholly owned for-profit subsidiary.

For instance, Oxfam established Oxfam Trading as a commercial company and Save the Children founded Inclusiv Ventures to develop social ventures which bring sustainable solutions to poverty and exclusion through partnerships between the private sector, donors and development organisations.

Harnessing its recruitment and workforce development expertise in Australia for the people in the South Pacific, AVI set up Pacific People as a wholly owned for-profit subsidiary company operating from Fiji, whilst housing and homelessness PFO Kids Under Cover used its design expertise in tiny houses to start a commercial company called Nestd Homes.

In 2017, Camp Quality created the oranges toolkit as a wholly-owned subsidiary dedicated to delivering evidence-based, measurable and practical tools that build resilient and change-responsive workplaces.

On a larger scale, Bethel Funerals was set up to generate money for Bible translation in the face of declining donations. Recently, Daniel Flynn has led the growth of thankyou as a category killer in hygiene products outselling Procter & Gamble with the net profits going to international development.[230]

Setting up a commercial business or social enterprise is an opportunity to partner with business to acquire the appropriate commercial expertise, knowledge and attitudes,[231] including in the governance of the venture, whether it is a new joint venture, company, board or steering committee.

Be enterprising

With twenty thousand in Australia and growing,[232] social enterprises are businesses that trade to intentionally tackle social problems, improve communities, provide access to employment and training, help the environment, or make profits for a cause.

Taking the Chinese proverb, 'give a man a fish and you feed him for a day. Teach a man how to fish and you feed him for a lifetime', a social enterprise then builds and operates the fish cannery business, employing disadvantaged jobseekers and using the profits to fund its activities.

Established in 2001, Wise Employment's Clean Force is a great example, operating in Sydney, Melbourne and Bendigo and providing employment for people with disability, including mental illness. The business provides quality commercial cleaning services for offices, apartment complexes, entertainment venues and vacated residences, as well as roads and grounds maintenance.

Prime Minister Kevin Rudd's stimulus package in the Global Financial Crisis stimulated the social enterprise sector with hundreds of social enterprises launched. One that has gone from strength to strength is Mission Australia's Soft Landings in NSW which has recycled nearly a million mattresses.

As a social enterprise tragic, having established six in Melbourne over the last twelve years and chaired another, my favourite was Urban Renewal, run by former builder, Chris Hawken, which provided landscape and construction services and was the first social enterprise on the Victorian Construction Supply Register. Young, disadvantaged, unemployed trainees worked on a variety of projects under trades pre-apprenticeships, including building a $600,000 sports precinct for the Victorian government.

Social enterprises can be the answer to significant income diversification or profit generation, especially if the PFO is in a position to capitalise at scale from social procurement opportunities from government or corporates. Other commercial advantages, such as a rent-free location or the donation of goods sold, are also welcome.

At the same time, social enterprises can have outstanding outcomes for disadvantaged people as they enable people who have been welfare recipients all their lives, as their family probably have, to be treated from the first minute as a trainee or employee. I have seen this completely change their perspective, behaviour and expectation. Even if they don't progress into that industry, they feel more confident about employment and open up a discussion about what jobs they would like to do.

To achieve this, the social enterprise needs to be:

- strong commercially with quality and price competitive products/services so that it can, in time, generate a profit and that the work environment is as close as possible to businesses that the trainees would transition to as mainstream employment;

- staffed by a full complement of experienced commercial staff that can cope with a workforce that they would not otherwise employ or who occasionally do not turn up for work; and

- supported by fundraising to fund the support and training costs of the trainees that the business cannot absorb, unless the trainees are managed by another PFO or the business generates sufficient margins to cover the cost of employing trainees, as Good Cycles does.

A number of PFOs exist to support the establishment and growth of social enterprises, such as the Swinburne Social Startup Studio, Social Traders, Social Enterprise Finance Australia and Social Ventures Australia, as well as a number of dedicated trusts and foundations, such as the English Family Foundation and the Westpac Foundation.

Fundraising

Whilst only providing on average eight per cent of a PFO's income,[233] donations from individuals, corporates and their staff, trusts and foundations are vital for innovative programs and enabling additional outcomes to realise the PFO's purpose, as well as much needed untied income for evaluation and research, systems development and infrastructure.

The bad news first. The traditional fundraising model is tired and in decline. Australians are fed up of being pestered by mass direct mail, chuggers, calls and emails. The market is crowded with three thousand new charities joining the sector every year and Australians are becoming less charitable and less trusting of charities.[234]

The better news is that with an ageing population and as untied income, bequests should still be a main focus for PFOs, as are trusts and foundations, which have become more focused and transparent in their giving.

With 1,284 Private Ancillary Funds (PAFs) now in existence in Australia and growing at an annual rate of eight per cent, PAFs now distribute $457 million a year to charities, a distribution that has tripled in the space of six years. PAFs are a type of charitable trust designed to provide individuals, families or associations with an investment structure for philanthropic purposes. As well as creating a giving mechanism for life that allows the family to be involved, the main benefit of a PAF is to park the net proceeds of the sale of an asset so that is not subjected to capital gains tax. A PAF cannot solicit donations from the public and cannot accept donations totalling more than twenty per cent of the value of the fund at the previous 30 June from people other than the founder, associates or employees of the founder.[235]

Although PAFs have to distribute a minimum of five per cent of their net assets a year to charities that are deductible gift recipients, they are private and invisible to PFOs. However, there are a number of consultants that act as intermediaries between PAFs and PFOs, such as filantropia run by two former ANZ Trustees managers.

Having run febfast, the pause for a cause, and with the success of World's Greatest Shave, Run for the Kids, Movember and the Big Freeze, I know how tempting it is to come up with the next experiential campaign or event that raises funds whilst engaging new and existing supporters. This quest has led to some really innovative month campaigns, such as Veganuary, februDAREy, March Charge, Mindful in May, JulEYE, Dogtober and Decembeard (cleverly following on from Movember).

You will be pleased to know that colours are not left out with Big Red BBQ, Purple Day, Wear Green for Premmies,

March into Yellow, Go Blue for Autism, White Shirt Day, Teal Ribbon Day, Wear White at Work, White Wreath Day, Red Apple Day, White Ribbon Night, Red Nose Day, Gold Bow Day, White Balloon Day, Pink Ribbon Day, Bright Pink Lipstick Day and Orange Day, not to mention a myriad of designated days throughout the year, including National Condom Day on Valentine's Day.

So, on the 4 May, I'll be playing outside on a bicycle for the cure for diabetes wearing a Darth Vader costume whilst living below the line and carrying a respected chicken, on the way to the Sydney to Surfers Ride.

For me, the winner is WaterAid's learning on the loo, which invites you to dedicate your toilet time during November to learning a new skill and ask friends to sponsor you. So, while you are spending a penny, you could be raising them too.

Just in case anyone feels left out, there is International Charity Day on 5 September, or should that be the fifth of Liptember or Steptember?

For PFOs that don't have significant fundraising resources, crowdfunding platforms can both raise funds for a project or start-up activity, as well as (re)access and (re)engage existing and new supporters. It is now legal in Australia to use crowdfunding to raise equity for PFOs (or their subsidiary companies) that are private (i.e., not publicly listed) companies limited by shares.

Some platforms run all-or-nothing campaigns where the funding target must be met within the timeframe before funds are released. Others, like Indiegogo, allow fundraisers to withdraw whatever funds they raise. All-or-nothing campaigns tend to be more successful, with more funds raised due to the sense of urgency that the chosen timeframe creates.

Supporters can also use these platforms, such as GoFundMe or Everyday Hero, to fundraise for their PFO through their own network. The fee charged is often a percentage of the money raised successfully and some crowdfunding websites only charge fees for successful campaigns that reach the target.

ChangePath gives a good comparison of the crowdfunding platforms on their website. It is usual to offer a reward to donors depending on their gift amount. This can be done at minimal cost, such as a special visit to the PFO or signed thank you cards.

Lastly, it is now legal in Australia to give a donation via text/ SMS on a mobile phone. This is particularly useful to access a large audience at supporter events, such as Cure for MND during the Big Freeze event at the MCG during an AFL match.

Cause related marketing (CRM)

In 1984, American Express donated one cent to the restoration of the Statue of Liberty every time someone used its charge card, introducing mass market cause-related marketing to the world as the promotion of a company's product or service to raise money for a not-for-profit organisation.[236]

As well as cents donated per product or service purchased, customers can make a donation or round up the price at the checkout, buy on a certain day when the company donates its profits to a cause, or buy a product so the company can donate the same product to those in need.

This can be powerful where the PFO's cause fits with the corporate's brand and customer base, leading to increased product sales for the company and new or reactivated supporters for the PFO.

The most successful CRM is the breast cancer PFOs' pink ribbon and colour theme during Breast Cancer Awareness Month in October which has seen over 150 products and services align to the brand—from Ford Mustangs to ball point pens. However, companies do risk a backlash over 'pink-washing' and the commodification of breast cancer as the contribution to breast cancer charities can be as little as two per cent of sales or capped so that extra sales generate no additional money for the PFO. It has also left the eighty-eight per cent of other cancer sufferers feeling forgotten and invisible and their PFOs fighting for attention and funds.

For *R U OK?* day on 10 September 2020, Nestlé launched its special KitKat bars to encourage its customers to 'take the time to have a break and check in with someone can have more of an impact than you might think'. In a win-win partnership, the PFO R U OK? gained valuable promotion and new supporters.

R U OK? has amassed an impressive range of partners— for well-being (Anytime Fitness), conversation (Twinings), sport (QBE), campaign (mtaa Super), small business (Yellow), community (Flight Centre Foundation), neighbourhood (Stockland Care Foundation) and workplace (avis budget group).

With fifty-seven per cent of consumers' purchasing decisions being belief-based, Foodbank promotes its CRM partnerships, including Subway Australia's biggest event of the year, the Subway Live Feed, which in 2019 donated fifty cents for each sub purchased on World Sandwich Day in November.

However, misalignment between the charity and the corporate sponsor can create wasted resources, customer cynicism and damage to reputations.

In 2017, South Australian brewery, Coopers, created a batch of ten thousand cartons of its light beer cans to commemorate the Bible Society's two hundredth year with the evangelical Christian organisation's logo and by-line 'Live light: Happy 200th birthday to Australia's longest-living charity, from Australia's longest-living family brewery. Bible Society 1817–2017'.

The subsequent release of a video posted on Facebook by the Bible Society featured Liberal MPs Tim Wilson and

Andrew Hastie sipping Coopers Premium Light and having a 'light discussion on a heavy topic', the former making the case for same-sex marriage and the latter defending traditional marriage, whilst its host thanked the Coopers family. The campaign website said the men were able to enjoy the debate because there was 'both a Bible and good beer on the table'.

Within minutes all hell broke loose with a massive social media backlash about Coopers sponsoring a religious organisation to make an explicitly political point. #boycottcoopers drinkers vowed never to drink the brand again, posted videos throwing Coopers' beer bottles in the bin and pubs around the country turned off their Coopers taps.

Two company press releases later failed to halt the controversy until Coopers Brewery directors Melanie Cooper and Dr Tim Cooper posted a video apologising and giving their support for marriage equality.

Mergers and joint ventures

If PFOs were businesses, we would have seen many more joint ventures, mergers and acquisitions, especially to create larger PFOs as the market consolidates around larger government service contracts. However, because of the absence of trust between PFOs in a fiercely competitive market, risk of affecting their precious charitable tax status, CEO and board personalities, and reliance on its name and supporter base for fundraising, we have seen limited mergers or joint ventures in Australia.

This doesn't mean that there shouldn't be consideration of mergers or joint ventures, especially where PFOs have worked together well previously, have built a relationship of mutual trust and respect, and can demonstrate better outcomes for their constituents.

In 2015, the Australian Institute of Company Directors found that thirty-two per cent of Australian not-for-profits had discussed a possible merger at director level and fourteen per cent had completed or were in the process of a merger.[237]

Three examples of successful mergers in the last five years are:

- In 2016, three Western Australia-based PFOs (Care Options, Volunteer Task Force and Community First) decided to merge. The new entity, Chorus, has more than $30 million in revenue, one thousand staff and volunteers, and supports ten thousand Western Australians in the community.

- Creating 'one united, for-purpose organisation, committed to the human rights and well-being of all people with a disability' with a combined five thousand staff supporting five thousand clients across Eastern Australia, House with No Steps merged with the Tipping Foundation in 2018 creating Aruma.

- In December 2020, Link Housing and Wentworth Community housing announced they are merging to create Link Wentworth, one of the largest housing providers in NSW managing sixty-three hundred houses with ten thousand residents in order to expand the supply of housing and related services and so respond to the growing demand for affordable housing in the state, as well as a stronger advocate for vulnerable people.

Starting Guides

Gender Equality - Women's Rights	
Rationale	*Globally, despite 143 countries guaranteeing equality between women and men in their constitutions:* • 1 in 3 women across the world experiencing violence • At least 200 million girls and women alive today living in 30 countries have undergone female genital mutilation • 250 million girls were married before they were 15 • Women make up less than 1 in 4 of all parliamentarians • Bringing women's wages into line with men would add US$28 trillion to global GDP • 130 million girls are out of school *In Australia:* The full-time gender pay gap is 14 per cent, or women earn on average $243 a week less than men • Australia is ranked 44 in the Global Gender Gap Index 2020, behind Laos and Bolivia. New Zealand is 6th • More than 1 in 3 Australian women has experienced physical or sexual violence in her lifetime and 1 in 2 experiences sexual harassment • Women comprise less than 1 in 4 of board directors across ASX listed companies • More than half of women aged 18 or older have experienced sexual harassment in their lifetime

Gender Equality - Women's Rights	
	• Women retire with 47 per cent less superannuation than men • Half of Australian women have experienced violence, partner emotional abuse or stalking since the age of 15 • On average, one woman a week is murdered by her current or former partner • 1 in 3 women will experience violence in her lifetime and 1 in 5 will experience sexual violence • Domestic violence is the single biggest cause of homelessness. A shortage in crisis accommodation for domestic violence victims often results in many women being turned away or put on waiting lists • Male intimate partner violence contributes more to the disease burden for women aged 18 to 44 years than any other well-known risk factor like tobacco use, high cholesterol or use of illicit drugs
Sustainable Development Goal	SDG3: Good health and well-being SDG5: Gender Equality SDG17: Partnerships
Belief	To achieve gender equality where women have the same rights, responsibilities, access to resources and opportunities as men. An Australia free of violence against women and their children, which is, in turn, an Australia where women are not only safe but respected, valued and treated as equals in private and public life.
Benefits to organisation	• Attraction and retention of talented employees • Inclusive workplace • Employee engagement • Broader customer/client market • Different perspectives • Increased creativity and innovation • Better decision-making • Strengthened reputation and brand

Gender Equality - Women's Rights	
Examples of specialist agencies (national unless otherwise stated)	• United Nations Women (international & national) • IWDA (international) • Action Aid (international) • Plan International (international) • Australian Human Rights Commission • Workplace Gender Equality Agency • Chief Executive Women • White Ribbon Australia • Rize Up Australia • Fitted For Work and Dressed for Success • Women's Legal Services Australia • YWCA • Our Watch • Australia's National Research Organisation for Women's Safety Homelessness Australia • Australian Women Against Violence Alliance
Actions	
Commit	• Use Workplace Gender Equality Agency's (WGEA) Gender Equality Diagnostic Tool, including gender equality strategy and action plan
Join	• Obtain White Ribbon Australia workplace accreditation • Gain a WGEA Employer of Choice citation • Global Compact Network Australia • Shared Value Project • Pledge 1% • Australia's CEO Challenge
Engage	• Wear a White Ribbon on the last Friday before 25 November • Participate in the International Day for the Elimination of Men's Violence against Women on 25 November
Employ	• Women comprise at least 50 per cent of board directors and at least 50 per cent of management

Gender Equality - Women's Rights	
Train	• Implement workplace equality and respect standards with tools from Our Watch • Take up Domestic and Family Violence workplace training with Australia's CEO Challenge
Buy	• Purchase from social enterprises supporting women, such as Who Gives a Crap (toilet paper and tissues) and thankyou (handwash, hand sanitiser) • Buy Fair Trade tea and coffee
Give	• Volunteer at women's NFPs • Donate women's sanitary products to Share the Dignity • Workplace giving to women's NFPs • Fundraising events for women's NFPs

Diversity and inclusion	
Rationale	*Globally* • Article 2 of the Universal Declaration of Human Rights states that 'everyone is entitled to all the rights and freedoms set forth in this Declaration, without distinction of any kind, such as race, colour, sex, language, religion, political or other opinion, national or social origin, property, birth or other status' • 71 million are displaced worldwide, comprising 41 million internationally displaced people, 26 million refugees and 4 million asylum seekers • 37,000 people a day are forced to flee their homes because of conflict and persecution • The 1951 Refugee Convention, ratified by 145 States, outlines the rights of those displaced • More than 1 billion people in the world live with some form of disability, of whom nearly 200 million experience considerable difficulties in functioning, with a higher disability prevalence in lower income countries • 163 nations are signatories to the United Nations Convention on the Rights of Persons with Disabilities

Diversity and inclusion

In Australia:

- Stigma around being LGBTQI is still prevalent with 44 per cent and 34 per cent hiding their sexuality or gender identity in public and when accessing health services, respectively
- LGBTQI people have the highest rates of suicidality[238] are at least 5 times more likely to attempt suicide and twice as likely to self-harm
- 6 in 10 experience homophobic abuse
- Unlike other countries, Australia's Constitution does not contain a bill of rights and only contains some limited rights protections
- A signatory to the *International Convention on the Elimination of All Forms of Racial Discrimination*
- Section 9 of the *Racial Discrimination Act 1975* makes it unlawful to discriminate against a person because of his or her race, colour, descent, national origin or ethnic origin or immigrant status
- Over 300 cultural backgrounds and languages are spoken in Australia
- Nearly a half of Australians have at least 1 parent who has born overseas
- 7 in 10 students experienced racism during their childhood, most of them in school
- 1 in 5 Australians has experienced racism in the last 12 months and a third experienced racism within their workplace or education facility
- Although those who have non-European and Indigenous backgrounds make up a quarter of the population, they only account for 5 per cent of senior leaders
- The *Disability Discrimination Act 1992* requires people with disabilities to be given equal opportunity to participate in, and contribute to, the full range of economic, social, cultural and political activities. The Act also makes it unlawful to discriminate in the provision of goods and services or facilities on the basis that the they have a disability

Diversity and inclusion

	• 1 in 5 Australians have a disability, with a third, or 1.4 million, of those having a severe or profound disability • Ranks last out of OECD countries for the relative income of people with disabilities • 9 in 10 women with intellectual disabilities have been sexually abused • 1 in 3 women and 1 in 5 men with disability have experienced emotional abuse from a partner • Less than half of working age people with disabilities are employed, compared to 79 per cent of those without disabilities • A third of adults with disability experience high/very high levels of psychological distress
Sustainable Development Goal	SDG3: Good health and well-being SDG5: Gender equality SDG8: Decent work and economic growth SDG10: Reduced inequalities SDG16: Peace, justice and strong institutions SDG17: Partnerships
Belief	People identifying as LGBTQI have the same rights, responsibilities, access to resources and opportunities as heterosexual people. All Australians, no matter their ethnic background, have the same rights, responsibilities, access to resources and opportunities. The full realisation of all human rights and fundamental freedoms for all persons with disabilities without discrimination of any kind on the basis of disability.
Benefits to organisation	• Attraction and retention of talented employees • Inclusive workplace with employee engagement • Broader customer/client market • Different perspectives • Increased creativity and innovation • Better decision-making • Strengthened reputation and brand

Diversity and inclusion	
Examples of national specialist agencies	• United Nations High Commissioner for Refugees (UNHCR) (international) • Human Rights Watch (international) • cbm (international) • Amnesty International (international and national) • Australian Red Cross (international and national) • Refugee Council of Australia • Australian Human Rights Commission • SisterWorks • Adult Migrant Education Service (AMES) • All Together Now • Equality Australia • Minus18 • Edge Effect • Diversity Council of Australia • The Equality Project • QLife • Lifeline • ACON • Headspace • Reach Out • National Disability Services • Australian Federation of Disability Organisations • National Disability Insurance Scheme • Australian Network on Disability • Disability Australia Hub • People with Disability Australia • Action on Disability within Ethnic Communities
Actions	
Commit	• Develop, implement, monitor a 'Diversity and Inclusion' policy and plan, including targets • Enact a Disability Action Plan
Join	• Join Australians Against Racism • Sign up to the *#YearOfWelcome* • Sign up to *I Choose Humane* • Become a member of Diversity Council of Australia

Diversity and inclusion	
Engage	• Take part in Refugee Week (in June) • Celebrate IDAHOBIT (International Day Against Homophobia, Biphobia, Intersexism and Transphobia) Day (in May) • Take part in Wear It Purple Day (in August) • Take part in the *International Day of Persons with Disabilities* (on 3 December) • Take part in specific disability days and weeks
Employ	• People with disabilities through Disability Employment Services providers • Refugees through Refugee Talent • Jobseekers through Job Active providers • Disadvantaged jobseekers with the Brotherhood of St Laurence's *Given the Chance*
Train	• Disseminate *Let's talk race: A Guide on How to Conduct a Conversation About Racism* from the Australian Human Rights Commission • Cultural sensitivity and awareness training with Diversity Australia
Buy	• Buy from social enterprises, such as catering from the Asylum Seeker Resource Centre • Buy from disability social enterprises with *BuyAbility* • Buy Fair Trade tea and coffee
Give	• Volunteer with NFPs such as AMES • Donate household goods to support refugees settling into their new home • Workplace giving to NFPs • Fundraising events with NFPs

Indigenous Rights	
Rationale	*In Australia, Indigenous people:* • Comprise 761,300 Aboriginal and Torres Strait Islander people as at 30 June 2017, or 3 per cent of the total population • Are 32 times more likely to be hospitalised for family violence as non-Indigenous people

Indigenous Rights

	• Comprise 20 per cent of those experiencing homelessness • Account for 48 per cent of young people under youth justice supervision and more than half (59 per cent) of young people in youth detention • 42 per cent of all Indigenous children in their first year of full-time schooling were categorised as developmentally vulnerable, twice that of non-Indigenous children, and ten times as likely to be in out-of-home care • Child mortality rate is twice the rate for non-Indigenous children • Employment rate was around 49 per cent compared to around 75 per cent for non-Indigenous Australians[239] • Will die, on average, 8 years before non-Indigenous Australians • Every second Aboriginal Australian experiences racism at sports events
Sustainable Development Goals	SDG3: Good health and well-being SDG 8: Decent work and economic growth SDG 10: Reduced inequalities SDG16: Peace, justice and strong institutions SDG17: Partnerships
Belief	Indigenous Australians have the same rights, responsibilities, access to resources and opportunities as non-Indigenous people
Benefits to organisation	• Attraction and retention of talented employees • Inclusive workplace • Employee engagement • Different perspectives • Increased creativity and innovation • Better decision-making • Strengthened reputation and brand

Indigenous Rights	
Examples of specialist national agencies	• Reconciliation Australia • Australians Together • Australian Indigenous Mentoring Experience (AIME) • Australian Indigenous Education Foundation • SEED Mob • Gunawirra • Career Trackers • Healing Foundation • Yalari • Indigenous Literacy Foundation • Cathy Freeman Foundation • Indigenous Marathon Foundation • Aboriginal Benefits Foundation Trust
Actions	
Commit	• Develop and enact a Reconciliation Action Plan with Reconciliation Australia • Set an employment target of Indigenous people • Invite a welcome to country or carry out an acknowledgement of country before meetings and events • Recognise Uluru Statement from the Heart • Acknowledgement of country plaque on building • Make contact with the local Indigenous group
Join	• Reconciliation Australia
Engage	• Hold a smoking ceremony with the local Indigenous group • Take an Indigenous tour • Hold an event in National Reconciliation Week (in May) • Get involved in events in NAIDOC week (in July) • Take part in National Close the Gap Day (in March)
Employ	• Take on an intern with Career Trackers • Post jobs at Indigenous Employment Australia • Recruit with Job Active providers and the Aboriginal Employment Strategy

Indigenous Rights	
Train	• Get information and videos from Australians Together • Seek cultural appreciation training from the local Indigenous group
Buy	• Become a member of Supply Nation and buy from Indigenous suppliers
Give	• Become a mentor • Support Adam Goodes' Go Foundation • Encourage workplace giving to Indigenous NFPs • Donate goods

Environmental Sustainability	
Rationale	*Globally*: • Human activities are estimated to have caused approximately 1.0°C of global warming above pre-industrial levels. Global warming is likely to reach an average 1.5°C between 2030 and 2052 if it continues to increase at the current rate • Even if warming is limited to 1.5°C, instabilities in the Greenland and West Antarctic ice sheets could be triggered resulting in a multi-metre sea-level rise • Further temperature rise beyond 1.5°C would drastically damage the environmental systems on which humanity depends • If nothing changes, we are on track for a rise in temperatures of between 4–6 ℃ and the extinction of our species *In Australia:* • Australia's climate and the surrounding oceans has warmed by just over 1°C since 1910 • Australia is the second highest emitter of CO_2 emissions per capita in the world • We are the worst-performing country in the world on climate action

Environmental Sustainability	
	• CSIRO predicts with a very high confidence more frequent and hotter hot days, sea levels rising, oceans becoming more acidic and extreme rainfall events becoming more intense • There has been a long-term increase in extreme fire weather, and in the length of the fire season, across large parts of Australia
Sustainable Development Goals	SDG 7: Affordable and clean energy SDG11: Sustainable cities and communities SDG12: Responsible consumption and production SDG13: Climate action SDG14: Life below water SDG15: Life on land SDG17: Partnerships
Belief	To reduce and get to zero carbon emissions to prevent the world warming by more than the agreed 1.5°C target under the Paris Climate Agreement
Benefits to organisation	• Reduced operating costs and increased profitability • Attraction and retention of talented employees • Employee engagement • Strengthened reputation and brand • Customer loyalty
Examples of national specialist agencies	• Climate Change in Australia • Climate Works Australia • Climate Council • Climate Action Network of Australia • Climate Active • 350.org Australia • Australian Youth Climate Coalition • WWF Australia • Greenpeace Australia • Australian Conservation Foundation • Greening Australia • Beyond Zero Emissions • Australian Dream Foundation

Environmental Sustainability	
	• Climate Justice Union • Global Compact Network Australia
Actions	
Commit	• To net-zero emissions by at least 2050 through a sustainability policy and annual plan • Measure carbon emissions transition using science-based targets • Gain Climate Active recognition • Ban single use plastic in the workplace
Join	• RE100 • Global Compact Network Australia • Sign up to Not Business As Usual • Climate Active
Engage	• Get an energy assessment • Get involved in Earth Hour (in March) • March in the Global Climate Strike
Train	• Enable staff awareness and tools for their homes with the Australian Energy Foundation
Buy	• Purchase green energy • Purchase carbon offsets • Buy toilet paper from Who Gives a Crap • Buy recycled paper from Ethical Paper • Buy Fair Trade tea and coffee
Give	• Workplace giving to climate change and environmental NFPs • Volunteer for climate change and environmental NFPs • Volunteer for Clean Up Australia Day (in March)

Poverty & homelessness	
Rationale	*Globally*: • Article 25(1) of the Universal Declaration of Human Rights states that 'everyone has the right to a standard of living adequate for the health and well-being of himself and of his family, including food, clothing, housing and medical care and necessary social services'

Poverty & homelessness	
	• Although declining, it is estimated there will still be over 500 million people living in extreme poverty (less than US$1.90 a day) in 2030 • 4 billion people are not covered by any social protection safety net • 47 million children under 5 years of age are wasted, 14.3 million are severely wasted and 144 million are stunted. Nearly half of deaths among children under 5 years of age are linked to undernutrition • 15,000 children and adolescents will die today, mostly from preventable diseases • 785 million people lack even a basic drinking water service and 2 billion people use a drinking water source contaminated with faeces • More than 820 million people do not have enough to eat *In Australia:* • Has 16th highest poverty rate out of the 34 wealthiest countries in the OECD—higher than the average for the OECD; higher than United Kingdom, Germany and New Zealand • Is ranked 38 in the Sustainable Development Goal Index, behind Bulgaria and Costa Rica • 3.24 million people in Australia live below the poverty line, including 774,000 (or nearly 1 in 5) children under the age of 15 • Nearly 50,000 children live in out-of-home care and rising • Wealth inequality continues to increase. The average wealth of the highest 20 per cent rose by 53 per cent from 2003 to 2016, while that of the middle 20 per cent rose by 32 per cent, and that of the lowest 20 per cent declined by 9 per cent • More than half of people on unemployment payments are unemployed long-term

Poverty & homelessness	
	• 43 per cent of low-income rental households are in housing stress, spending. more than 30 per cent of their gross income on housing costs • Over 5 million tonnes of food ends up as landfill, enough to fill 9,000 Olympic-sized swimming pools • Over 100,000 Australians will experience some form of homelessness tonight, a number that is increasing with those aged 25–34 most prevalent • 26,500 children aged under 9 years old came into homelessness services due to domestic violence • Over 92,000 who contacted homeless services could not find help, most of them women • Over the last 5 years there has been a 75 per cent increase in older women sleeping in their cars • Domestic violence is the single biggest cause of homelessness. A shortage in crisis accommodation for domestic violence victims often results in many women being turned away or put on waiting lists • Over 8,000 Australians will sleep rough tonight • A shortage of affordable and available private rentals is forcing 80 per cent of very low-income Australians to live in unaffordable rentals • Over a million households are experiencing housing stress (pay over 30 per cent of their income on their housing)
Sustainable Development Goal	SDG1: No poverty
	SDG2: Zero hunger
	SDG10: Reduced inequalities
	SDG3: Good health and well-being
	SDG17: Partnerships

Poverty & homelessness	
Belief	• In an affluent country with the 14th largest economy in the world, there is no excuse for people, let alone children, to live in poverty and be hungry in Australia, and everyone should have a safe and secure place to call home. • To end homelessness in Australia.
Benefits to organisation	• Attraction and retention of talented employees • Employee engagement • Strengthened reputation and brand
Examples of specialist agencies (national unless otherwise stated)	• Oxfam (international) • World Vision (international) • CARE International (international) • Action on Poverty (international) • Save the Children (international & national) • Brotherhood of St Laurence • The Smith Family • Salvation Army • Australian Red Cross • St Vincent de Paul • Council to Homeless Persons • Women's Community Shelters • Homelessness Australia • StreetSmart Australia • National Shelter • Mission Australia
Actions	
Commit	• To ending poverty and homelessness
Join	• Sign up to Raise the Rate • Become a member of Global Compact Network Australia • Join *Everybody's Home* campaign for a better, fairer housing system for everyone
Engage	• Engage in Anti-Poverty Week (in October) • Take part in the Vinnies CEO Sleepout • Get involved in National Homelessness Week (in August)
Employ	• Employ a disadvantaged jobseeker through a Job Active provider or the Brotherhood of St Laurence's Given a Chance

Poverty & homelessness	
Buy	• Buy toilet paper from Who Gives a Crap • Buy washroom handwash from thankyou • Buy Fair Trade tea and coffee • Buy from social enterprises
Give	• Volunteer at homelessness NFPs • Workplace giving to homelessness NFPs • Donate goods, such as women's sanitary products to Share the Dignity • Hold a food drive for your State's Foodbank

Health	
Rationale	*Globally*: • 11 per cent of the world's population or 792 million people live with a mental health disorder • More than 70 per cent of people with mental illness receive no treatment from health care staff • Mental disorders are on the rise in every country in the world and will cost the global economy $16 trillion by 2030 • Noncommunicable diseases (NCDs) kill 41 million people each year, equivalent to 71 per cent of all deaths globally with cardiovascular (18 million), cancers (9 million), respiratory diseases (4 million), diabetes (2 million) and dementias (2 million) • As the deadliest animal in the world, mosquitoes spread malaria, dengue, lymphatic filariasis and yellow fever, which together are responsible for several million deaths and hundreds of millions of cases every year • Out of the 10 million people who will contract tuberculosis this year, 1.6 million people will die. TB is a treatable and curable disease with a standard six-month course of four antimicrobial drugs • Today, 15,000 children under five will die, largely from preventable diseases

Health	
	In Australia:
	• 3 million Australians live with anxiety or depression
	• Nearly half will have a mental disorder in their lifetime and 1 in 5 have had a mental disorder in the last year
	• 600,000 children and adolescents have had a mental health disorder in the last year
	• Every day, 8 Australians die from suicide and a further 30 people will attempt to take their own life
	• Suicide remains the leading cause of death for Australians aged between 15 and 44
	• Untreated mental health conditions cost Australian workplaces approximately $10.9 billion per year comprising $4.7 billion in absenteeism, $6.1 billion in productivity and $146 million in compensation claims
	• 91 per cent believe mental health in the workplace is important, but only 52 per cent of employees believe their workplace is mentally healthy and only 56 per cent believe their most senior leader values mental health
	• Three-quarters of people feel uncomfortable telling their employer they were experiencing a mental illness
	• Collectively, chronic conditions account for 87 per cent of deaths, 61 per cent of total disease burden and 37 per cent of hospitalisations
	• Every day over 400 new cases of cancer are diagnosed and 48,000 die from cancer annually
	• 34 Australians will die today from bowel cancer, prostate cancer, breast cancer or pancreatic cancer
	• Every day, 20 Australians die of heart attack
	• Two-thirds of adults are overweight or obese
	• 1.2 million adults have diabetes which contributed to 11 per cent of deaths
Sustainable Development Goal	• SDG3: Good health and well-being • SDG17: Partnerships

Health	
Belief	• All Australians with mental health illness have a right to participate meaningfully in individual and community life without discrimination, stigma or exclusion. • We can cure chronic diseases and save millions of lives.
Benefits to organisation	• Attraction and retention of talented employees • Inclusive workplace • Employee engagement • Reduced absentee days and increased productivity • Better decision-making • Strengthened reputation and brand
Examples of national specialist agencies	• World Health Organisation (international) • MSF (international) • The Global Fund to Fight AIDS, Tuberculosis and Malaria (international) • Bill & Melinda Gates Foundation (international) • Cancer Australia • Cancer Council • Breast Cancer Network Australia • Heart Foundation • Diabetes Australia • National Mental Health Commission • Mentally Healthy Workplace Alliance • Mental Health Australia • Australians for Mental Health • Lifeline • Beyond Blue • Black Dog Institute • Sane Australia • Mind Australia • Headspace
Actions	
Commit	• Support employees and stakeholders with health issues, including suitable employment arrangements and an Employee Assistance Program • Enact an Employee Well-being strategy and plan, including reporting

Health	
Engage	• Take part in Mental Health Week, including World Mental Health Day on 10 October • Host an event to shine a light for those affected by suicide and mental illness (in June) • Take part in World Cancer Day (on 4 February), wear a teal ribbon in Ovarian Cancer Awareness Month (in February), purchase a virtual ribbon for Bowel Cancer Awareness Month (in June), and wear a pink ribbon for Breast Cancer Awareness Month (in October) • Form a team and take part in an organised run or mini-triathlon • Run lunchtime Mindfulness classes
Employ	• People with disabilities through Disability Employment Services providers
Train	• Access employer resources at Heads Up • Understand mental health in the workplace • Run lunchtime mindfulness classes • Undertake a mental health workplace assessment • Ensure a suitable Employee Assistance Program is in place • Enable employees to check their heart age during Heart Week (in May) • Run lunchtime Pilates classes
Buy	• Buy from disability social enterprises with BuyAbility • Buy pink buns for staff from Bakers Delight for BCNA (in May)
Give	• Fundraise and volunteer for mental health NFPs • Take part in the Big Aussie Barbie with a BBQ lunch at work for prostate cancer • Register and fundraise for the Biggest Morning Tea (in May) • Grow a 'mo' for Movember (in November) • Grow a beard for Decembeard for bowel cancer (in December) • Pause for a cause with febfast (in February)

Animal Welfare

Rationale	*Globally*:
	• With a value of between $7 billion and $23 billion each year, illegal wildlife trafficking is the fourth most lucrative global crime after drugs, humans and arms
	• 100,000 whales, dolphins, porpoises, seals, sea lions and other marine mammals die every year as a result of plastic pollution
	• Animals are still suffering and dying to test shampoo, mascara and other cosmetic products. Terrified rabbits, rats, guinea pigs and mice have substances forced down their throats, dripped into their eyes or smeared onto their skin before they are killed
	• In defiance of the ongoing global ban on commercial whaling, Japan has commenced their new commercial whaling programme putting hundreds of whales at risk of suffering long and painful deaths from exploding harpoons
	• 55 African elephants are killed each day for their ivory
	• There are at least 12,000 bears in bear bile facilities today. Bears are kept in "crush cages," which are deliberately too small for animals to stand or move much. In order to extract the bile—often daily—workers make permanent holes or fistula into the bear's gall bladder to extract the bile which is sold for Chinese medicine
	In Australia:
	• To maximise their production of milk Australia's 1.6 million milk cows are kept almost continually pregnant. The resultant male calves are usually slaughtered at 5 days of age
	• Each year, endangered scalloped hammerhead sharks are killed in their thousands throughout the Great Barrier Reef because of industrial-sized gillnets stretched out for up to 1.2 km

Animal Welfare	
	• Puppies and breeding animals kept on puppy farms (also known as puppy mills or puppy factories) live in appalling conditions. • 9 million egg laying hens spend their entire lives in metal cages with 3–7 other hens. Basic normal behaviours such as perching, nesting, foraging, stretching and flapping aren't possible
Sustainable Development Goal	SDG12: Responsible consumption and production SDG13: Climate action SDG14: Life blow water SDG15: Life on land SDG17: Partnerships
Belief	The humane treatment of all animals. Eliminate poaching and trafficking of protected species (SDG15 Target 15.7).
Benefits to organisation	• Attraction and retention of talented employees • Employee engagement • Strengthened reputation and brand
Examples of national specialist agencies	• World Animal Protection (international) • Thin Green Line (international) • Humane Society International (international and national) • People for the Ethical Treatment of Animals (international and national) • World Wildlife Fund (international and national) • Sea Shepherd (international and national) • Animals Australia • RSPCA • Voiceless
Actions	
Commit	• To protecting animal rights
Train	• Disseminate Choose Wisely

Animal Welfare	
Engage	• Sign a petition to end the Global Wildlife Trade • Take part in World Animal Day (on 4 October) • Help stop puppy farms with the RSPCA • Take part in Bring your Dog to Work Day (in June) • Sign a petition to stop mass diary calf slaughter with Animals Australia
Give	• Fundraise and volunteer for animal protection NFPs • Enact workplace giving to animal protection NFPs

Acknowledgements

Over the last eight years, it has been an absolute privilege to work and talk with so many inspirational and talented people.

As the saying goes, 'I fall in love with people's passion; the way their eyes light up when they talk about the thing they love and the way they fill with light'.

I am indebted to these special people that have helped me with this book, including the wonderful Ali Hooper, Alison McClelland, Andrew Davies, Andrew Mahar AM, Dr Catherine Brown OAM, Chris Hawken, Conny Lenneberg, Craig Fitzgerald, Darrell Wade, David Taylor, David Thompson, Daniel Flynn, David Gonski AC, Di Clark, Digby Hannah, Frances Horton, Helen Maisano, Ian (Macca) McDonald, Ipsita Wright, Ivan Deveson AO, Jaison Hoernel, Kathy Townsend, Kristian Dauncey ,Kylee Bates, Lyn Swinburne AM, Margot Franssen OC, Melanie Gow, Michael Perusco, Murray Chapman, Paul Little AO, Paul Ronalds, Peter Walton, Quig Tingley, Richard Dent OAM, Rohan Garnett, Ruth Oakden, Sam Biondo, Sam Mostyn AO, Sarah Davies AM and Stephen Bird.

References

Introduction

1   Charity Commission for England and Wales (2019) *Statement of the Results of an Inquiry into Oxfam*, p.134

2   The British Academy (2019) *Principles for Purposeful Business. How to deliver the framework for the Future of the Corporation An agenda for business in the 2020s and beyond*, November 2019, ISBN 978-0-85672-646-0

3   Beyond Bank Australia (2019) *Changing Lives. 2019 Corporate Report*

4   Said at the Shared Value Project Asia/Pacific virtual conference on 10 June 2020

5   Cohen R (2020) *Impact. Reshaping Capitalism to Drive Real Change*, Ebury Press, London, p.183

6   Deloitte Access Economics (2020) *A new choice Australia's climate for growth*, p.iii

7   Fisk P (2010) *People, Planet, Profit*, Kogan Page Limited, London

8   McKinsey and Company (2020) *The Board's Role in Embedding Corporate Purpose: Five Actions Directors Can Take Today*, November 2020

9   YouGov Omnibus research at https://au.yougov.com/news/2018/01/04/businesses-and-environmental-damage/

10 Committee for Economic Development of Australia (2020) *2019 Company Pulse: A Nationwide Survey of the General Public and Business Leaders on Expectations of Business and Business Priorities*, ceda, Melbourne

11 PwC (2016) *Putting Purpose to Work: A study of purpose in the workplace*

12 Zeno Group (2020) *The 2020 Zeno Strength of Purpose Survey*

13 Harvard Business Review (2015) *The Business Case for Purpose*, Harvard Business School Publishing

14 Edelman (2021) *Edelman Trust Barometer. Trust in Australia*, p.11

Why PurposeFull?

[15] It took me fifteen years to stop wearing leather-soled shoes

[16] Toffler B L (2003) *Final Accounting. Ambition, Greed and the Fall of Arthur Andersen*, Crown Publishing, New York, p.219

[17] Pfau B N (2015) *How an Accounting Firm Convinced Its Employees They Could Change the World*, Harvard Business Review, 6 October 2015

[18] Hannan E (2016) *How KPMG Gave 6,000 Employees a Higher Purpose*, BOSS, Financial Review, 6 May 2016

[19] Friedman M (1970) *The Social Responsibility of Business is to Increase its Profits*, The New York Times Magazine, September 13, 1970

[20] Schumpeter J (1942) *Capitalism, Socialism and Democracy*, Harper & Brothers, USA

[21] Commonwealth of Australia (2018) *Interim Report: Royal Commission into Misconduct in the Banking, Superannuation and Financial Services Industry*, Canberra

[22] KPMG (2019) *Shareholder value: Shareholder Values: What Motivates Australian Retail Investors*, September 2019

[23] Davis GF and White C J (2015) *The New Face of Corporate Activism*, Stanford Social Innovation Review, Fall 2015

[24] Business Roundtable (2019) *Statement on the Purpose of a Corporation*

[25] Edelman (2020) *Edelman Trust Barometer 2020*, p.17

[26] Harvard Business Review (2015) *The Business Case for Purpose*, Harvard Business School Publishing, p.2

[27] SSRS (2018) *A View from the Top: U.S. Fortune 1000 CEOs and C-Suite Executives on Social Purpose and Its Impact on Business*, Covestro

[28] Zeno Group (2020) *The 2020 Zeno Strength of Purpose Survey*

[29] Deloitte (2020) *The Social Enterprise at Work: Paradox as a Path Forward*, Deloitte Global Human Capital Trends

[30] Gartenberg C and Serafeim G (2019) *181 Top CEOs have realised Companies Need a Purpose Beyond Profit*, Harvard Business Review, 20 August 2019

[31] Development Dimensions International Inc, The Conference Board and EY (2018) *Global Leadership Forecast 2018*

[32] Collins J C and Porras J I (1994) *Built to Last: Successful Habits of Visionary Companies*, Century Limited, London, p.4

33 Harvard Business Review (2015) *The Business Case for Purpose*, Harvard Business School Publishing

34 Crutchfield L R and McLeod G H (2012) *Forces for Good: The Six Practices of High Impact Nonprofits*, USA

35 Brotherhood of St Laurence (2014) *Tony Nicholson Speech on the Future of the Community Welfare Sector 27 May 2014*, Melbourne

36 Collins J (2006) *Good to Great and the Social Sectors. A monograph to Accompany Good to Great*, UK

37 Drucker Peter F (1990) *Managing the Non-Profit Organization. Practices and Principles*, New York

Begin with Belief

38 Leading Teams Australia (2014) *Mission Statement and Values study*

39 Hamilton C and Denniss R (2005) *Affluenza: When Too Much is Never Enough*, Allen & Unwin, Sydney

40 NCD Risk Factor Collaboration (2016) *Trends in adult body-mass index in 200 countries from 1975 to 2014: A pooled analysis of 1698 population-based measurement studies with 19·2 million participants*, The Lancet 2016; p.387: pp.1377–1396

41 Mackay H (2010) *What Makes Us Tick? The Ten Desires That Drive Us*, Sydney

42 For instance, Proverbs 19:17, *Whoever is kind to the poor lends to the Lord, and he will reward them for what they have done*

43 Kerr J (2013) *Legacy. What the All Blacks Can Teach Us about the Business of Life*, London, p.33

44 Kerr J (2013) *Legacy. What the All Blacks Can Teach Us about the Business of Life*, London, p.35

45 Dunant J H (1863) *A Memory of Solferino*

46 Zhang, L (2020)"An Institutional Approach to Gender Diversity and Firm Performance," *Organization Science* 31, no. 2 (March–April), pp.439–457

47 Robert W (2013) *Building A Business Case for Gender Diversity*, Centre for Ethical Leadership, University of Melbourne

48 McKinsey and Company (2018) *Delivering Through Diversity*

49 ClimateWorks Australia (2020) *Decarbonisation Futures: Solutions, Actions and Benchmarks for a Net Zero Emissions Australia*, p.8

50 UTS (2020) *Do Better—Independent review into Collingwood Football Club's Responses to Incidents of Racism and Cultural Safety in the Workplace*

51 Merkus A (2019) *Mapping Social Cohesion 2019, The Scanlon Foundation Surveys 2019*, Scanlon Foundation Research Institute

52 Merkus A (2020) *Mapping Social Cohesion 2020, The Scanlon Foundation Surveys 2020*, Scanlon Foundation Research Institute

53 Biddle N, Gray M and Yung Lo J (2020) *The Experience of Asian-Australians during the COVID-19 Pandemic: Discrimination and Wellbeing*, ANU Centre for Social Research and Methods

54 Hunt V, Layton D and Prince S (2015) *Why Diversity Matters*, McKinsey & Company, January 2015

55 Hunt V, Prince S, Dixon-Fyle S and Yee L (2018) *Delivering through Diversity*, McKinsey & Company, January 2018

56 Wilson T and Shalley F (2018) *Estimates of Australia's Non-Heterosexual Population*, Australian Population Studies 2, no. 1, pp.26–38

57 National LGBTI Health Alliance (2020) *Snapshot of Mental Health and Suicide Prevention Statistics for LGBTI People*

58 Hindle K, Noble J and Phillips B (1999) *Are Workers with a Disability Less Productive? An Empirical Challenge to a Suspect Axiom*, paper submitted to the refereed stream of the ANZAM 99 Conference, University of Tasmania), p.5; Graffam J, Shinkfield A, Smith K and U Polzin (2002) *Employer Benefits and Costs of Employing a Person with a Disability*, Journal of Vocational Rehabilitation 17, pp.251–263

59 Diversity Council Australia (2015) *Building Inclusion: An Evidence-Based Model of Inclusive Leadership*

60 United Nations (2020) *Sustainable Development Goals Report 2020*, p.3

61 Credit Suisse Research Institute (2019) *Global Wealth Report 2019*

62 Oxfam (2019) *Public Good or Private Wealth?*

63 OECD (2015) *In it together: Why Less Inequality Benefits All OECD*, Paris

64 Australian Council of Social Service and University of New South Wales (2018) *Inequality in Australia 2018*, p.14

65 Australian Council of Social Service and University of New South Wales (2018) *Inequality in Australia 2018*, p.16

66 Australian Council of Social Service and University of NSW (2020) *Poverty in Australia 2020: Part 1 Overview*, Sydney, NSW, p.9

67 Foodbank (2019) *Foodbank Hunger Report 2019*

68 McClelland A (2000) *No Child…Child Poverty in Australia*, Brotherhood of St Laurence, Fitzroy, pp.13–16

[69] Australian Institute for Health and Welfare (2019) *Specialist Homelessness Services Annual Report 2018-19*

[70] Australian Institute for Health and Welfare (2020) *Australia's Children*

[71] Australian Institute for Health and Welfare (2019) *Housing Assistance in Australia 2019*

[72] United Nations General Assembly (1993) *Declaration on the Elimination of Violence against Women*

[73] PwC (2015) *A High Price to Pay, The Economic Case for Preventing Violence against Women,* p.5

[74] Australian Bureau of Statistics (2013) *Personal Safety Survey 2012*

[75] Webster K (2016) *A preventable burden: Measuring and Addressing the Prevalence and Health Impacts of Intimate Partner Violence in Australian Women*, ANROWS, Sydney

[76] Henderson C, Evans-Lacko S and Thornicroft G (2013) *Mental Illness Stigma, Help Seeking, and Public Health Programs,* American Public Health Journal 5, no. 103

[77] Australian Bureau of Statistics (2007) *National Survey of Mental Health and Wellbeing: Summary of Results*

[78] The Australian Senate (2010) *The Hidden Toll: Suicide in Australia*, Report of the Senate Community Affairs References Committee, Commonwealth of Australia, Canberra

[79] PwC (2014) *Creating a Mentally Healthy Workplace: Return on Investment Analysis*

[80] TNS (2014) *State of Workplace Mental Health in Australia*, Beyond Blue

[81] Australian Institute for Health and Welfare (2020) *Mental Health Services in Australia*

[82] Australian Institute for Health and Welfare (2019) *Overweight and Obesity*

[83] Australian Institute for Health and Welfare (2019) *Cardiovascular Disease*

[84] Australian Institute for Health and Welfare (2019) *Cancer in Australia 2019*

[85] Roddick A (2000) *Business as Unusual*, HarperCollins, London, p.174

[86] Cable D (2019) *Helping Your Team Feel the Purpose in Their Work*, Harvard Business Review, 22 October 2019

[87] Australian Institute for Disaster Resilience (2020) *Our Word, Our Say: eNational Survey of Children and Young People on Climate Change and Disaster Risk*, Victoria

88 Australian Government (2018) *Report on the Implementation of the Sustainable Development Goals*, Canberra

89 United Nations (2015) *Paris Agreement*, Article 2(a), 12 December 2015, Paris

Live the Dream

90 Senge P M (1990) *The Fifth Discipline: The Art and Practice of a Learning Organisation*

91 Shearer M (2015) *T2: The Book*, Penguin Random House Australia, pp.1–2

92 Lui S (2016) *The World We See: Leadership Lessons from Australia's Iconic Change Makers*, The Dream Collective

93 Shearer M (2015) *T2: The Book*, Penguin Random House Australia, p.156

94 T2 (2018) *People and Planet, Impact Report 2018*

95 Green N (n.d.) *Black and Bloody Beautiful*, Honours Thesis Harvard University, USA

96 Australian Institute of Health & Welfare (2020) *Alcohol, Tobacco and Other Drugs in Australia*

97 City of Yarra and the Aboriginal Cultural Signage Reference Group (2002) *Snapshots of Fitzroy*

98 Reconciliation Australia (2019) *2018 Australian Reconciliation Barometer*

99 Booth G, Huggins J, Thodey D, Rigney L-I, Ganley L, Glanville J, Pearson L and O'Leary T (2014) *Making the Connection: Essays on Indigenous Digital Excellence,* Fontaine Publishing Group, p.60

100 Kelly A (2013) *An End to Racial Profiling in Sight*, Crime and Justice Insight 8, VCOSS

101 Australia Post (2017) *Diversity and Inclusion Annual Report 2017*

102 Commonwealth of Australia (2019) *Final Report, Royal Commission into Misconduct in the Banking, Superannuation and Financial Services Industry*, vol. 1, p.1

103 Accenture (2020) *PurposeFull Banking: Can Trust Create Win-Win Banking Relationships?*

104 Roy Morgan Research (2003) *ANZ Survey of Adult Financial Literacy in Australia*, Melbourne, Australia, p.2

105 Roy Morgan Research (2003) *ANZ Survey of Adult Financial Literacy in Australia*, Melbourne, Australia, p.4

[106] Brotherhood of St Laurence (2003) *Banking on the Margins: Promoting a More Financially Inclusive Community*, Melbourne, Australia

[107] Russell R and Nair A (2005) *Evaluation of MoneyMinded: An Adult Financial Education Program*, RMIT University, Melbourne, Australia

[108] Russell R, Kutin J, Stewart M, Welwood M and Marriner T (2019) *MoneyMinded Impact Report: A Report Prepared for ANZ*, RMIT University, Melbourne, Australia, p.2

[109] Russell R, Kutin J, Stewart M and Godinho V (2016) *MoneyMinded Report 2015*, RMIT University, Melbourne, Australia, p.4

[110] Russell R, Kutin J, Stewart M, Welwood M and Marriner T (2019) *MoneyMinded Impact Report: A Report Prepared for ANZ*, RMIT University, Melbourne, Australia, p.4

[111] Roslyn R, Stewart M and Cull F (2015) *Saver Plus: A Decade of Impact*, RMIT University, Melbourne

[112] Roslyn R, Kutin J and Stewart M (2016) *Saver Plus: Pathways to Wellbeing*, RMIT University, Melbourne, p.2, 9–10

[113] Faulkner N, Zhao K, Kneebone S and Smith L (2019) *Measuring Social Inclusion, Inclusive Australia*, Monash University, BehaviourWorks Australia

[114] Priest N, Perry R, Ferdinand A, Paradies Y and Kelaher M (2014) *Experiences of Racism, Racial/Ethnic Attitudes, Motivated Fairness and Mental Health Outcomes Among Primary and Secondary School Students*

[115] Blair K, Dunn K, Kamp A and Alam O (2017) *Challenging Racism Project: 2015-16 National Survey*, Western Sydney University

[116] Soutphommasane T, Whitwell G, Jordan K and Ivanov P (2018) *Leading for Change: A Blueprint for Cultural Diversity and Inclusive Leadership Revisited*

[117] McIntosh P (1988) *White Privilege and Male Privilege: A Personal Account of Coming to See Correspondences through Work in Women's Studies*, Working Paper 189, Wellesley Collage Center for Research on Women

[118] See https://www.thehrsource.com/post/5-types-of-unconscious-bias-in-the-workplace

[119] Australian Institute of Health and Welfare (2019) *People with Disability in Australia*

[120] Australian Institute of Health and Welfare (2019) *People with Disability in Australia*

[121] OECD (2010), *Sickness, Disability and Work: Breaking the Barriers: A Synthesis of Findings across OECD Countries*, OECD Publishing, Paris

122 World Economic Forum (2020) *Global Gender Gap Report 2020*, p.9

123 Chief Executive Women (2020) *Chief Executive Women ASX200 Senior Executive Census*

124 McKinsey and Company (2017) *Women in leadership Lessons from Australian companies leading the way*

125 Centre for Australian Ethical Research (2006, March) *The State of Sustainability Reporting in Australia 2005*, p.31

126 Skarbek A (2020) *Ways to Shift to a Net Carbon Emissions Future*, Company Director April 2020, AICD, Sydney

127 ClimateWorks Australia (2020) *Decarbonisation Futures: Solutions, Actions and Benchmarks for a Net-Zero Emissions Australia*, pp.9–11

128 The Climate Council (2017) *Factsheet: Transport Emissions: Driving Down Car Pollution in Cities*

129 International Labour Organization, Walk Free Foundation and International Organization for Migration (2017), *Global Estimates of Modern Slavery*, pp.10–11

130 *Maslow* A H (1943) *A Theory of Human Motivation*, Psychological Review 50, no. 4, pp.370–396

131 Australian Council of Social Service and University of New South Wales (2018) *Inequality in Australia 2018*

132 https://www.firststep.org.au/about_us

133 PwC (2015) *A High Price to Pay: The Economic Case for Preventing Violence against Women*

134 Our Watch (2015) *Change the Story: A Shared Framework for the Primary Prevention of Violence against Women and Their Children in Australia*

135 Australian Institute for Health and Welfare (2019) *Overweight and Obesity: An interactive insight*

136 Australian Institute for Health and Welfare (2018) *Australia's Health 2018*

137 Australian Bureau of Statistics (2007) *National Survey of Mental Health and Wellbeing: Summary of Results*

138 TNS (2014) *State of Workplace Mental Health in Australia*, Beyond Blue

139 Barraket J, Collyer N, O'Connor M and Anderson H (2010) *Finding Australia's Social Enterprise Sector: Final Report,* Australian Centre for Philanthropy and Nonprofit Studies, p.4

140 The State of Victoria (2018) *Victoria's Social Procurement Framework,* Melbourne

[141] Wigglesworth C, Exon J, Chandgothia N and Dal A (2020) *Buy Social Corporate Challenge: Year 3 Impact Report*, Social Enterprise UK

[142] Schmidt-Burbach J (2017) *Taken for a Ride: The Conditions for Elephants Used in Tourism in Asia*, World Animal Protection

[143] Lencioni P (2002) *Make Your Values Mean Something*, Harvard Business Review, July 2002

[144] Greenleaf R K (1977) *Servant Leadership. A Journey into the Nature of Legitimate Power and Greatness*, Paulist Press, New Jersey, p.27

[145] Baldoni J (2009) *Humility as a Leadership Trait*, Harvard Business Review, 15 September 2009

[146] Kerr J (2013) *Legacy: What the All Blacks Teach Us About the Business of Life*, Great Britain

[147] Collins J (2001) *Good to Great: Why Some Companies Make the Leap… and Others Don't*, London

[148] Fowler A (2000) *The Virtuous Spiral. A Guide to Sustainability for NGOs in International Development*, London, p.173

[149] Brown B (2018) *Dare to Lead*, Penguin Random House, UK, p.4

[150] Scott K (2017) *Radical Candor. How to Get What You Want by Saying What You Mean*, Pan Macmillan, London, p.9

[151] Koda Capital (2018) *Snapshot of Australian Giving*

[152] LBG and Volunteering Australia (2018) *Corporate Volunteering in Australia: A Snapshot*

[153] Accenture (2016) *A 2020 Vision for Employer-Supported Volunteering*, p.4

[154] Volunteering Australia (2016) *Help Create Happiness: State of Volunteering in Australia*, p.19

Demonstrate Impact

[155] Cohen R (2020) *Impact: Reshaping Capitalism to Drive Real Change*, Ebury Press, London, p.12

[156] Association of International Certified Professional Accountants, Black Sun and International Integrated Reporting Council (2018) *Purpose Beyond Profit: The Value of Value—Board-Level Insights*

[157] Institute of Community Directors Australia (2019) *NFP Governance Survey 2019, ICDA Spotlight Report: NFP Impact & Data*, June 3, 2019

[158] Commonwealth of Australia (2008) *The Road Home: A National Approach to Reducing Homelessness,* Canberra

[159] Charities Aid Foundation (2019) *Australian Giving 2019: An overview of Charitable Giving in Australia*, p.14

[160] Community Council for Australia (2019) *The Australia We Want: Second Report*

[161] Subramaniam N (2019) *SDG Measurement and Disclosure by ASX150: Research Report*, RMIT, Global Compact Network Australia

[162] Australian Council of Superannuation Investors (2019) *ESG Reporting by the ASX200*, p.14

[163] T2 (2108) *People and Planet: Impact Report 2018*

[164] International Integrated Reporting Council (2013) *The International Framework*

[165] Serafeim G, Robert T Z and Downing J (2020) *Impact Weighed Financial Accounts: The Missing Piece for an Impact Economy*, Harvard Business School

[166] Cohen R (2020) *Impact: Reshaping Capitalism to Drive Real Change*, Ebury Press, London, pp.110–111

[167] Social Ventures Australia Consulting (2012) *Social Return on Investment: Lessons learned in Australia*

[168] Social Ventures Australia Consulting (2011) *Food Connect Brisbane: Forecast Social Return on Investment Report*, May 2011

[169] Social Ventures Australia (2015) *Baseline Social Return on Investment analysis of Mirabel's Victorian activities,* Sydney, Australia

[170] Financial Services Council and Australian Council of Superannuation Investors (2015) *ESG Reporting Guide for Australian Companies*

[171] ASX Corporate Governance Council (2019) *Corporate Governance Principles and Recommendations*, 4th edition, February 2019, Recommendation 7.4, p.27

[172] PwC (2020) *ESG Reporting—Are We Keeping Pace? PwC's Analysis of ESG Reporting in Australia*

[173] See https://www.csi.edu.au/media/Ganging_up_on_the_Problem_-_Andrew_Hocking.pdf

[174] See https://www.worldvision.com.au/docs/default-source/seed-docs/youth-livelihoods/world-visions-youth-livelihood-and-empowerment-theory-of-change.pdf?sfvrsn=2

[175] See https://www.thinknpc.org/resource-hub/ten-steps/

[176] See https://www.thinknpc.org/resource-hub/understanding-impact/

[177] Carbon Market Institute (2019) *Australian Climate Policy Survey 2019*

Work for Change

[178] Crowe, David M (2013) *War Crimes, Genocide, and Justice: A Global History*, Palgrave Macmillan

[179] Perry M (2008) *Gold Prospects: Business Case FOR Whole-Of-Community Planning and Development 2008/2016*, Central Goldfields Shire Council

[180] State of Victoria (2015) *Go Goldfields Alliance Evaluation Report 2012-2014*, Central Victorian Primary Care Partnership (CVPCP), Go Goldfields Evaluation Working Group

[181] Commonwealth of Australia (2009) *The Way Forward: A New Disability Policy Framework for Australia,* Disability Investment Group

[182] Productivity Commission (2011) *Disability Care and Support*, report no. 54, Canberra

[183] United Nations *Convention on the Rights of Persons with Disabilities*, Article 3(a)

[184] Centre for Applied Disability Research (2019) *State of the Disability Sector Report 2019*, National Disability Services

[185] Carey G, Weier M, Malbon E, Dickinson H, Alexander D and Duff G (2018) *How is the Disability Sector Faring? A Report from National Disability Services' Annual Market Survey*, ISBN: 987-0-7334-3852-3

[186] Chatterji A K and Toffel M W (2018) *The New CEO Activists*, Harvard Business Review, January–February 2018

[187] Walker S (2018) *You're a CEO—Stop Talking Like a Political Activist,* The Wall Street Journal, 27 July 2018

[188] Sammut J (2019) *Corporate Virtue Signalling: How to Stop Big Business from Meddling in Politics*, Connorcourt Publishing

[189] Daniel J. Edelman, Inc (2020) *Edelman Trust Barometer 2020*

[190] Chief Executive Women (2020) *CEW ASX200 Senior Executive Census 2020*

[191] Australian Institute of Company Directors (2020) *Gender Diversity Progress Report, October 2019 to January 2020*

[192] The Constellation Project (2019*) Year in Review*

[193] Ronalds P (2014) *The Change Imperative. Creating the Next Generation NGO*, USA

[194] Janneke Berecki-Gisolf J, Hassani-Mahmooei B, Clapperton A, and McClure R (2017) *Prescription Opioid Dispensing and Prescription*

Opioid Poisoning: Population Data from Victoria, Australia 2006 to 2013, Australian and New Zealand Journal of Public Health41, no. 1

[195] Australian Bureau of Statistics (2018) *Drug-Induced deaths in Australia: A Changing Story*

[196] Create Foundation (2010) *What's the Answer? Young People's Solutions for Improving Transitioning to Independence from Out of Home Care*

[197] UNICEF Cambodia and Division of Data, Research and Policy, UNICEF New York, A Statistical Profile of Child Protection in Cambodia, United Nations Children's Fund, New York, March 2018

[198] ReThink Orphanages (2018) *Inquiry into Establishing a Modern Slavery Act in Australia: Submission 23*

[199] van IJzendoorn M H, Palacios J, Sonuga-Barke E J, et al. (2014) *Children in Institutional Care: Delayed Development and Resilience*, Monogr Soc Res Child Dev. 76, no. 4, pp.8-30, doi:10.1111/j.1540-5834.2011.00626.x

[200] Business Council of Australia (2019) *A Plan for a Stronger Australia*

[201] Heiman J and Timms H (2018) N*ew Power: How Power Works in Our Hyperconnected World—and How to Make It Work for You*, Penguin Random House, New York, p.59

[202] Heiman J and Timms H (2018) N*ew Power: How Power Works in Our Hyperconnected World—and How to Make It Work for You*, Penguin Random House, New York

[203] Parliament of Victoria, Drugs and Crime Prevention/Committee (1997) *Inquiry into the Victorian Government's Drug Reform Strategy: Interim Report*, December 1997

Partner with Purpose

[204] Allen T (2010) *The Lord's Resistance Army: Myth and Reality*, London, UK

[205] Edelman (2020) *Edelman Trust Barometer 2020*

[206] Barrakett J (2008) *Strategic Issues for the Not-for-profit Sector*, UNSW Press, Sydney, p.18

[207] Porter M E and Kramer M R (2011) *Creating Shared Value. How to reinvent capitalism-and unleash a wave of innovation and growth*, Harvard Business Review, January–February

[208] Commonwealth of Australia (2017) *Giving Australia 2016 Business Giving and Volunteering*, May 2017

[209] State of Victoria, Department of Human Services (2011) *Human Services: The Case for Change*, Melbourne

[210] PwC (2017) *Reimagining Public Private Partnerships*

[211] Autesserre, S (2012) *Dangerous Tales: Dominant Narratives on the Congo and their Unintended Consequences*, African Affairs 111, no. 443, pp.202–222, doi:10.1093/afraf/adr080

[212] Human Rights Watch (2002) *The War Within the War: Sexual Violence Against Women and Girls in Eastern Congo*

[213] As guest speaker at the Committee for Melbourne Annual Dinner on 22 May 2019

[214] VicRoads (2012) *Cycling to Work in Melbourne 1976–2011*, State Government of Victoria

[215] Beyond Bank Australia (2019) *Changing Lives: 2019 Corporate Report*

[216] Gahan P, Adamovic M, Bevitt A, Harley B, Healy J, Olsen J E and Theilacker M (2016) *Leadership at Work: Do Australian Leaders Have What It Takes?* Melbourne Centre for Workplace Leadership, University of Melbourne

[217] Commbank (2018) *Not-for-Profit Insights Report*

[218] Australian Institute of Company Directors (2020) *Director Sentiment Index: Research Findings Second Half 2020*

[219] Gladwell M (2006) *Million Dollar Murray*, New Yorker, 0028792X, 2/13/2006, vol. 82, no. 1

[220] Global Impact Investing Network (2020) *2020 Annual Impact Investor Survey*

[221] International Finance Corporation (2020) *Growing Impact. New Insights into the Practice of Impact Investing*

[222] Responsible Investment Association Australasia (2020) *Benchmarking Impact: Australian Impact Investor Insights, Activity and Performance Report 2020*

[223] Traill M (2016) *Jumping Ship, From the Heart of Corporate Australia to the World of Social Investment*, Sydney

[224] Commonwealth of Australia (2020) *Social Impact Investing Taskforce Interim Report December 2019*, p.3

[225] Cohen R (2020) *Impact: Reshaping Capitalism to Drive Real Change*, Ebury Press, London, p.169

[226] Commonwealth of Australia (2020) *Social Impact Investing Taskforce: Interim Report*, December 2019

[227] Australian Institute of Health and Welfare (2014) *Australia's Health 2014*, Australia's Health Series no. 14. Cat. no. AUS 178. Canberra: AIHW.

[228] Australia Post (2020) *Inside Australian Online Shopping: 2020 eCommerce Industry Report*

[229] Collins J (2001) *Good to Great: Why Some Companies Make the Leap... and Others Don't*, UK, p.96

[230] Flynn D (2016) *Chapter One*, NSW

[231] Light P (2000) *Making Nonprofits Work: A Report on the tides of Nonprofit Management Reform*, Washington, p.17

[232] Barraket J, Mason C and Blaine B (2016) *Finding Australia's Social Enterprise Sector 2016: Final Report,* Melbourne, VIC. Centre for Social Impact Swinburne and Social Traders, p.3

[233] McLeod J (2018) *The Support Report: The Changing Shape of Giving and the Significant Implications for Recipients*

[234] Knowles D (2018) *A Snapshot of Australian Giving*, Koda Capital

[235] Australian Tax Office, *Private Ancillary Fund Guidelines 2009*

[236] Rozensher S (2013) *The Growth of Cause Marketing: Past, Current, And Future Trends*, Journal of Business and Economics Research 11, no. 4 (April)

[237] Australian Institute of Company Directors (2015) *2015 NFP Governance and Performance Study*

Starting Guides

[238] Rosenstreich G (2013) *LGBTI People: Mental Health and Suicide.*, 2nd rev. ed., Sydney, National LGBTI Health Alliance

[239] Commonwealth of Australia (2020) *Closing the Gap Report 2020*, p.65

Index

www.purposefull.com.au

www.ingramcontent.com/pod-product-compliance
Lightning Source LLC
Chambersburg PA
CBHW020528270326
41927CB00006B/483